AGAINST THE WIND
The Story of Louie

By
Louie Brighton

Copyright © Louie Brighton 2012

All scripture quotations, unless otherwise indicated, are taken from The Holy Bible, New International Version®, NIV®.

Copyright ©1973, 1978, 1984, 2011 by Biblica, Inc.™

Used by permission of Zondervan.

All rights reserved worldwide. www.zondervan.com

The "NIV" and "New International Version" are trademarks registered inthe United States Patent and Trademark Office by Biblica, Inc.™

COVER ILLUSTRATION BY JOAN MCKENZIE

I WOULD LIKE TO DEDICATE THIS BOOK TO:

GRANDMA BAKER WHO SAVED MY LIFE,

AND

TO THE PLASTIC SURGEONS WHO TREATED ME

AND

TO THE NURSING PROFESSION FOR ENABLING ME TO BECOME A PROFESSIONAL NURSE.

Contents

Early Years 1
Myrtle Street Hospital, Liverpool 7
Chester Royal Infirmary 9
War Is Declared 11
Britain's Darkest Hour 15
School Days 22
Sir Harold Gillies 28
Gloucester Royal Infirmary 31
Chepstow Hospital 44
Back To Hospital 51
The Teenage Years 56
Confirmation 63
A Visit To Chepstow Hospital 65
The Start Of My Working Life 72
Stoke Mandeville Hospital 74
My Career As A Nurse 76
Time Off From Nursing Duties 84
Bristol Hospital 93

Stoke Mandeville Hospital 101
Back to Hospital Again 104
Christians! 109
Back To Bristol 139
My First Exam Success 148
Moving To Croydon 152
A New Hospital 234
Louie Brighton SRN at Colchester Hospital 241
West Bromwich 278
Marriage And Family 280
Life without David 315

Early Years

'My thoughts are not your thoughts

Neither are your ways my ways, declares the Lord'

Isaiah chapter 55 verse 8.

It is strange how one can feel the agony of certain painful earlier experiences many years after they have happened. The memories of those former days seem to remain crystal clear.

We have all had earthly fathers and we have all had to come to terms with what our fathers were like. The fruits of today are rooted in yesterday and this has been so from the beginning, from Adam.

Our forms and our features are cast in the moulds of those from whose seed we have descended. The ways and mannerisms which we may have thought are unique and peculiar to us may have lived generations ago perhaps through our parents, grandparents and our great grandparents. The slight tilt of the head, the gestures, and the ways in which our minds operate may have been characteristics of others even before we were born.

My Grandfather, David Baker was from Birmingham. When he was young he was employed in the stables on my Great Grandparent's estate in Stafford. That is where he met my Grandmother who was from a very well-to-do family called the 'Countys'. My Great Grandparents were not pleased when my Grandfather showed an interest in their daughter. But my Grandfather won the interest. He fell in love with my Grandmother whose name was Louisa Jane.

They were very young – just seventeen years old at the time and her parents were furious about the relationship. They told her that if she didn't give up David Baker they would disinherit her from their will, property and estate. David and Louisa decided to elope and went to Redditch. Soon after their eldest son was born, they moved to Rhyl, North Wales and then moved to Fforddisa, Prestatyn.

Louisa Jane became the mother of thirteen children, although sadly, four of them died. One of her five boys was my father – Phillip Baker. Louisa Jane didn't like children so the maids who looked after other children brought hers up as well.

Louisa Jane called herself Louie from an early age and she told her children that the first grandchild to be born in her house, whether a boy or girl, was to be called Louie. Little did my father know that it would be him or that his first child would be a girl.

My Grandmother, Louisa Jane
(Sitting front row the fifth adult from the left)

My Mother's Father was born in Rhyl. His name was Richard Evans and he was the youngest son of the former Registrar of Rhyl, Sylvanus Parry Evans.

On 4th August 1914 at 11:00pm Great Britain declared war upon Germany. Richard, my Grandfather was aged forty five at the time but he falsely declared his age because the upper age limit was forty one years to join the North Wales Pals Battalion Rhyl, Royal Welsh Fusiliers and he wanted to join up. On 5th March 1916 my Grandfather was killed while on duty on trench work.

My Grandfather's platoon Commander (Vivian Jones) wrote a letter to my Grandmother as follows:

> "His sad death has cast a great gloom over his fellow men who held him in the highest respect and amongst whom he was exceedingly popular. He was the oldest man in the platoon and did everything in his power to set up a cheerful tone and whenever we were heavily worked and everyone greatly fatigued his cheerfulness would come in front and inspire the lads in the platoon. As his platoon officer I found him always willing and nothing asked of him was too much for him to do and I feel I have lost one of my best men".

My Grandfather was buried in France. He never saw his youngest child, a baby girl who was my mother – Phyllis Evans.

My paternal Grandmother, Catherine Jones, was born in 1876 in Llandyrnog on a farm called Tan-y-Onnen. Catherine had an illegitimate son called Richard but he died at the age of twenty.

Catherine's parents, who were from Denbigh, raised Richard. Her father was Morgan Salisbury Jones and her mother was Winifred. Richard's father was Lord Mostyn who was a cousin of Queen Victoria.

At some point Catherine Jones moved to Rhyl and took service in the household of Vivian Hewitt, the famous aviator who was the first man to fly the Irish Channel, when he lived in St Asaph Street, Rhyl. There, Catherine met up with Richard Evans and together they went on to have six children. Following Richard's death in the First World War, Catherine married again and had two other children. My mother was the youngest child of Catherine and Richard Evans. Apparently Catherine didn't like children so the girls were given away to relatives, including my mother who was given to. My mother, who was born in Rhyl was the youngest of 8 children. When she was a baby she was often left unfed. She was taken by an aunt and uncle, Sarah and Arthur Denning who lived in Rhyl. Sarah took care of her. Arthur owned the milk dairies in Rhyl. He was a very cruel man and he was cruel to his wife. They had maids and Arthur treated them badly too. He also used to beat the horses until they went mad. Arthur's wife, Sarah Denning died of cancer.

My Father and Mother

My mother, who was clever, went to Rhyl Grammar School and she played the piano. While she was at Grammar School her friend, Lucy Baker, who was the youngest sister of my father, used to take her home to her house in Prestatyn and that is where Phylis Evans met Philip Baker, my father. They also married very young, perhaps 17 or 18 years old.

At some point when she was a young adult my mother became involved with fortune telling and tarot cards. My mother, Phylis Evans was 22 when her mother Catherine Jones died in 1939.

My Grandma Baker had two boarding houses on Marine Road in Prestatyn and my parents lived there for a while. My father was a slater and tiler. My mother had a miscarriage because she fell down a flight of stairs, but soon afterwards she became pregnant again with me. If the baby that she miscarried had lived I might never have been born. My father was very good to my mother and always showed her love but his character changed later once they had a family.

Louie about 8 months old on Prestatyn beach

My father, Philip Baker was born in Fforddisa, Prestatyn, one of Grandma Louie Baker's thirteen children, the third from the last. He was born in 1912, the year the Titanic sank, the same year that Robert Falcon Scott lost his life in the Antarctic Expedition and the suffragette movement was in progress for the women's vote.

Myrtle Street Hospital, Liverpool

In 1936 while my mother was expecting a baby, the whole country was waiting to hear whether King Edward 8th was going to abdicate the throne. Britain was facing its biggest constitutional crisis of the 20th century when King Edward 8th announced that he intended to marry an American divorcee. His love affair with Mrs Wallis Simpson threatened to bring down the Conservative government. It divided the nation and caused a rift with his own family, including the Queen Mother, which was never truly healed. The King decided to abdicate on 10 December 1936. He spent the rest of his life in exile abroad, leaving his brother to become King George 6th.

On 1st April 1936 my mother gave birth to me. A lady from Prestatyn delivered me (but she was not a midwife). She told my mother that I would not live because I was born with a double cleft lip and palate. I had no upper lip or gum in the front of my mouth. I do not know what my parent's reaction was to this news but I do know that as a child my father did not seem to want to know me. He wanted a boy, but he felt as though he had gained a lot of trouble instead!

However, my prayer now is:

'Even so, Heavenly Father, for it seemed good in Thy sight'

When I was a baby no-one was allowed to touch me. My mother later informed me that I had stopped crying after 3 days as she was unable to feed me because my mouth was so open. My father's mother, who didn't like children, decided to pay me a visit. She climbed up two flights of stairs to see yet another grandchild. She took one look at me and said, 'This baby is dying'. She told my mother that she would get her doctor in to have a look at me. In those days you had to pay for a doctor.

When he examined me he told my mother that I was seriously ill and he transferred me from my home to Myrtle Street Children's Hospital in Liverpool. When I was admitted to the ward the doctor told my mother to go back to Prestatyn and bring a box to put my body in as I wouldn't last the night.

I believe now that God had his hand upon my life, even then as my mother arrived back at the hospital to find out that I was still alive. The doctor told her that as I was dying she could come in for a moment although in those days parents were not usually allowed to be with their children on the ward.

My mother said that I was black with pneumonia.

I had Pneumonia, Gastroenteritis and Malnutrition all together. At that time the hospital had no drugs to help me. An emergency christening was arranged because they believed I was dying. My mother wanted to call me Pamela but my Grandma Baker insisted I was to be called Louie. The ward Sister who was in charge called me Rosebud. She was very protective of me and she wouldn't let anyone else touch me but she nursed me through the illness.

The specialist told my mother he had never seen anyone so close to death and yet live and he said: 'There must be a purpose for her.'

When I was eventually moved out of the ward they started to repair my palate but apparently it broke down and, after three attempts, they gave up. At that time my parents were living with my paternal grandmother.

Chester Royal Infirmary

At the age of three I was admitted to Chester Royal Infirmary to have another operation on my lip and palate which also broke down, I found out later.

When I was discharged from the hospital my mother put me in a cot and left me there for most of the day. One day I was standing up in the cot and one of the rods at the end of the cot caught in my palate. I could not get myself free and needed someone to come to free me. Eventually someone came and set me free but I remember that my mouth was very sore after that incident.

During that time I recall that my mother's mother, Catherine Jones, came to see me. Therefore, my memory must go back to the age of three. It may not have happened that way but this is how I remember my past. Whilst I was living in Grandma's house in Marine Road, Prestatyn, and my Grandma's daughters were also living with Grandma and Granddad Baker.

My father's sisters were very good to me and I think that I was quite spoilt, but my father didn't seem to have any patience with me. Often when I was downstairs with his sisters my father would pick me up and carry me back up three flights of stairs on his shoulder with my Aunties following saying, 'Philip, bring her back downstairs' but he used to take no notice of them and would drop me back in my cot.

Around that time in 1939 my maternal grandmother, Catherine Jones, died. My Father and mother were expecting their second child by then bought a house in Bristol where my sister was born.

Grandma Baker wouldn't let me go with them to Bristol so I stayed with Grandma Baker and her family who all spoilt me. I was taken to Bristol for a short time but not for long as my parents sent me back to my Grandma Baker's house in Prestatyn. My sister was a beautiful baby who apparently had no problems at birth. She had thick red curly hair and big eyes and everybody used to admire her because she was so pretty. She became my father's favourite and turned out to be very clever. My Grandma Baker, however, did not make a fuss of any of any of the children.

War Is Declared

In 1933 Adolph Hitler became chancellor of the German Reich. It was becoming noticeable that Hitler intended to get rid of the Jewish people in Germany and that anti-Semitism was spreading rapidly through the country of Germany. Hitler wanted a superior race of Germans.

In Britain in 1938 Neville Chamberlain had negotiated a peace deal in Munich with Adolph Hitler. Keen to avoid a second war with Germany, he returned from the talks in Munich to declare, "I believe in peace in our time."

In 1934 one man spoke out against the Nazi aggression, Winston Churchill. He was labelled a warmonger. Neville Chamberlain's speech to the commons on 2nd September following the previous afternoon's invasion of Poland would announce an ultimatum to withdraw from Poland. The failure to do so divided the House of Commons and, following late night talks in the cabinet, the demand was delivered to Berlin at 9:00am on 3rd September with a deadline for compliance set at 11:00am of the same day. When the regime in Germany failed to suspend the attack on Poland, Britain declared war with Germany.

By the morning of 3rd September war was inevitable. And Prime Minister Neville Chamberlain broadcast to the nation at 11:00am, 'Britain is at war with Germany'. At that time Hitler and Mussolini threatened not just Europe but the whole world. Their military build-up and Hitler's rantings and ravings would plunge the whole world into a holocaust.

Louie with her sister Josephine

When the war started my parents lost their house in Bristol due to the bombing so they returned to Prestatyn to live with my Grandparents and my sister Josephine. I didn't like her and I was very naughty. When my mother put Josephine outside in the pram I would take her out of the pram and carry her to Victoria Park. Victoria Park had been built for Queen Victoria's Coronation Day and had opened in 1911. On this particular occasion I had left my sister under the bushes there. My mother had returned to the pram to pick Josephine up for her feed and was horrified to find that her baby had disappeared!

My mother became increasingly upset as I refused to tell her where I had taken baby Josephine. However, one of my relatives had found her under the bushes in Victoria Park and the baby had been quite happy there. Needless to say, I was in a lot of trouble and I was given a good hiding which I deserved on that occasion.

My mother took me back to Chester Royal Infirmary and while we were waiting in the corridor my mother was talking to a lady who was crying. The lady had asked my mother if she was upset that I was being admitted to hospital but my mother replied, 'No, I am not upset. I am glad she is coming into hospital'.

The Sister on the children's ward came and took me away from my mother and into the ward. My mother did not attempt to come with me she just said goodbye and told me to be good. I was put into a cot and shortly afterwards the Nurses cut off all of my white-fair curly hair. I was just 4 years old at the time and I did not see my mother again for 4 months.

I used to sit up in my cot and I would not lie down, even when I was told to. I used to watch the children going through the ward to the theatre for their operations. The children were always crying for their mothers but I did not cry at all. I remember two men with a long trolley who came to collect me but I refused to lie down. When we arrived in the anaesthetic room four people held me down. I started to scream as the man who was standing at the top of my head put a black mask on my face. The next thing I remember I was standing up again in the cot!

The operations were repeated twice but all failed. When the specialist used to come to do his ward round I would refuse to open my mouth unless he gave me a penny. I had collected lots of pennies by the time I went home from the hospital! When my mother came to collect me from the hospital and to take me home she asked the ward Sister, 'Where has all this money come from?' To which Sister replied, 'From the specialist. It was the only way he could examine inside her mouth'.

My parents had moved to a house in Dyserth and took me home there from Chester Royal Infirmary.

I was very weak and kept falling over. I grew stronger but I also became very naughty and I would run off with my sister in her pram. One day my sister was in the garden in her pram so I had thought that I would take her for a walk. I took the pram out into the road. It was a big pram and far too heavy for me to handle. I pushed the pram down the steep hill which led down to the Dyserth waterfalls.

I lost control of the pram completely. Suddenly a man appeared, he took hold of the pram and took us home. My mother was very cross and I ended up with another well-deserved hiding!

At home, my father would hardly ever speak to me and I always had to be out of his sight. He would ignore me completely for most of the time. I was always running off to the house of an old lady, Mrs MacWeeny, who lived down the hill in a cottage. I became friends with her and I would often turn up in her kitchen. Mrs. MacWeeny was always very kind to me although she could not understand what I was saying due to the nature of my cleft lip and palette.

I remember on one occasion that my mother took me to the dental department in Chester Infirmary. I do not remember feeling afraid of the dentist but I did resent what he was doing as I was having alterations made inside my mouth. My mother took me out of the dentist's chair and started to give me a good hiding with the hair brush which made me scream loudly. The dentist said to my mother, 'Oh, do not hit her!' as he picked me up off the floor. He sat me on his knee and calmed me down and then he told me a story. Once he had calmed me down he proceeded with the treatment.

He was a very kind man.

Britain's Darkest Hour

Once again I was admitted to Chester Royal Infirmary for further treatment. I was put into a cot but unfortunately I wet the cot on this occasion. A Nurse gave me a good hiding for doing this. I never wet any cot or bed again after that incident. I remember that the Nurses put me in a bath with a little boy but I started shouting, 'He is not my brother!' and flatly refused to get into the bath with the little boy. The Nurse slapped me across the bottom and put me in the bath so I started to attack the little boy and then he started crying. Suddenly we all heard a very strange noise that I did not recognize. The Nurses pulled us both out of the bath and quickly wrapped towels around us. I remember that we ran through a dimly lit corridor into a room down the stairs until another the strange noise occurred. I later learned that these noises were the air raid siren and the 'all-clear.' The Battle of Britain had begun.

It was 1940. It was Britain's darkest hour. Winston Churchill warned Parliament of Germany's growing military ambitions and air might. He also warned that Britain was not prepared for a possible attack. In 1935 a new government was elected but the Prime Minister, Stanley Baldwin excluded Churchill from office because of his outspoken views about the German threat. In 1934 Chamberlain became Prime Minister and Churchill continued to severely criticize the government's policy towards Germany.

Germany occupied Austria and Czechoslovakia in 1934. Chamberlain visited Munich and signed a peace agreement with Hitler. Churchill called it an unmitigated defeat and warned that it was the prelude to war. He said that Britain must arm immediately but he was ignored by the government.

In 1939 Hitler invaded Poland and Britain and France declared war against Germany. Churchill was appointed First Lord of the Admiralty.

In 1940 Hitler invaded Norway and Denmark and then Belgium, Holland and France. Chamberlain resigned and King George 6th appointed Churchill as Prime Minister. On 10th May he formed a national government of all the main parties. I praise the Lord for Winston Churchill! The Spirit of the Lord was in our country – in the time of war God reigns.

Churchill delivered his famous speech in the House of Commons.

> *"The battle of France is over. I expect the Battle of Britain is about to begin. Upon the battle depends the survival of Christian civilization. Upon it depends our own British life. We shall defend our island whatever the cost may be. We shall fight on the beaches; we shall fight on the landing ground; we shall fight in the fields and in the streets; we shall fight in the hills; we shall never surrender."*

Winston Churchill, affectionately known as 'Winnie' was famous for his cigar and for his two-fingered 'V' gesture which was the sign of victory and symbol of the unconquerable will of the people.

The occupied territories of Europe were sure that so long as they continued to refuse to collaborate with the invader a fate awaited the Nazi tyranny and that his cause would perish and Europe would be liberated. Churchill's speech was so inspirational that it gave hope and strength to the British people in the face of the terribly uncertain time of World War Two.

I personally thank God and praise Him for 'Winnie' who was sent as our saviour. If Britain had lost the battle in the air Germany would have invaded our country and the Nazi doctors would have invaded our hospitals, killing children such as those with cleft lip and palate and all other abnormalities including spina bifida and also other people who they did not consider to be 'normal.'

I had returned to Prestatyn with my Grandma Baker. I clearly remember that on one particular occasion she had given me an orange to eat. I had gone outside of the house to play and had gone into Morley Road, near the park where there was a row of terraced houses. At the first house there was a pram with a baby girl in it who was around six weeks old. I placed a piece of the orange into the baby's mouth. Just at that moment Mrs Roberts, the baby's grandmother, came out and she shouted at me. Fortunately, she took the orange out of the baby's mouth. However, she left the baby again and went back into her house at which point I took the baby to the park. I took her out of her pram and played with her as though she were a toy doll. After a short time I returned the baby to her pram although I left the pram in the park!

Louie sitting on the bench in Dyserth (4 – 5 years old)

When the mother of the baby girl went out of her house to attend to the baby she was shocked to find that the baby and the pram had gone and apparently everyone had panicked. The baby's mother and grandmother came to my Grandma's house, but no one else knew anything about the baby and once again, I could not tell them where the baby was. Everyone went out of their houses to search for the baby and eventually my aunty found the baby sleeping safely in the pram in the park. Someone called for a doctor who then examined the baby girl. The doctor gave the baby the 'all clear' and said that no harm had come to her. A terrible row ensued between my grandma and the baby's grandma. I was just five years old.

I became much attached to a man who repaired shoes and I always wanted to see him. I kept pulling the buckles off my shoes so that I could go and see him. I asked my Grandma if I could go and see him but she said that he was closed as it was Sunday. I did not believe her so I went to see anyway and it was closed!

I went for a walk and ended up at the Methodist Church off Station Road (opposite the park). I walked into the church in a really filthy state, covered in jam and dirt, and sat down between the middle-aged ladies. At the end of the service they were concerned and wondered where I had come from so they called the Minister over. He came and picked me up and asked my name and where I lived but I did not answer. People were all around as he carried me down the steps of the church and outside. There I saw some of my relatives looking for me. My Aunt Lucy and my Mother asked what I was doing there. The Minister was very nice and smiled a lot but I was taken home and shouted at!

The men used to play bowls in the park and I used to run on the green and take their bowls which must have annoyed them considerably! They used to shout at me and would threaten to tell my Father if they saw me again.

When my Uncle returned home from the war he brought me a doll which I used to take to the park and on one occasion some of the local boys took it off me, ran off with it and threw it into a bush of nettles. I went in after it and was stung all over. The boys did it three times, after which they took the doll from me altogether and went away with it. I felt...when my Grandma said it was my fault as I should not have taken it to the park.

It was around this time just before Christmas that two of my aunts, Margery and Lucy were making Christmas cake. One day in the park a girl fell over and was crying so I said I knew what would stop her crying and I went to my aunt's house and took their newly baked which I remember was quite heavy for a little girl! When I returned to the park the two of us started to eat the cake and we were soon joined by several other children. Apparently, I was informed later that my Aunt went to the pantry where she had left it to cool so that she could put icing on the top of it and the whole cake was missing! My aunty began to accuse family and friends who were around at the time until she spotted some cake crumbs outside the door. Aunty followed the trail of cake crumbs to the park where she found me and my newly found friends tucking in to her cake! I was in a lot of trouble with her but she forgave me, eventually.

I got into a habit of stealing things from outside shops in Prestatyn High Street but my Mother would always make me return them and apologise to the shopkeeper who was always very pleased when I did. I was afraid of upsetting my mother because she regularly lost her temper with me and it was very unpleasant when this happened.

One day when I was about six years old I went to the park and there was a man who sat me on his knee and felt my body all over and molested me. This happened on many occasions but I didn't tell anyone as I thought that I would be punished although I knew he was wrong to do it.

It was around this time, when I was six years old that I had to return to Chester Royal Infirmary when I had two more operations which both failed.

Soon after we moved to Dyserth, just after my brother was born. We lived on top of the hill in a cottage. I was very naughty and kept going into the farm and banging on the shed door where the bull was kept. The farmer came out and threatened to give me a good hiding if I did not stay away. I kept running away and trying to get to Grandma's house because I did not like it in Dyserth. My Father used to come after me and hit me with his belt. Sometimes my mother would take us out for a picnic in the fields which was nice.

Sometimes when we were at home, my mother used to put the three of us in the bath and throw cold water over us. It seemed as though she was always in a temper. Sometimes mother would tell my Father what we had been doing and then he would hit us with the belt. In general those were not happy days.

Eventually we went back to Grandma's house because my Father could not pay the rent until we moved on to a bungalow in Eaton Avenue in Rhyl. My Mother's temper got worse. When my sister had tantrums my Mother would throw cold water over her and grab our hair and bang our heads together. I remember the time when my sister, brother and I caught the measles and we were put into a dark room with a very hot poultice put on each of our chests. When we began to get better my Mother told us not to go outside but we disobeyed her instructions and decided to go on the beach and build a sand castle together.

In those days the sea defences had not been built and there was no sea wall. Sometimes the sea would come right up and would flood the bungalow. On one occasion I asked my sister to go and get some water because she had wellington boots on. However she got stuck in quick sand and it went up to her chest as I turned to look around I saw a rock. So, I lay down flat on the rock and pulled my sister up to safety by her hair although she came right out of her wellingtons because they were too big for her. After this we returned home crying and my Mother went berserk but my Aunt told her not to hit me. I felt very guilty about this incident.

My Mum said that she didn't want us anymore so my sister and I went to my Grandma's house. When I arrived there I took my Aunty Lucy's wages out of her handbag and decided to go on the bus to Rhyl. I also took my other Aunt's high heeled shoes. The bus was full of people but the bus conductor soon realised that I was on my own. He asked me if I belonged to anyone on the bus. A lady was on the bus who was my Aunty Lucy's friend and she said that she knew who I was and the bus conductor asked her to take me home. When I got home I was in trouble again as my Grandma was not very pleased with what I had done and I remember how that had upset me.

When we returned to the bungalow in Rhyl my brother became seriously ill with Gastro-enteritis and my Mother went for the doctor. She said to me, 'If Philip is sick, just wipe his face' and she gave me a flannel to use for this purpose. However, instead of just wiping his face I put him in a cold bath and washed him and his hair; the doctor did not seem at all impressed with this but thankfully Philip survived. My Mother was yet again in a foul temper.

It was around this time that my Father left Wallasey where he worked as a slater and tiler and returned home. Whilst he was at home I had to keep out of his sight as I knew by then that he did not like me.

My Father also had a small holding where he used to keep hens. A young lad called Jimmy Butler worked for him who used to hold the hens down while my dad cut off their heads. They would then run around headless which often used to give me nightmares as it was not a nice thing to watch them do.

School Days

When I was around seven and a half years old my Grandma decided to send me to a convent school on Russell Road. My Mother took me to the school but we were late going in. as we approached the school, I skipped along quite happy about going into the school but that was soon to change. My new teacher took me along to meet a little boy called Richard who was tall and blonde and had fair white hair. Richard looked me up and down and asked me how old I was but he could not understand what I said due to my due to the nature of my cleft lip and palette. He said that I looked more like five years old than seven years old. Later on, I needed to go to the toilet but the teacher and Richard did not understand what I was saying. When the teacher told us to play outside I stood up and realised that I had wet myself; Richard pointed this out and said to me, 'Take your pants off and I'll do what Mummy does'. He took my pants from me and then he washed them. He told me to go outside while he did that and when I got outside I was surrounded by other children. They pushed me against a tree and the older ones called me 'devil child' and 'witch'. At that point Richard came out and chased them away from me.

At every opportunity the kids made fun of me. I didn't understand why they couldn't understand my speech because it sounded plain to me. I made the big mistake of running home to the bungalow and asking my mother what was going on. Unfortunately my Father was there and when I tried to ask him what was the wrong with me he slapped my face so hard that I lost my balance and fell over. I just stared at him and then I ran back to school.

At this time I had obtorator in my mouth but I did not like wearing it. However, my Father had said that he would punish me if I took it out. During the Sports day at school, while I was taking part in the sack race the obtorator fell out. As I was last in the race, I stopped to look for it in the grass meanwhile the other children went back into the school to change out of their sports clothes and to drink their milk. I was crawling on the ground looking for the obtorator when I looked up to see Richard standing near to me. I tried to tell him what I was doing but he could not understand me. However he found it in the grass but it was broken. By that time I had become very cold and I was shaking as I was only wearing a vest and pants. Richard took me inside and dressed me and then we went back to the classroom. The teacher gave us some milk to drink but mine just poured down my face. I was afraid to go home but Richard walked with me.

Richard had sisters at the school and they told his parents what he was doing for me (no-one else at the school helped me). I used to call for him in the morning. When I knocked on his door, his father came to the door. He was tall and wore grey clothes. He put his hand up and told me that I could no longer play with Richard. I felt devastated and as I walked to school alone I covered my face with my hand. The other children soon heard about what had happened and they treated me in a worse way as Richard was not at hand to defend me. Once when we were in the school grounds playing Richard sat on a wall with two boys. He suggested that they all played planes to distract their attention from me. The next day a little girl called Catherine pushed her way through the children and said she would play with me. But after that things got worse because the other children began to attack her. She was badly bruised. Catherine's parents told her that she was to stay away from me. I wanted to know what was wrong with me and so I asked Richard who said that I had a tunnel in my mouth.

There used to be a man who wore dark clothes and a raincoat who we would see walking near to the school. One day Catherine was walking home with me and the man followed us. He asked us what colour our pants were and so I pulled my dress up and said that they were navy blue. He did not understand what I was saying so he asked to see Catherine's pants but she took hold of my hand and we ran away from him! When I arrived home there was a knock on the door and there was a policeman was standing on the step. Catherine had told her parents about the incident and they had reported it to the police. Again my Mother lost her temper with me and threatened me that I was going to prison.

Near to where I lived there was a little girl called Eileen who I often played with. I remember on one occasion my Mother told me to go and get some bread from a small local shop and Eileen came along with me. Unfortunately that same man followed us again. He asked us if we would go down to the sea with him and have our photo taken. I said 'no' but Eileen went off with him.

When I returned home from the shop my Mother was very angry with me because I had bought the wrong items and she hit me. I was so frightened that I did not dare to tell her about Eileen. Soon afterwards Eileen's Mother came to our house to look for her but I would not tell her where Eileen was because I was so afraid of my mother. Later on that day the police came to our house to tell us that they had found Eileen's body in the barbed wire near the beach.

Soon after these events I went back to Chester Infirmary for a new obtorator. My Mother was not pleased with my progress and she asked to see another Specialist. I had to go yet another operation which turned out to be unsuccessful.

I used to see my Grandma quite often and I would always speak with her and tell her if I was not happy. Grandma encouraged me to continue with my education and to stay on at school. There was one day at school when I was feeling particularly sad because Richard was no longer my friend, when a tall girl with very dark hair was making fun of me along with a group of other girls. I decided that she should have a hiding. During the school dinner hour, I went home, when I knew that my parents would not be there to get my Father's belt. I ran back to school. Later on at the end of the school day as the children were all leaving the school and some of them were walking in the road the dark-haired girl started to attack me. I told her that I was going to thrash her. I could feel the belt in my pocket. She started to laugh and threw her head back laughing so I moved in first to start hitting her. She began to scream and fell into the gutter, crying. As I was hitting her across her legs the girl's Mother arrived and came to her rescue as she shouted at me

'What's going on here?' but I was feeling pleased that I had won the victory over her.

Granddad Baker had a newspaper agency for Rhyl, Prestatyn and Dyserth. All the Aunties and Uncles and children helped deliver the Sunday papers. My Father delivered the papers in Dyserth and although we were living in Rhyl he made me walk to Prestatyn. He would ride his bike with my sister and brother and even though I use dot get very tired he would insist that I walked and he would threaten me with a hiding. I delivered the papers up the steep hills of Dyserth, by the waterfalls, to the cottages on the right.

One Sunday as I was delivering papers I arrived at the cottage where two elderly ladies lived, (they were very pretty and sweet and they always wore pretty dresses). One of the ladies asked me what was wrong with my mouth. I was not able to explain to her so I returned home to tell my Father and told him what the ladies had asked me. He turned almost purple with rage; he marched up to their cottage taking me with him and banged on the door with his fist. I was just seven years old and I felt very frightened. When the ladies came to the door he started shouting at them and he told them to ask him and not me however, he would not tell them what was wrong with my mouth. The next Sunday I felt apprehensive going to deliver the papers to their cottage but the ladies were very kind to me and told that they had a present for me. To my surprise and delight they gave me a box and when I took the lid off there was a little kitten with a red ribbon round her neck. I went back to my Father and I showed him but to my dismay he said, 'No cats!' When we got back home to Rhyl, I begged my Mother to let me keep the Persian kitten who I had called 'Fluffy.' My Mother said that if it was a Tom then we would keep it. We found out it was a female cat but my Mother said we could keep her anyway.

We moved back to Dyserth where we experienced a harsh winter with heavy snow storms. My parents would throw Fluffy out every night but she would climb up the drainpipe onto my bed. One night I watched Fluffy give birth to five kittens which were very beautiful but my Father threw them out into the snow. However Fluffy carried them one at a time up the drainpipe into my bedroom. Eventually my Mother gave them all away. One day, after a hard day at school, I got home to learn that Fluffy was missing and when I asked my

Mother what had happened to her she said that she did not know. I looked everywhere but I could not find Fluffy. I learned later on that my Father had drowned Fluffy and that my Uncle had helped him. Fluffy was a very big cat so they must have found it hard to drown her. I was very upset and I never really got over it. I missed her so much as she was my only comfort in those days.

Yet again I had to go back to Chester Infirmary for another operation. It was the usual routine and again it was not successful.

Throughout this time the war was progressing. On the beaches of Dunkirk in May 1940 the balance of the Second World War shifted and for the first time losing became a distinct possibility.

I was back home in Dyserth and after a time of illness I went to live with my Grandma again in Prestatyn. My cousins also lived there and they told me stories of rats in the cupboard under the stairs. My cousin Rolland said that the rats had eyes like saucers and teeth like razors. The day after that whilst we were playing, my Grandfather lost his temper with me. He hit me and locked me in the cupboard under the stairs. I was terrified because of what my cousins had said about the rats and I said, 'God, help me'. I sat down with my chin on my knees asking God to help me. I suddenly felt an unusual sense of peace. Eventually my Mother came to take me out of the cupboard but again she was in a temper and I had to go to bed for the rest of the day.

We continued to deliver the papers in Dyserth with my Father who was in his usual bad temper.

Sometimes we would visit my Father's smallholding in Dyserth, down the Dell, where he kept pigs and hens. We used to play down at the Dell, and we would ride on the sow's back. I always had to try my best to keep out of my Father's way because he would just freely hit us with the belt. Once whilst I was delivering papers in Upper Foel Road in Dyserth that I took a wrong turning and got lost and I came across a big old house. I knocked on the door but there was no answer. As I came away from the house I looked up and I saw a lady looking at me with a very angry face. I felt very frightened and I ran back down the lane. I eventually found my Father but he was furious with me as I told him what had happened.

He said that the old house was derelict and no-one had lived there for many years. My father hit me across my head because I had somehow lost the papers. I was around 7 years old at the time, I think.

When I was staying in Prestatyn my Grandfather used to hit me with the belt and put me in the cupboard under the stairs. I used to feel hurt because I loved him. On one occasion when he hit me I said, 'Don't hit me, I love you', but he took no notice.

We left my Grandma's house and returned to Dyserth where we lived in a cottage at the top of the second hill opposite what was the Infants School. My sister went to that school and I remember that she had to wear clogs because there was no money available for shoes.

I was still attending the Convent School in Rhyl but I missed a lot of schooling due to illness and operations. As part of the uniform, I had to wear gaiters to school.

At Christmas time we were usually given very poor presents but one particular Christmas time while we were staying at Grandma's house in Prestatyn, I noticed that one of my cousins had been given lot of lovely presents. On our return to Dyserth a young boy who helped my Father asked me and my sister what Father Christmas had brought us. When we told him what we had received he responded by saying, 'Father Christmas doesn't like you' and from that time onwards we did not like Christmas.

Sir Harold Gillies

My Mother's elder sister, who was a music teacher, had a friend who was a doctor, and together they decided to make an appointment for me to see a Sir Harold Gillies.

During that era plastic surgery was considered to be the domain of quacks and make-up artists and those involved in it were accused of turning operating theatres into beauty shops. A judgement which in my opinion is unfair as plastic surgery is vital to many people. It was even used in the treatment of bullet wounds during the Great War.

Sir Harold Gillies had trained at Aldershot in a unit set up to treat facial casualties from the Somme in 1916. Gillies had learned much from the Somme casualties and he made many discoveries of his own. One of the most important of his discoveries was that of the tube pedicle. The pedicle attached skin from parts of the body and by this tube Gillies was able to graft skin from parts of the body in stages.

Eventually we received an appointment to see Sir Harold Gillies in Harley Street, London. We stayed at Grandma's house the night before we caught the train to London.

I recall the train to London was full of soldiers from Kinmel Camp in North Wales. They were kind to us and offered my Mother a seat. The soldier near the window sat me on his knee and gave me candy sweets. Some of the soldiers were Americans as by that time the Americans had joined the war due to the Japanese bombing Pearl Harbour. As we were travelling near London one of the soldiers went into the narrow corridor of the train to watch a Luftwaffe plane which he said had lost its way back to Germany. I watched the plane too as it flew over our train. After a long journey, we arrived in London and went to Harley Street.

As I remember it we were shown into a room where Sir Harold Gillies was sitting behind a brown desk. All of the furniture in the room was brown.

Sir Harold Gillies, a tall, thin man who had a bow at his collar was very polite to my Mother and informed her that the operations would cost over £100 to which my Mother responded, 'No!' in those days £100 was a lot of money and we did not have the National Health Service. He suggested that I should be referred to a Mr Emlyn Lewis who had trained under Mr Gillies and had operated on badly burned American and British fighter pilots. My Mother agreed to his proposal.

I do not remember how long we waited for the appointment to see Mr. Emlyn Lewis but I had to go back to the usual routine of school and of being made fun of. At home one of my Aunties was also very unkind to me and would constantly say that if I cried they would chop off my head. She was married to my Father's youngest brother and they would come to see my parents a lot. This aunty would even wake me up during the night and tell me my head would be chopped off. What she said frightened me a lot as I actually believed her. My Mother also acted strangely during the night as she would wake me up, take me downstairs and hold me tight when my Father was shouting at her. I think that they must have been drinking during these times. During the day times my Mother continued to give the three of us ice cold baths because she had the idea that they were good for us but I do not think that they were because my sister ended up very ill with Pneumonia. However she did recover despite there being no Penicillin in those days.

At Christmastime I was in the school Carol Service. I stood on the stage wearing a lovely yellow organza dress and shiny black patent shoes which Grandma had bought for me. Previously, Grandma and my father had argued because he would not buy me anything. On the stage, I held hands with Richard and he did his best to prevent the other children making fun of me. While we were all singing the Christmas carol 'We three Kings of Orient are' I looked down from the stage at the audience where I saw Richard's Father. I immediately let go of Richard's hand but the teacher told Richard to continue holding my hand, which he did. After the service had ended, I sat alone on the stage steps. An older girl walked passed me and called out to me, 'You are a devil child'. Fortunately I didn't know then what that meant. After that day I never saw Richard again.

Gloucester Royal Infirmary

We received a letter to say that we had an appointment to see a Mr Emlyn Lewis which arrived just before Christmas. We were living in Dyserth in a cottage on the second hill. It was snowing very heavily and my Father even fell into a seven foot snow drift!

Soon after the letter arrived, my Mother took me to Gloucester Royal Infirmary. We travelled from Prestatyn on the train and I made friends with a little girl and we ran along the narrow train corridor to the end where we reached the last door which was open and we looked out onto the railway line. We had a terrible fright and we ran back to my Mother in the carriage and tried to tell her what had happened. Once again my Mother was not very pleased and told me I could have been killed.

We arrived at the hospital to see Mr Lewis who was surrounded by a lot of different people including doctors and students. Mr Lewis was sitting on a chair and pulled me towards him. He was a short, broad man with black hair which was parted at the centre and he had thick rimmed glasses on. He peered into my face and then asked me my name. I told him my name and he asked me again. I repeated my name but he started to make fun of me. He then asked where I lived and I told him 'Dyserth' but he said he had never heard of the place so he asked me again but when I tried to tell him he just made fun of me and asked sharply, 'What kind of a place is that?'

Even now, I can still feel the shock of his responses to me.

I expected school kids to make fun of me but I did not expect the Specialist to make fun of me. However, I could not cry because my

Mother had already threatened me with the hair brush if I cried. Mr Lewis turned to my Mother and asked, 'Who did this surgery?' my Mother said, 'Chester and Liverpool'. Mr Lewis said, "I think they operated with a knife and fork, I have never seen such a mess!"

I will admit her into hospital and I will put the whole lot down'. He also told my Mother that I had a double Irish man's lower lip. He kept pulling me backwards and forwards like a doll. Then he told me to go out with the Nurse who then took me into another room. I was on my own for a few minutes and then the door opened and some people came in and I saw the worst facial sights.

The men who came in were burns victims; two of the men had no noses at all and one had his arm attached to his forehead. They were all very badly scarred. I found out that they had been fighter pilots.

In those days we didn't have television and I had never seen anything like this before so it was a terrible shock to me to see such awful sights. One of the men asked me, 'Have you been to see the big chief?' I thought that their injuries did not hurt them because they were laughing and they spoke very kindly to me. At that moment the Nurse came back into the room with my Mother who told me that I was to stay in the hospital. I was eight years old at the time and I was taken straight to the children's ward. My Mother told me to be good and not to cry and then she left me and I was put into bed by the Nurse.

I started to think about the burned pilot that I had seen at the clinic so the next morning I decided to find him. The Ward Sister Shannon was busy with the other Nurses doing dressings on other children and one little girl was screaming because the Nurses were holding her down and she was shouting, 'Don't hurt me. I'm only little'.

I crept away through the ward door and made my way to the men's ward. I walked down the ward in my night clothes and I found him sitting in a chair by his bed. I said 'Hello' to him and sat on his knee. At that moment the Ward Sister came down the ward talking to each man. When she saw me sitting on a patient's knee she was shocked and asked "Well, what are you doing here?" I didn't answer but the man said, 'Leave her, Sister. I'll take her back to the ward'.

The patient had his arm attached to his side by a pedicle graft. In the men's ward there was a terrible smell of burnt flesh and awful sights. But there was music playing on a gramophone and some of the patients were playing cards and generally the men seemed to be quite happy. One man was covered from head to toes in white bandages.

Back on the children's ward, the children seemed to be crying all of the time. I do not remember seeing any of the Mums or Dads, as they were only allowed to visit at weekends. I did not have any visitors at any time.

Whenever the parents had been to visit their children they would bring presents for them. After the parents had left then I would go and take away any toys hide the presents away. One weekend a little girl was given a very pretty little doll's pram. After her parents had gone, I stole it from her and she became very upset. When the Staff Nurse found it in my locker with all the other things I had taken, I got into trouble. I still kept leaving the ward to visit the men's ward and on one occasion the pilot brought me back to the children's ward after the Nurses had been looking everywhere for me. The Children's ward Sister was very strict and she sat me on a tall cabinet and told me that if I left the ward again she would put me in a cot. The pilot was going to have his operation that day and I never saw him again.

Mr. Emlyn Lewis continued to make his ward rounds with his entourage and he would ask me my name and continued to make fun of me. On the Christmas Eve that I was there a Nurse sat on my bed and asked me what I wanted for Christmas. I said that I wanted the burnt man and I wanted to go to the men's ward but the Nurse said that I couldn't have that. There were a lot of people singing Christmas Carols and I just felt that I wanted to cry but I was frightened in case I got a hiding. When Christmas Day arrived the Nurses seemed very happy. There was a lot of kissing going on. We all had Christmas dinner and then the visitors arrived. Parents were giving their children Christmas presents but I only had what was in a little stocking.

Later on during the operation I had a lot of teeth removed. I began to feel so unwell that I had to be moved to the women's ward. It turned out that I had Chicken Pox. I felt quite happy to be on the women's ward because the women spoiled me. However, I saw some awful sights there too, such as victims of burns. I tried to go on 'walk - about' from there but a Nurse caught me trying to find my way to the men's ward and I got into trouble with the Ward Sister.

One day I heard all of the patients talking about a person who was going to be hanged for murder. I did not know who they were talking about so I asked one of the patients who told me that I was going with the person who was to be hanged. I was very upset and frightened and I thought that it was because of my mouth and I thought that no-one liked me, except the fighter pilot.

At last my Mother came to take me home. I was very weak on my legs. I began to have nightmares because I was worried in case I would be taken away and hanged. I slept with my sister and I told her that they were going to hang me so we decided to run away. We took some things and some food in a small case. We walked out in the dark and decided to go to my Grandma's house in Prestatyn.

Soon my Mother discovered that we were missing and caught up with us by the Dyserth Waterfalls. I got a hiding and I cried to my Mother, 'I do not want to be hanged'. My Mother didn't know what I was talking about so I told her what the patient had said to me and my mother explained that she had been teasing me and told me not to be so silly.

Another day we went to Grandma's in Prestatyn but I did something to upset Grandfather so he belted me and locked me up in the cupboard. My Grandfather and my Mother's temper were frightening.

Later, we moved to live in a cottage in Dyserth called RAXANA, Bryn y Felin. It was during this time I began to feel very ill and I stopped going to school. Suddenly, one day, I collapsed and I could not move my arms or my legs. I was diagnosed as suffering from Poliomyelitis (Infantile Paralysis). I didn't go into hospital but I was in a bed downstairs in the front room and a Nurse visited every day to attend to me. I felt ill and frightened because I could not move. My Father used to come downstairs early to shave but he would not speak to me. I tried to get him to speak but he would not, he just ignored me completely. I remember feeling very hurt by that.

I remember hearing people having conversations about the war and at that time Guy Gibson, a pilot, was busy bouncing bombs in 1943. The Dambusters were a hurriedly assembled squadron of young pilots who had been training for two months. They were then told that their mission was to bring the industrial powerhouse of Hitler's third Reich to a standstill. Their weapon was to be Barnes Wallis revolutionary bouncing bomb and the only way it could be used effectively was by flying no more than 60 feet above reservoirs lined with anti-air craft defences. It was a success.

While I was still recovering from Poliomyelitis we moved back to live in Prestatyn with Grandma. Her daughters were not very pleased about that because it meant more kids in the house making a lot of noise. I was determined to walk again and someone brought me some callipers. I refused to put them on but my Father took no notice and ignored me. I did not realise it at the time but he did me a good turn. If he had been a loving father he would have encouraged me to put the callipers on. I dragged my body around the furniture and no-one took any notice. I kept massaging my legs at the top of the stairs and then I would fall down continually. Someone used to carry me to the clinic and I would have physiotherapy but I remained very weak in my limbs. I missed school for a whole twelve months.

I started having nightmares again. I dreamt that I was running along the sea wall and the moon turned into a burnt face and I could hear a man's voice saying, 'Look at my face'. I turned around to see a RAF pilot with a badly burned face. Then I would wake up and shout to my Mother. On one occasion my parents came to me and I said, 'Please put the light on because I'm having a nightmare' but my Father had his belt and slapped me and said 'No!' He said that if I did not stay in bed I would get a good hiding. As they went out of the bedroom my Mother said something to my Father but he replied that I had to learn to sleep in the dark. I realise now that even during that incident the Lord was with me. I was crying under the bed clothes and suddenly the room was filled with light because the people next door were going to bed and their bedroom light shone straight into my bedroom. I know that the Lord hears the cries of children. Now, I am reminded of the words of James Montgomery written in 1818 'Prayer is the burden of a sigh, the falling of a tear. The upward glancing of an eye, when none but God is near.'

Conversations about war continued around me and I heard that Mussolini had brought Italy into the war on Hitler's side. With forces controlling almost the whole Mediterranean he was threatening Egypt next.

Eventually, I was well enough to go back to school but I discovered that Richard had left. Some of the children there continued to make my life feel like hell and I actually missed being in hospital very much. I cried to Grandma and told her about the children at school and she told my Father but he took no notice.

Soon we received a letter asking us to go back to the hospital and I was over the moon with excitement. My Mother took me in and I was admitted to the children's ward. Mr Emlyn Lewis examined my mouth and he continued to make fun of me but by then I did not mind. I made a private, conscious decision that I was going to fight Mr. Emlyn Lewis.

Some of my memories of the hospital include a little boy of about five years old who was admitted to the ward. I asked him if the children at his school made fun of him and he said 'yes'. He was crying because his Mother had left him so I told him that Mr Lewis would also make fun of him. When he heard that he started to cry out even more, crying, 'Mummy, Mummy, Mummy' but I told him that he would not see his Mother for a long time. By that time he was falling on the floor crying. I said to him, 'If you cry when Mr Lewis makes fun of you I will give you a good hiding - we have got to fight Mr Lewis'. The poor boy was almost hysterical and I started to feel sorry for him so I told him, 'You will not want Mummy by the time you go home. I will take you everywhere with me.' I even used to take him into the men's ward to see the RAF pilots.

I had two more operations but I got into a lot of trouble because I kept going on what the staff called 'walk-about' and I even removed the rubber sheets out of the other children's beds for some reason. The Sister-in-charge found out that I was the one who went into the other wards. Sadly, one day a Nurse gave me a bath and told me that I would be scarred for life.

In the forties burns victims were not separated from other patients. I remember on one occasion lying on my back between two little girls called Shirley and Sheila. They had been burnt because they had been wearing inflammable nighties. All night long they were crying and moaning. For those children there was the dread of daily dressings. The children were usually held down by the nursing staff and their screams were terrible.

For some time after my operations I would have to lie down flat on my back with splints on my arms. Lying down for long periods of time like this would make me very weak as I could not eat food and I could only have fluids.

Eventually I went home but I did not want to leave the hospital because I felt so happy there. Grandma would not allow me to go back to the Convent School and so I was sent to Bodnant School in Marine Road, Prestatyn. This felt like going from the frying pan into the fire! My life felt like it was almost intolerable! The school was mixed and I was continually made fun of, kicked and hit by the other children. Sometimes the Welsh and English children would fight each other and then they would leave me alone. My sister and brother also attended the same school. However, my sister had a lot of friends and she was also very clever. At that time my brother was only five years old.

I hated going to that school and on one occasion I nearly had a stand-up fight with one of the teachers, Miss Ceri Ellis. I had not wanted to go to school at all that day because it was cold and I was experiencing discomfort from chilblains. During the morning play time all of the children went outside but I stayed in the class room near to the cast iron stove which had a metal guard rail around it. Miss Ellis saw me in the classroom and told me to go outside but I would not move away from the stove. She started to pull me away but I resisted her so she sent someone to get Mr Jones, the headmaster. He walked in with the cane which they used in those days. I still would not move away from the stove and he threatened me with the cane. I pushed my hands into the wire of the fireguard and suddenly I saw the faces of the pilots and I could smell the burns and I started to cry. By that time playtime was over and the children came back into the classroom.

I had one friend there at that school and she would help me in class but I refused to write. One day we were each given our school report to take home for our parents. On the way home, I opened mine and then threw it over the railway bridge. When I got home my Father was already reading my sister's report which was very good, as she had got 100% in all subjects. My Father turned to me and asked me for my report but I told him that they hadn't given me a report. He said that I was lying and thrashed me so hard that I could not sit down for a week.

In the year 1944 the war in Europe was over. On the 30th April that year Hitler committed suicide. The Prime Minister, Winston Churchill spoke to the nation, no longer steeling us for yet more hardships and not thundering threats against the Nazis. The voice that had given strength to defy Hitler was with deep emotion as he told us all that we wanted to hear. After six long years of hardship and misery the war with Germany was over. My relatives went to celebrate at the Victoria pub leaving Granddad in charge of the children. During the night I got very thirsty and went downstairs for a drink. Granddad belted me for getting out of bed. I was very upset and tried to pull tears into my mouth.

One day the Headmaster Mr Jones came into the classroom to announce the death of Frank Gilmore who had been killed by a bull. The bull was kept in the farm on Gronant Road by the duck pond. Apparently Frank's Grandfather had brought the bull up from birth. Mr Jones told the class that no-one was to go to the farm, but guess who went to the farm after school? We did! As children, we had usually played in that area. There was a small holding by the duck pond and we used to look through the bars of the building where the bull was kept. There was a horrible noise like an electric generator. The bull was put down. I missed seeing the bull with his huge head.

Around Christmas time in 1945 when I was nine years old I was running down Marine Road after the school day had ended because some children were trying to catch me. As I went through the front door into the hall there was a very big Christmas tree, well over six feet tall. The ceilings of our house were very high. I stared at the tree and thought to myself, 'I wonder if Father Christmas will visit me?' When it was bedtime on Christmas Eve I wondered again if Father Christmas would come to me. On that night we went to bed with my Father's socks with the usual hole in them. I was lying awake when the door opened and Father Christmas appeared! He was quite well built and had a very pleasant face. I knew that it wasn't my Father because of his figure. He smiled at me and then he left the room very quietly. We didn't have many presents (usually second hand things). After this event, I asked my uncles if they were Father Christmas but they responded to me by saying "Don't be daft!" The Father Christmas that I saw I now believe was the Spirit of the Lord and I believe he was an angel.

However, we didn't have a very pleasant Christmas day that year. My Mother had a row with my Grandma so she told my Mother that only Louie was to go to her party. Every year Grandma would have a big party at Christmas but on this occasion my Mother said, 'If the others cannot go then Louie cannot go' so we ended up with just bread and butter to eat.

As the New Year unfolded, my Mother was expecting another baby. I remember suffering with the pain of very bad and broken chilblains. One of the teachers in school lined four of us up for the cane because we had been talking in class. She struck two of the children and then it was my turn. I was asking God not to let her hit my hands, only my legs but when I reached up to her she said, 'Hands out'. When I held my hands out, the teacher exclaimed, 'Oh, your hands!' and immediately told me to sit down. She wrote a note to my Mother instructing her to take me to the doctors with regard to my chilblains. When my Mother read the note she told me to go to the surgery.

There was an early evening surgery on Victoria Road, Prestatyn which was run by Doctor Tudor John Griffiths and his son, Dr John. All the children were nervous of Dr Tudor, the old doctor, because he was very strict and he had a very deep voice and was often what was then described as 'four ways to the wind' through having too much alcohol to drink. I had asked my Mother if I could see the young doctor but my Father said that if I went home without seeing the doctor I would get a good hiding. So I ran down Victoria Road to the surgery. In those days the doctor's surgery did not have a receptionist to organise the people and related administration. Patients would just have to wait until it was their turn.

On this occasion, the room was full of people but I found myself a corner seat. Then the door opened and a farm worker came out and said, 'Four ways to the wind' and walked out. Then I heard the doctor's deep voice shouting, 'Next, I haven't got all night!'

A mother who was looking very anxious along with her son went in to see the doctor. Then I heard the doctor shout, 'Where is your sense, boy, in your big toe?' The boy came out shuffling in his boots followed by his mother, looking nervous. Eventually all of the people had their turn at seeing the doctor except for me. I was still sat in

the corner. The doctor came out to lock the main door. He was bending down to pull the lower bolt across when he turned his head and saw me. He said, 'What on earth are you doing here?'

As he came towards me I thought that he was going to hit me but instead he lifted me up and sat me on a high chest of drawers. Then he told me to open my mouth but I was trying to tell him about my hands. Then he said, 'I will see your mother'. As I left the surgery he shouted after me, "'Snow fire' for your chilblains! 'Snow fire' was a kind of green soap but I did not think it helped relieve the chilblains at all. Sundays were especially difficult with the painful chilblains on my hands as we had to deliver newspapers in the bitter cold and rain or even snow sometimes

It was soon to be my tenth birthday and I had wanted a doll for a long time but there never seemed to be any money available. I don't remember any of us in my family having birthday cards or presents and I have never really liked birthdays. I have never enjoyed singing the 'happy birthday' song. However, at the end of March my Mother came home with a baby girl and told me that it was the doll that I had always wanted. I took Stephanie off her and took her up three flights of stairs and I just believed what my mother said and I treated her like a doll. I didn't want anyone else to take her away. I wanted to take her to show Grandma and I also wanted to show the children in the park so I took her outside and my Mother was cross with me.

My baby sister had to sleep in a drawer while the four of us slept in one bed with my Mother. Soon after this we moved to a flat opposite the Fish and Chip Shop at the top of Prestatyn and then I became very ill. An Irish family lived next to us. They had a lot of children and at first we would all fight with each other but one little girl called Noreen made friends with me because she thought I was a good fighter. We both took our baby sisters out in their prams and we also tipped the poor babies upside down in their prams! The main reason that happened though was because the second hand pram that my Mother got for my sister was far too big and too heavy for me to handle. Fortunately the babies survived without any injury.

My Mother had suffered from Arthritis since she had been 19 years old during the time that she was expecting my sister. Mother often had to use two walking sticks. I was very afraid of my Mother as she would lose her temper and she seemed to lose it quite frequently.

My Mother's temper grew steadily worse. On day she sent me to the shop called E. B. Jones for some groceries but because they could not understand what I was saying, they gave me the wrong items. When I arrived back home with the wrong items my Mother gave me a good hiding.

It was around this time that I became friends with a girl called Elsie Corbet who lived in Penisadre Farm, opposite the Scala Cinema in Prestatyn. The farm was built in 1575 and it was demolished in 1963 to make the shopping precinct which still makes me feel sad.

I loved the farm and we would often play on the poor old horse. One day I took my brother to the farm and I put him in the haystack while I was playing with Elsie. My brother fell asleep and meantime the farm worker started to remove the hay with a pitchfork. He felt a bump and pulled my brother out of the hay. He was very cross with me because he could have seriously injured my brother.

On another occasion I had been instructed to go to the shop for some fish but I forgot to go. When I returned home my Mother was very cross with me and gave me another hiding. We were sent to Sunday school at the Church of England Church in Prestatyn High Street. I did not like that place but my Father insisted that we should go so that they could go to bed on Sunday afternoons. So I had to go to Sunday school or I would get a hiding from my parents. My Father would give us each a penny to put into the Church collection. During one of my visits there I tore up the hymn books in the church and I also spat on one of the teachers and told her that I hated her.

The teacher reported me to the Sunday School Superintendent who was Miss Roberts. She came to talk to me just as I was about to tear up another book. I said to her, 'Don't tell my Father or he will thrash me' and she said, 'I want to take you home with me.' Miss Roberts was very kind to me and I got on well with her. I did some jobs for her and she gave me sixpence and told me that I was to be an angel in the Christmas nativity play. I didn't want to be in the play but when I told my Mother she said that I would get a good hiding if I didn't do as I was told.

One day I woke up with a sore throat and I was shivering but my Mother made me go to the shop. Once again I came home from the shop with the wrong items and my Mother lost her temper with me and hit me across the face. By this time I was beginning to feel really ill and I started to cry. My Father said that if I didn't stop he would give something to cry about. I was supposed to go to church for a rehearsal for the play but I told my Mother that I did not want to go because my throat felt as though it was on fire. I was told that if I didn't go I would get the belt so off I went. At Church the lady told me to get undressed but I felt too ill to move. The other children had got undressed and were ready. Then the lady looked at me and said, 'Louie Baker, you are still not undressed'. She started to undress me but when she took my dress off she shouted, 'Oh my goodness, child, whatever is the matter with you? You are covered in a rash all over your body'. A lady took me home to the flat at the top of Prestatyn High Street and told my Mother that I seemed to be ill. Mother was not very pleased but contacted the District Nurse (at that time you still had to pay to see a doctor). The Nurse arrived, put me into bed and then sent for the doctor who told my Mother that I had Scarlet Fever. By that time I was very ill. The doctor told my Mother to light a fire in the grate. When the doctor came the next day I was much worse (we did not have the benefit of Penicillin then). I was taken to St. Asaph Isolation hospital in an ambulance on the Doctor's orders. The hospital seemed strange to me and I did not like it. The ward was stark because everything was white and the ward Sister was very strict. The children there were quite different from the children that I had met in Gloucester. The Nurses sang a song to us that I have never forgotten:

"I had Scarlet Fever, I had it very bad.

They wrapped me up in blankets; they put me in a van.

The van was very rocky, I nearly tumbled out.

When the door was opened I gave a shout.

Mummy, Mummy, take me home, I have been here a bit too long.

A Nurse comes in with a red hot poultice

And slaps it down and takes no notice.

'Oh', said the patient, 'that's too hot',

'Oh', said the Nurse, 'I am sure it's not'. Goodbye, Isolation ward,

Goodbye, all the Nurses and the jolly doctor too.

The Nurses also told me that I was from 'Press my hat in' not Prestatyn. My Mother came to see me just once and I remember her looking at me through the window outside.

At last I went home but I was very weak and could hardly walk. The school told my Mother that I was not able to sit the 11+ exam and I did not attend school for long time after my illness. It was at this time that my Father was taken ill with a burst Duodenal Ulcer. The doctor would not come to see him at home so my Mother went to tell Miss Ceri Ellis, the teacher at my school. She came to see my Father and then she persuaded her own doctor to visit my Father at home. He immediately arranged for my Father to be admitted into St. Asaph hospital. I was ten years old. On one occasion, I was feeding my baby sister with the bottle while at the same time I was watching my Father lying on the floor in agony. I stopped feeding my sister and I went upstairs and knelt down and I said to God, 'If I say gentle Jesus six times will you make my Father better?' I repeated 'Gentle Jesus, meek and mild, look upon a little child, suffer me to come to Thee'. The Lord heard my prayers because my Father recovered. I believe that the Lord hears the prayers of little girls.

Chepstow Hospital

Soon afterwards, we received a letter from St. Lawrence Hospital in Chepstow, South Wales. Mr Emlyn Lewis had transferred from Gloucester to Chepstow. I was very excited as we stood on the platform at Prestatyn Station watching the old steam train coming in. As usual the train was full of soldiers from Kinmel Camp. When we arrived at our destination, I was admitted to the children's ward and then my Mother returned home to Prestatyn. The nursing staff at Chepstow had changed but they soon discovered what I was like as I went back to my old ways. I went on walk-about, wandering off to look for the pilots. The wards smelt strongly of antiseptic and there were flowers on the tables, their scent fighting a losing battle with the hospital smells. I found the men's ward which smelt of ether mixed with a different kind of odour, burns. There were horrifying rows of beds with mummy like forms on drips and sling pulleys and cages. There was also a piano wireless. The men's ward was in a Nissen hut. Some of the men had no proper features left. They had raw, red flesh with flaps of skin hanging loose. There were patients with pedicle grafts and swollen, misshapen features, holes where there should have been eyes; an opening gap was all that was left of one mouth. One day when a Nurse caught me wandering about she took me back to the children's ward where I received a good telling off from the ward Sister.

Once again I was in a bed between two little girls, one called Shirley and the other Valerie. I remembered Valerie from the last time I had been in hospital. Soon I became so ill that I was transferred to the women's ward. The women patients were kind to me and listened to my singing at night. They each gave me a penny and I would go around to each of the patients in the beds to collect my money.

But one night I had a terrible shock! I saw a lot of commotion at the end of the ward. There were screens around the bed nearest to the door but I wanted a penny from whoever was in that bed. As I walked towards the bed the other patients told me not to go behind the screens but I did not listen to them. Suddenly I was looking down at the worst sight I have ever seen in my life. I cannot describe what I was looking at it was so awful. The patient had a badly burnt face, chest and arms. She had no nose or eyes, just slits and holes in her face and all of her colours were grey and red.

As I stood looking at this female patient with horrific injuries I heard a voice which came from somewhere within her say,

'Don't be frightened'. She had no lips, only a big gap and would not have been able to speak in the usual ways.

At that time I was eleven years old and I had very little understanding. I thoughtlessly asked her, 'Can I have my penny?' One of the Nurses quickly came to the bed and shouted at me to go back to my bed.

Later on, I discovered that the patient's name was Francis. She had been a ballet dancer and had been engaged to an RAF pilot. Francis had received a telegram to say that her fiancé had been killed in action. On receiving the telegram she had passed out with shock at the awful news and then had fallen into the fire where she had been very badly burned.

I saw Francis many, times during my stay in hospital.

I became friends with a young girl called Joyce who was also on the women's ward. We went 'walk-about' together to the other wards, much to the disapproval of the ward Sister. One day the ward Sister informed me that I was to be moved back to the children's ward. I received this news quite badly as it would be so much harder for me to get to the pilot's ward from there. So I told Sister that I did not want to leave the women's ward and she said, 'You are only eleven years old' but I argued with her. I asked "So why can't Joyce go as well?" Sister had replied "Joyce is older than you. She is thirteen."

I felt very annoyed and I also felt jealous because Joyce would be able to get to the men's ward and I would not. I was also furious because I would miss the singing of lots of wartime songs including: 'Run, rabbit, run', 'Blue moon' and 'You are my sunshine.'

During the morning I had another shock because the patient in the bed next to me lost her temper when Mr Lewis came with his entourage to examine the patients. She was not happy about the surgery that Mr Lewis had performed on her face and she shouted at him. Mr Lewis took a step back and said, 'Do you think I am God?' Then she pulled the pedicle graft from her side and threw it across the floor. The Nurses ran to her with screens.

Next it was my turn. Mr Lewis came to inspect me and he asked me if I was pleased with what he had done. I replied that I was not a bit pleased. The Sister was very cross and sent me off to the children's ward. When I arrived on the ward the Sister told me told me that I was not to leave the ward and then, what was even worse, she told me that I was to join the other children for afternoon school.

The teacher of afternoon school was a tall lady with a dark costume and wore her hair in a bun. I hated her on sight and I refused to take up my pen. She told me again to start writing but again I refused and then she became very cross with me. By that time none of the children were writing. The teacher pulled me to my bed and started to shake me. Then I clenched my fist and punched her in the face. She was so furious with me that she slapped me so I kicked her, bit and scratched her. Fortunately for me the Doctor came to my bed, although I thought that he was going to thrash me with his stethoscope. So I said, 'If you thrash me I will tell my Father and he is a policeman'. The Doctor turned to the Sister and asked what was wrong with me. Sister told him that whenever any of the children had spent any time on the women's ward they were always disturbed when they returned to the children's ward. Then the Doctor explained to me "I only want to examine your chest because you are going to theatre in the morning." I did not realise then that it would be one of the worst operations of my life.

I recall one morning, when Mr Lewis had examined me and started asking me questions. He had imitated every word I said and then he had told me that I had a double Irish man's lower lip and that he was going to take my lower lip and attach it into my upper lip because my top lip was very small and too tight.

When I came round from the anaesthetic I couldn't breathe and I had stitches everywhere. Mr Lewis had stitched my lips together and also taken my lower lip into my top lip with what he called an Abbe flap. I also had Elastoplast all over my head and around my face. I had splints on my arms and I couldn't move or breathe and I was very uncomfortable. The Sister and the Doctor tried to help me to breathe. The next morning when Mr Lewis and his entourage came to do the ward round he told the Doctor that the plaster around my face was not tight enough. It was really painful when the Doctor took the plaster off and I dreaded every morning because Mr Lewis kept saying that the plaster was not holding my jaws up.

The poor Doctor used Ethanol to remove the plaster every morning. The staff told me that I was really good because I did not need to be held down while he did this.

My lips were stitched together for five weeks and I had to lie flat on my back until the stitches were removed. By the second week I started to feel very hungry because I had only been given fluids through a very small gap in my lips. I remember that one good thing about being in that situation was that I did not have to go to afternoon school and whenever the teacher came anywhere near me I pretended to be asleep.

Eventually I was encouraged to get up and I was put in a wheelchair. The day came for me to have my next operation which was to open my lips. I made a fuss in the anaesthetics room because I wanted Uncle Norman to put me to sleep as he always made a fuss over the children. Because I did know the anaesthetist who was there, I did not want him to put me to sleep and I told him so. However, the anaesthetist did not put up with any nonsense from me and so I was held down while he put me to sleep.

When I came round from the anaesthetic my mouth was open but I had lots of stitches in my lower and my top lip. I had to lie flat on my back again with splints on my arms and once again I was on fluids. When I was allowed to get up I was very weak and I had to be put in a wheelchair. I remember feeling very hungry and a night Nurse took pity on me and gave me a piece of Fry's Chocolate cream bar.

My bed was between a little boy and a ten year old girl called Sheila Johns. She had been burnt all over her face and body because of her nightdress catching fire. After her operation she was continually moaning. The little boy on my other side had his cleft palate repaired. He was crying because he was hungry so I decided to find him some food. I found some bread and an apple in the kitchen and I told him to swallow it quickly. I was still in the wheelchair and he had splints on his arms so I had to bite the bread and apple for him. I realise now that I could have done a lot of damage but it all turned out well and his operation was a success. On our ward there was a very pretty Staff Nurse called Ann Yates who had jet black curly hair. Unfortunately for me she discovered that I was stealing from the other children. Usually, after visiting time had ended I would take the other children's belongings and hide them away.

The other children used to have a lot of visitors who would bring them nice gifts and I did not have any. One day the Staff Nurse asked me if I would write a letter to my Mother because she was also writing to my Mother but I replied, 'No, I won't write'.

When the little boy was up and about I told him to go to the men's ward and find out if any RAF pilots had come into the ward. He found one new pilot who was covered in bandages from head to toe. I would still go looking for the pilot who I had met when I was eight years old. On one occasion we saw Francis walking around the huts. She was so disfigured in her face that all of the other children started to scream so I hit them.

One day during Mr Lewis's ward round he said that my top lip was too long but he decided to discharge me and let me go home anyway so that I would get stronger for the next operation. However, I had very mixed feelings about going home! When my Mother arrived to take me home she brought me a navy blue coat from Grandma. On my arrival at home I was very restless and kept running round the flat until my Father showed me his belt and sent me to bed. I was having terrible nightmares so my Mother sent me to Grandma's house on Marine Road, Prestatyn.

Grandma always stayed in bed all day as she liked to drink and even had a cupboard beside her bed to keep her drinks in. Once when I was about seven years old Grandma gave me a drink of sherry. Grandma would usually only get out of bed to go to the Victoria pub opposite the park where she would take her dog, Tony. Often, I would go with her too although she would leave me at the door of the pub and then I would go to play in the park. During one of Grandma's visits to the pub, I was in the park playing with some children and we were making houses with the grass. A group of boys were making fun of me just as Grandma was returning home along the path. Grandma often returned home by taxi but on that particular day she had decided to walk. Grandma heard the boys making fun of me. She picked up a stick and hit the boys across the legs which made them jump about and cry out to her saying, 'Sorry, Mrs Baker'.

Most of the children would make dens to play in amongst the hedges in the park. One day when we were playing in the dens that we had made a girl started to make fun of me so I went back to Grandma's house, I found a belt then I went back to the park and gave her a good hiding with the belt.

On another occasion a terrible thing happened. A girl and I were on the swings in the park and we were watching a steam train leaving the station. In those days we played a childish game as whenever a train passed the park all the children would shout, 'Hands off, iron feet off the ground'. On that day we were very high on the swings when we heard the train coming. We took our hands off the swings but the girl went over the top. As the train passed she crashed down on her face and her face was smashed and there was blood everywhere. At that moment my Mother arrived as she was coming to the park to look for me. She thought it was me who had fallen as the girl and I both had the same dresses on.

The family who lived next door to Grandma's house had a daughter called Christine Ash. She was my friend and we played together a lot. Christine's Mother often gave us clothes for my sister and me to wear. I had returned to Bodnant School and I would be sent there wearing Christine's clothes. The other children laughed and made fun because the dresses were too big for me. I was full of hate for the school and refused to co-operate with anyone. My friend Noreen lived next door in the flats at the top of Prestatyn. When bonfire night came Noreen, her sister and I went to the top of the hillside. The girls had new coats on and when we arrived the fire was started. The girls took their coats off and left them on the ground but some boys picked the coats up and threw them on the fire. I was upset and I asked Noreen to give me some punishment because I felt guilty about the girls losing their coats. Noreen slapped my face hard and we then started to fight on the stairs and I won. Noreen decided that I was a good fighter and wanted to start a gang. We decided to call it the 'Baker Gang' and when we met up with the 'Taylor Gang' we did nothing but fight. I was always stealing people's apples, climbing the tree in people's gardens, stealing out of shops and breaking into warehouses and generally getting into a lot of mischief.

Back To Hospital

A letter arrived recalling me to hospital and we followed the usual routine. Mr Lewis examined my mouth. He asked me my name and then imitated every word that I said. He decided that my top lip was too long and that I would have to have two more operations. Francis was still in the women's ward. She had had several operations and pedicle grafts to her face but it still looked horrific. Francis and the pilots still walked around the grounds but if they went too near the children's ward the children used to scream. I couldn't understand why they screamed, this upset me and so I would hit the children.

In between operations I used to go walk-about and I would take the children who could walk with me. We went to some old Nissen huts and I told the children that they were haunted by ghosts. We frightened the life out of each other! I got into a lot of mischief and trouble with the ward Sister. The teacher on the children's ward left me alone after all the trouble she had with me previously. She just gave me a pencil and paper to do what I wanted.

In the year 1948 Aneurin Bevan was in the Labour government and he formed the N.H.S. That was good news for the people of Britain because it meant that they no longer had to pay for medical treatment and it was good news for my Grandma and for my Aunty, who was a music teacher, who no longer had to pay for my operations.

My Mother came to take me home from hospital and told me that I would be going to the Emmanuel Secondary School in Rhyl. I described it as 'my third pit of hell.' I was very unhappy and I did not want to go. But my Mother took me to the school and we went into the Headmaster's office. His name was Mr. Jones and at first he seemed to be a very kind man. My Mother explained why I was so late in the term going to school and he sat me on his knee and talked to me. However, his kind influence was to be short lived because he retired fairly soon afterwards and was replaced by the new headmaster, Mr. Dan Owen. I took an instant dislike to him. I was always late going to school in the mornings and I did not like the prefects. I spat and swore at them and they often reported me to Mr. Owen. I was very unhappy because the other children made fun of me. I missed hospital so much and I refused to co-operate with any of the teachers which got me into more trouble and made me feel that I hated them.

Louie aged 11 years

One day when I arrived home at Grandma's my Mother told me that we were going to live in a new house on the Bryn Rhosyn estate in Prestatyn. The council houses were built in the early 1940's and some of the houses were still being built. The estate was very stark. There were no fancy windows or fancy doors, no television or phones, no trees and no cars. When my parents, two sisters, one brother and I arrived at our new home it was a very stormy night with gales blowing hard. We arrived on a horse and cart from Mr Roberts in Station Street. We only had a very few belongings which included three beds. My sister and I slept together in a small bed which was tied up with string.

At school a new girl arrived in our class. When the teacher called her out I almost fell in love with her! She was beautiful – golden hair done in ringlets and very blue eyes. Her name was Rebecca Cane. I said to God, 'Please let Rebecca become my friend.' The problem was that she was very popular with all the other children in the class, especially the boys. One day some boys were making fun of me and I ended up down on the ground. Then I saw Rebecca walking along with a gang of children.

When Rebecca saw me on the ground she put her hand into my hand and pulled me up and asked, 'What's going on here?'

Then she said, 'From now on you will be my friend' and from that day on Rebecca would stay with me in the playground. The other children were not pleased because Rebecca was very popular and the boys were around her like wasps round a jam pot!

Another girl in my class at school who lived in the same avenue became my very good friend. Her name was Shirley Williams. One day in class a teacher called me up to the front to do a sum and to write it on the board. I could not do it but then Shirley held the correct number of her fingers up to help me. I did not understand so the teacher got cross and then I decided to get undressed. I took off my gymslip, then my blouse, then my vest and I was just about to take down my knickers when the teacher lost her temper with me and showed me the cane. At the same time the boys were going berserk and the noise was terrible. The poor teacher sent for Miss Lewis, the Headmistress, but I ran into the toilets and Shirley came to find where I was. When she found me I cried out, 'I miss hospital so much, I want to go back'. Shirley told me that I could not go back but that she would help me in any way that she could.

Grandma had taught me how to knit and crochet. I enjoyed knitting and I took it to school. We had a Welsh teacher called Glyndwr Richards, who I felt I hated. Whenever it was Welsh class I used to take my knitting out of my bag which would make him furious and then he would send me to Miss Lewis. On my way home from school, after causing a disturbance in the classroom, one boy who was in my class called Grenville Williams was riding towards me on his bike and I said, 'Don't hit me, Grenville, I have had enough for one day'. His answer was, 'Did anyone tell you that you have a nice pair of legs?' He was good friends with Shirley and they tried to help me. They told me, 'You must go to school or your father will belt you'.

One day, as I was walking home from school along the Dyserth railway line three boys grabbed hold of me. Two of the boys held me while the third boy threw stones at me. They wanted to know what the blood was like in my lips. They hit me everywhere but my lips. I managed to get away but my neck and head were bleeding. I shouted at them, 'You've hit me everywhere but my lips. You can't aim right or straight'.

When I arrived home I was washing my face at the kitchen sink when my Mother came in and when she saw the state I was in she lost her temper. I refused to tell her who had attacked me and she shouted, 'Your Father will get it out of you', so I told her who it was. My Mother was in such a rage because my Aunt and my Grandma had paid a lot of money towards my last operations. She grabbed hold of me and took me to the boy's house on the estate. The boy's father came to the door and let us in. My Mother told him what had happened and he was very cross. He called the boy to him and told him to lean over a chair. He pulled the boy's trousers down, took off his belt and thrashed him for a long time. After what seemed like a life time he told the boy to go to his bedroom until the next day. After this, I told my Mother that I thought the boys would kill me but my Mother sent me to school the next day and the boys ignored me.

Usually, on a Saturday afternoon, my friend Shirley and I would go to the pictures at the Scala in Prestatyn High Street, opposite Penisadre Farm. In the days of the silver screen, the Liverpool born pioneer cinematographer Saronie ran the Scala cinema. His real name was James Roberts and he was born in 1972. Apparently, he changed his name by deed poll in 1912 because he felt 'Saronie' would sound a better name in the world of entertainment. He gave his first film show in Prestatyn in January 1899 in Caradoc Community Centre. Eventually in 1913 he took over the Town Hall and converted it into what we now know as the Scala Cinema.

There used to be queues for the performances up Prestatyn High Street. The problem for me was that at the Saturday afternoons shows all the children would not leave me alone. Because there was so much noise and disturbance in the cinema Saronie would turn me out and I would go home. I told my Father but he did not want to know. He hissed at me and told me to get out of his house so I sat in the gutter and waited until someone let me into the house. My father could not stand me in his sight; I was like a red rag to a bull.

One Saturday afternoon Shirley and I went to the Scala Cinema and there was a long queue. Mr Saronie came out to inspect the queue and all the children in it. All the boys shouted, 'Here she is, Mr Saronie'. He took one look at me and said, 'You cannot come in because you cause too much trouble'.

At that moment Shirley said, 'If Louie can't come in then I won't come in', and said to me, 'Come on, we will go to the Palladium Cinema'. (The Palladium was built in 1920, across the road from the Scala and, sadly, was demolished in 1979 and Boots, the Chemist, was built there.) Shirley and I no sooner sat down in the Palladium than all the children from the Scala ran through the doors. I felt my heart drop but they stayed quiet so Mr Saronie lost out.

One Saturday afternoon when we were in the Palladium a message came to me saying a girl called Elsie was going to thrash me. We left the cinema and were walking up the High Street and there was Elsie, waiting for me. I knew by her body language that I was in for a fight so, as usual, I started to ask God to help me win the fight. Elsie proceeded to punch me and hit out at me and all the other children were shouting. I started to realise that I was losing the fight so I sent an SOS to God to help me. Then suddenly, I felt her body relax under me and then I made one last attempt and with all my strength pushed her through a shop window. The shop was opposite a church and there was glass everywhere. Two ladies ran from across the road towards us and wanted to know what on earth was going on. Elsie was crying and I was thanking God because I had won the fight!

The Teenage Years

At that time my Mother was expecting another baby which I didn't feel pleased about. I heard my mother discussing how to have a miscarriage but she didn't terminate the baby. Poor Charles, he was a Christmas baby and my Father woke me up at 4:00am to help clear up after the birth. I was fourteen years old. Charles was born in the front room in the house My Mother kept wanting chips late at night and my Father always sent me to get them.

I remember the Ffrith in Prestatyn was a very popular bathing and pleasure centre when I was a teenager. There were Pierottes in the open air or in a marquee. One day two friends and I went to the Ffrith to see the show but we had no money to pay the entrance fee. I decided to get into the show for free and after we had sneaked in we sat on the grass at the side of the chairs. At the end of the show a man asked if anyone would like to say a little act or do a dance but no one responded so I ran up on the stage to say a rhyme:

> *"Incy wincy spider*
>
> *Went up the water spout,*
>
> *Out came the raindrops*
>
> *And washed the spider out.*
>
> *Out came the sunshine and*
>
> *Drove the rain away*
>
> *So incy wincy spider went up the spout again."*

The problem was no one could understand what I was saying. The manager ran up onto the stage and shouted at me to leave immediately. I will never forget the expressions on the adults' faces and all the children were falling about laughing.

One evening, after school, my friend Shirley asked me to go with her to a lady's house that lived on the estate. We went to a dancing class run by Mrs Ivy Kay who had come from Liverpool during the war. Her father's hairdressing shop had been hit and completely destroyed by a German bomb. Ivy never left Prestatyn and ran a successful dancing school for all the children of the town, including children on my estate. As we arrived at the house Mrs Ivy was in the middle of teaching the little girls to do a back bend right over until your hands touched the floor.

The teacher wanted a girl to bend right over in the shape of a 'C'. However, no one in the class could back-bend in the way she wanted. I was watching the girls trying to do it from the corner of the room and decided to have a try myself. I managed to bend immediately into the shape that Mrs Ivy had requested although she did not seem very pleased with me. I got the impression that she could not even see that I was there judging by her attitude as she chose to ignore what I was doing. Mrs. Ivy kept on instructing the rest of the class, 'Oh, no, repeat the exercise again'. My friend Shirley kept asking her to 'Look at Louie'. Eventually, Mrs Kay decided to take me home while the other girls continued to practice. On arrival she explained to my Mother that she wanted me in the dance team, including acrobatics and dancing. My Mother refused this because she couldn't afford the shilling for lessons. In response Mrs Kay said, 'never mind the money, I want her in the team'. So I started my dance lessons for free. After some weeks we started lessons in the dance hall in Bastion Road Scout Hut, Prestatyn. I learned to dance quickly and loved every minute of it. In addition to this I also did Morris dancing at the carnivals and I was able to do the splits at my first attempt. I could also do high kicks so that my legs touched my nose. We also did concerts and carnivals at the Lido central beach, which is known now as the Nova Centre. I was placed at the front of the Morris dancers because of having a nice pair of legs.

As time went by I was enjoying the shows and concerts. On one occasion I had a big boil on my nose and while I was on stage dancing, the boil burst and the discharge went all over everyone during the acrobatics. On another occasion, I was performing acrobatics with the team at the Lido one night when I made a terrible mistake in the air and everyone came tumbling down like a pack of cards. I could never remember my right hand from my left hand and the teacher, Mrs Kay, was so cross with me that she asked me to leave the dance team for good.

Often, my brother and I would go stealing apples from the trees in people's gardens. Sometimes we would go during a thunderstorm. I would put the apples inside my clothes and we would run home down the railway line and then hide the apples, usually at my cousin's house.

After school I would usually go on the bus to Woolworths and steal anything that I could get away with. I hid the things that I stole and no-one found out so I got away with it, for a time. One night my Father found some of the things that I had hidden away in an old shed and I got into a lot of trouble and I also got a good hiding.

I would also steal from most shops and on one occasion, my cousin and I entered a warehouse and stole a lot of invoicing papers.

I used to travel to school on the bus and that was very difficult because all of the children from Prestatyn were on the Rhyl bus which usually meant trouble. The bus conductor didn't want me on the bus either because I usually caused a disturbance although I do have one fond memory of the day I gave an old man my seat and he gave me a sixpence for my trouble. However, on many occasions I had to walk to school because I was put off the bus because of my bad behaviour. Sometimes, I would help myself to my Father's drink before going to school and so I would start to argue and fight with the prefects as soon as I arrived. Because they could not understand the awful things that I was saying, I often got away with it! One morning as I arrived at school I swore at a prefect and she said to me, 'You are swearing! I will report you to Mr. Cowen, the Headmaster' so I ran out of the school and headed down to the beach. As I was walking along I met a girl who was from the same school as me and she was smoking a cigarette. The girl taught me to smoke and we both played truant from school for many days.

On another occasion I was in a music lesson and I did well in the test which was a quiz. The teacher came to my desk and asked me how I knew the answers to the questions. I tried to explain but he walked away as I he could understand what I was saying. There were two boys behind me who started to make fun of me so I grabbed them by their hair and banged their heads together! One boy screamed and the teacher came back with his cane and brought it down with a terrific force. He then told me to get out of his class so I went to the toilet and smoked a cigarette. After some time my friend Shirley came to look for me and said, 'What are you doing?' I said, 'I want to go to the hospital', but we decided not to go in the end.

I used to do a lot of knitting and I often took my knitting into the Welsh class because I hated the teacher. But on this occasion, as he began to teach I brought out my knitting along with a cigarette, which I had done just to annoy him. He became furious with me and told me to go to Miss Lewis, the Headmistress. I went to her but she did not look very pleased to see me and told me off severely.

One day when I arrived home from school there was a very pretty tailor made coat waiting for me. A man used to go around the estate with clothes in a suitcase to sell. He charged two shillings in old money. I asked my Mother if I could have the coat but she said, 'NO'. I asked God to let me have the coat and then I asked my Mother once again if I could have the coat. She refused again and told me to speak to my Father. On the Saturday I was alone in the house and I was looking at the coat and then my Father came in 'four sheets to the wind' as he had been drinking too much.

As my Mother had told me to ask my father about the coat I had said a prayer and I had asked God to make my Father say 'yes' about the coat. Later on, as he had come through the door and he was drunk I had made sure that there was a safe distance and enough space between us before deciding to 'take the bull by the horns' and ask him 'Can I have that coat?' He grabbed hold of me and to my amazement he said, 'Yes!' In addition to this he took a wad of notes out of his pocket and gave me half of them. I think he must have also won a bet on the horses! After this, I went outside to wait for my Mother. When I told her about the coat and the money that my Father had given me she was surprised but she took the money off me and told me that I needed pants, vests and socks and said, 'Never mind the coat'. Then we went off to the shops in Prestatyn. Later on when we were at the table having our tea my Father woke up after he had been asleep in the armchair. He came to the table, hung his belt over his chair and asked my Mother if she had taken his money out of his pocket as he couldn't remember giving it to me. My Mother said no but as I was beginning to tell him that he gave me the money for the coat my Mother gave me a kick on my legs so I shut up. I believe that God had heard me and had let me have the coat.

Around that time my Grandma made me a black velvet dress. It was very pretty with long sleeves, tight in at the waist and a circular skirt. It was finished off with a wide round collar trimmed with red velvet. I thought that I was like the 'cat's whiskers' in that dress. Then, one day, my brother and I were fighting over the biscuits, as usual. Then he got the scissors, went upstairs and cut my lovely dress and I couldn't stop him. When my Mother came in we got a good hiding. I was broken hearted but my Grandma never made me another dress.

One day, I was on my way to take the wages for a man called Bill Taylor who worked for my Father. I always opened the wage and took some money out for myself. The Taylor gang intercepted me and started to throw stones at me. Bill Taylor saw all this from his bedroom window and he took his belt off and gave them a good hiding. Little Amy who hadn't throw any stones was also beaten even though I said she was innocent. Bill said, 'She has to learn'. My Father eventually found out about me opening the wages and I received traditional chastisement!

Some houses at the end of our street were still being built and I was on my way to my friend's house when four boys grabbed hold of me as they wanted to throw me in the lime pit. A man who was coming out of his house saw what was going on and shouted at them to leave me alone. Usually, my brother, my sister Shirley and Grenville escorted me to school because if I could, I would bunk off and go to the beach instead.

We did not have much money in our family and I arrived home from school one day to find my sister having a big row with our Mother.

Shirley was upset because she was invited to go to a party and needed a new dress. She was told that there was no money and so she had to go in her school uniform. We never had birthday parties or received cards or presents in our house.

When my sister was thirteen she wanted to invite some of her friends to our house for tea and surprisingly, my Mother said 'Yes!' When the girls came round we decided to go for a bike ride to Dyserth. The bike I rode had no brakes, mudguards or chain! It was a miracle that I returned home alive! However, when we got back my sister ended up in tears as my Father was in a temper.

My Father did not like parties and this had made him cross. He got his belt out to me because I wasn't helping my Mother with the preparations. Shirley intervened and shouted at him that it was not my fault so Dad relented and sent me to bed instead.

A boy called Andrew used to come round on Sundays to help Dad with the papers. He wanted to go out with me and asked me if I would go round to his house. I did not feel comfortable about this. However, my father sent me round to his house to give him a note. He invited me in saying his mother was in the living room and wanted to see me. Again I did not feel comfortable but I went in to find that his mother wasn't there. He then grabbed hold of me and I knew that he wanted to do something bad to me. I managed to break free and ran home in tears. I told my Mother what had happened and she shouted at me and slapped my face. She told my Father who became even angrier and got out his belt. Later my parents reported the attack to the boy's parents who came to our house with Andrew. He denied everything and my father remained cross and, of course, I was very upset about the whole thing.

During that time I started to develop my own interest in my future. I would often go to the arcade and get lucky charms and cards out of the machines that would supposedly tell me my personality and my future destiny. The devil can only guess at such things but the person who chooses to open up their soul to such messages can leave themselves wide open for self-fulfilling prophecies of doom and destruction in that person's life. As my interest in these types of thing grew, I started to go to more experienced clairvoyants in Rhyl and also in Liverpool. I wish I had realised the dangers then of becoming involved in such practices as these activities attracted demonic influence into my life which brought a lot of harm rather than good. The Bible warns us about this. As I reflect now on the levels of pain and violence in my own family I realise that it is all evidence of how opening doors to the occult affects the family line in a negative way, not just for today but for generations to come.

Confirmation

One day the local vicar came to our house and told my Father that I wasn't attending Sunday school. My Father, as usual, was very angry with me and I got a good hiding and I was sent to bed early.

A few weeks later my Mother informed me I was to be confirmed by the church. I didn't want to be confirmed but my Mother told me that if I got confirmed I would not have to go to church anymore, so I was very pleased to hear that good news. Then I had to attend some lessons at the Church of England in Prestatyn High Street. I didn't like the study or going to the church. At last the day arrived but I fell ill and I was told by my Mother that I could not go to the Cathedral as I was ill. I felt very upset at this news because I wanted to get it over with. Also my Auntie had made me a white dress for the occasion so in my mind I decided to make my own way. On the evening of the confirmation I was supposed to be in bed at the right time. I got up and dressed and climbed down the drain pipe outside my bedroom window. I made my way to the church, wearing my white dress, and joined the others. We went on the transport to St Asaph Cathedral. I remember the Bishop or someone like a Bishop putting hands onto my head. I remember feeling very ill but eventually I would arrive back at home and told my Mother that I had been confirmed. My mother could not believe what she was hearing. There was an awful row and that was the end of that. I never went near a church again for many years.

In the meantime I was still getting into a lot of mischief, stealing from shops. One day, during a visit to the cinema with a boy, while we were in the queue, waiting to go in, another boy was making fun of me. I had made a decision to 'get him back.' The next day, I took my Father's roofing knife with the intention of cutting that boy's face open so that he would have to have stitches. Fortunately for everyone, he had gone home a different way. I dread to think what might have happened if I had caught him on the way home.

I feel now that the Lord protected us in that instance. However, that same boy very often exposed himself to me. He has since died.

During all this time I was having terrible nightmares. I also had to sleep with Mother who would attack me until she would finally fall asleep. My Mother and Father would drink a lot while they were out during the day and also during the evenings, which caused a lot of problems for us as children.

A Visit To Chepstow Hospital

At last we received a letter from St Lawrence hospital in Chepstow, South Wales. Oh, the excitement that I felt! I just could not wait! The day arrived when we caught the train from Prestatyn station. We arrived at the hospital and there I was admitted on the women's ward. My Mother slept overnight as the journey was too long to travel there and back to North Wales in one day.

During the four days following, I settled into the ward routine and I felt happy. I made friends with the other patients, two of whom I already knew. Sheila was in the ward having more operations. She had severe burns to her face and body, due to her nightdress catching fire. There was a girl called Valerie who was also a burns case.

The day came when the plastic surgeon, Mr Emlyn Lewis did his ward round. The usual performance: 'What's your name?' I told him as best as I could. Then he repeated the words back to me in the same way that I spoke. In other words, he made fun of me. One of the doctors, a Mr Philips, appeared to dislike the way Mr Lewis spoke to me. I could tell by his reaction but I didn't mind as I got used to it. After Mr Lewis examined my mouth and discussed it with his entourage, he then told me that my nose was very flat and that he was going to carry out some bone grafts. He would take some bones from my ribs. I was due to have my operation in two days' time. When I came to the hospital I was wearing the white dress that my Auntie had made for my confirmation. I was also wearing white tap shoes and I was doing tap dancing on the ward continually. I was also trying to teach the other children how to tap dance. In this hospital you did not stay in bed until after the operation, which was for many days at that time. The day arrived when I was to go to the theatre to have my nose repaired by Mr Lewis, who took a bone from my ribs. After the operation, when I awoke from the anaesthetic I was in a lot of pain and I was not allowed to lie down, which I found very difficult. One day, when I was eventually allowed to go out for a walk, I went with my friend Valerie with the idea of looking for the fighter pilot patients. As we walked along the grounds of the hospital we saw Mr Lewis and his entourage coming towards us. Mr Lewis looked at me, and then asked me my name which I answered. He immediately started to imitate every word I said.

When Mr Lewis left us we heard some laughing and making fun of me. It was the gardener who was working at the side of the ward Nissen huts. I felt very annoyed and went up to him and said, 'When children make fun of me at school, they get this': I clenched my fist and hit him in the face. He was not very pleased about what I had done to him. In his anger he grabbed hold of me and hit me across the legs. Val, who was watching all the commotion asked, "What's going on here? Stop it, leave her alone!" We walked away from him, back to the ward. The gardener shouted after us, "You are not too old for a hiding!" I was fifteen years old although I was very naïve in many ways.

Eventually, when I was up and walking about we would walk round to the men's ward to see the pilots. One day, while Matron was doing her ward round she came near to my bedside. Sister Morrison Davies, who was the sister on our ward, told Matron 'Louie does a lot of tap dancing'. The Matron asked me a lot of questions about my dancing. Then she told me she would like me to go on the hospital stage where they did hospital shows for the patients. I did not feel very happy about that. However, the Matron arranged a night and told me I would be on the stage. On the day that I was to perform, I felt very nervous but I was feeling hopeful as a miracle had occurred on the day before the show. The Anaesthetist had been to examine my chest and told me that I was on the list for my next operation. For the three days following, as I recovered from this operation, I was given Penicillin injections three times a day, was which were very painful. I don't think that penicillin tablets had been prescribed in the forties and fifties.

All the patients heard that Francis was coming back into the ward for more operations. I remembered Francis from a few years back. She had suffered burns to her neck, face and body.

During this time I used to help the patients go to the shop or do jobs for them and if they had pedicle grafts attached to their foreheads I would hold their arms up.

Mr Lewis also had a Speech Therapist working at the hospital. She was a very cruel person and none of the patients liked her. She would have all the cleft palate patients in tears. On the first day I had an interview with her, a patient came out of her office in floods of tears. When I went into the room she told me I had terrible speech and she recorded my speech on a record player (there were no tapes in those days!) Then she asked me "What are you going to do about it?" I thought inwardly "What could I do about it?"

I felt very upset at the unkindness of the speech therapist. Also she expected me to write. During that time in my life I was not able to read or write. One day she told me to do some written work before seeing her again. When the time came for me to have another session with her, she discovered that I had not done what she had asked me to do. She became very cross and locked me in a room all afternoon but I still did not cry. I remember that the gardener was looking through the window and was making me laugh. Mrs Bennett, the Speech Therapist did not realise that I had problems with reading and writing.

At the hospital there was a social club where all of the patients could meet which included males and females. My friend, Mary always came to the social club with me to mix with other patients. The trouble was Mary liked the boys. The Nurses told me to keep an eye on her which was not easy as the boys gave her a lot of attention. I would try to get her away from them and get her back to the ward.

I had a boyfriend called Arthur who was a good friend. We talked about many different things especially about the hospital. I was scheduled to have more operations. Mr Lewis decided that my top lip was too long and so he shortened it. He also made a 'cupid bow' by taking the skin from under my top lip. It was very sore! However,

Mr. Lewis appeared to be very pleased with the work that he had done.

Once I had recovered and I was on my feet again I decided to take to all the children from the children's ward to the pictures. I did not ask for permission. I took the children who could walk as we had to walk a long way down a big hill. Some of the children were crying and some could hardly walk but I insisted that they carry on.

When we arrived at the cinema the lady at the pay desk became suspicious and called the manager. He rang up the hospital and they came with transport to take us back to the hospital. I was in serious trouble. When I arrived on the ward the Sister gave me a good telling-off. I was put onto a specific diet and I was not allowed to leave the ward. The sister informed me that Mr. Lewis had done a ward round with an American plastic surgeon and to Mr Lewis' annoyance and amazement there had only been a few patients in bed!

During my stay in hospital in-between operations I was admitted to a Convalescent home with another young girl, where there were also some pilots. When I arrived at the home I went into the sitting room and there was a badly disfigured pilot playing on the piano. Suddenly I started to feel very upset and started to cry. The pilot stopped playing and told me to come over to him. He sat me on his knee and he asked me what was wrong. I told him that I hadn't seen my Mother for months. He then told me: 'When it will be time for you to go back to the hospital you won't want to leave. Here you will be happy'. Soon after I settled down and made friends but sometimes it was hard because the other patients had visitors and I didn't have anyone to visit me the whole time I was in the hospital.

When I eventually arrived back at the hospital I was to have two more operations. Mr Lewis told me he would attempt to correct my palate. I was so excited! Two other girls were on the ward to have the repair of their palates. On the day of the operation I was over the moon with excitement. I was first on the list. After the operation I was in the recovery ward. When I opened my eyes I put my tongue on the roof of my mouth. What a shock!!

I could feel the big hole in the top of my mouth. I started to cry. The Nurses came to me but I could not stop crying because I was devastated. Also I was having a blood transfusion. When I asked the other two girls who were with me about their palates, theirs had been repaired. I was pleased for the girls but I felt so disappointed for myself and I was in a terrible state.

Soon after this Mr Lewis came to visit us. He sat on my bed and took hold of my free hand. He tried to explain to me the difficulty in trying to repair my palate as he told me I had no flesh in the side of my palate so he did what was called a Pharyngeal flap. The next day we were transferred back to the ward and the usual routine helping the patients. I had to go to the dentist for a new plate for my palate but I felt very unhappy.

Then the day came when Mr Lewis came to do a ward round. When he spoke to me I started to cry, so he decided to discharge me from the hospital. Good news and sad news! I would miss the patients. Bad news, I would have to go back to school until I was sixteen. What a shock!

When I arrived at home, I was not a very happy child mostly because I would have to go back to school along with my feelings of disappointment about not having my palate repaired. My Father found the sight of me very unpleasant. The only time he spoke to me was to threaten me. I was also surprised to see how much my younger brother had grown and that he had begun to walk during my absence.

On my return to school I discovered that my friends, Shirley and Granville, were still at school. I immediately rebelled at the prefects and I felt that I hated them. One morning, when I arrived at school late, the prefect told me she was going to report me to Mr Owen the headmaster. I swore at her. Then she said,' you are swearing', so I swore a lot more. Then I ran out of the school down to the beach and lit up a cigarette. When I arrived home there was a terrible row between my parents. I was also put into another class for the very backward children. It was called 1Y. I hated it there and I refused to cooperate with the teacher, who eventually gave up on me. The kids made fun of me and I missed being in the hospital all of the time.

One morning Mr Owen came into the classroom to ask the girls who wanted to be a Nurse. I put my hand up with another girl. Mr Owen immediately put his hand towards me and said, 'You will never be a Nurse'. I felt furious and I replied, 'Yes, I will be a Nurse!' At this he just walked out of the class. I followed him and told him, 'I hate you'. Then I went to the headmistress and told her how I hated her. When I got home I told my Mother that I wanted to be a Nurse and she slapped my face and told me to stop daydreaming. There was a terrible row. I told my Mother that I was not going to school any more. My father said he would drag me to school if need be. My father tried to help me learn but it was a disaster because he threatened me with the belt and I was so nervous. In the end my mother went to the school to see Mr Owen, the headmaster, who apparently told my mother I would never be able to work although there was a possibility that I might be able to work in a factory. But I remembered what Mr Lewis, the plastic surgeon, said to me when I was in hospital, 'You have the makings of a good Nurse'. I had no encouragement from anyone.

In the end, after so many rows, my mother took me from school. I was 15 years old and I was so happy to be leaving school.

My mother got me a job in a convalescent home for sick men and boys from Liverpool. The home was somewhere between Rhuddlan and St Asaph. I was very happy to be working there but it was to be short lived as we were not allowed to speak to the patients who were all men.

One day, when I was washing up in the kitchen, a young man came to the window and asked me to go out with him to the pictures. I shook my head to mean the answer was 'no' but we still had a lot of fun amongst the staff. The matron was very nice but also strict with the staff. I made friends with a girl who was welsh but she was not there very long as she left to start her Nurse training in Chester. After that I became unhappy because I thought the rules were silly, so I left the home. My parents were very cross because I did not have a job. I was living at home and felt like a 'living hell.' My parents went out most nights, especially my father. During the evenings I had to look after my younger brothers and sisters and I would also have to feed my baby brother. When my mother went out she always came home 'tight' or drunk and she would often attack me. I had to sleep with my mother and she would pinch me and hit me until she fell asleep.

The Start Of My Working Life

After many rows about me my mother eventually found a job for me and we went along to the interview for me to work in a tobacconist's shop. The shop was in Bodfor Street Rhyl and the name of it was Clarke & Sons. The managers were two brothers, Mr Rupert Clarke and Mr Leonard Clarke and they were both very kind men. I was very happy working there. The only problem was that I could not read very well, or spell or add up and I was serving in the shop!

I had to ask customers how much change they should have and I also used to ask them to write down in the order book what papers and magazines they would like to order. One day Mr. Clarke took me into his office. I thought that he was going to tell me off or, even worse, that he might sack me. I said to him, 'Please don't sack me, Mr Clarke, because my father will thrash me'. He was very kind to me and he answered: "No, I won't sack you because you are a good and willing worker. I will put you to work in the warehouse and I will put Margaret to work in the shop." So, I worked in the warehouse. I got on well with the staff and we used to have a lot of fun and teased each other. During this time I was attending Broadgreen Hospital in Liverpool for plates and for my teeth. I still had a cleft palate. During one of my visits, whilst having treatment, I met a plastic surgeon called Mr Osborne. I asked him if he could repair my palate. He said, 'No!' I felt very disappointed.

At work a young man who I worked and got along quite well with, asked me if I would go out with him. His name was Gwylam. One evening he came to my house in Prestatyn to take me out to Rhyl roller skating. I was all ready to go out of the door when my father appeared and started to accuse me of drinking his best sherry. I told him I hadn't but he just got his belt and dragged me up the stairs and continued to hit me across the legs and arms, but I managed to bite his hand which was poured with blood. When he finally stopped beating me I ran out of the house. The poor boy went very white. I think he was in shock. We eventually arrived at the skating rink but my heart wasn't in it and I fell flat on my back as my legs were really hurting me. I apologised to Gwylam but he answered, 'I'm not surprised after what you went through. Let's go for a drink'. That night I decided that I was leaving home because I had had enough of my parents' tempers.

Stoke Mandeville Hospital

Stoke Mandeville Hospital

My mother spoke with Dr McLeod, my doctor, who then referred me to Stoke Mandeville Hospital, Aylesbury, Buckinghamshire, the largest hospital in Europe.

The day came at last for me to be admitted on to ward 6. My mother came with me. I was so excited because I believed I was going to have my palate repaired. My mother stayed the night as it was too far for her to travel back to North Wales in a single day. I settled down in to the ward and I felt very happy which lasted until the doctors told me that they could not repair my palate. I was very upset at that news. I was 17 years old at the time. I stayed on the ward for teeth, plates, or obturates where I made friends with some of the other patients, especially one girl. We used to go for walks to the men's ward, looking for fighter pilots. We met a few, but nothing like the pilots in Chepstow hospital. We also went to the pictures sometimes. The hospital seemed to be all Nissen huts.

After 3 months I was discharged but I did not want to go home. I felt very unhappy and the almoner wanted to send for my mother, but I was determined to go home on my own. I eventually had my own way but I felt very sad to leave my friends as I loved Stoke Mandeville hospital.

When I arrived home there was not a very nice atmosphere. My father wouldn't speak to me and when my parents went out during the evening I was expected to look after the younger brothers and sisters. Oh, how I missed the hospital!

During this time I was still working at Clarkes in Rhyl. I settled down to the usual routine and I felt happy in my work. There was also a lot of teasing and joking amongst us and it was a very happy atmosphere, although life at home was very different and very difficult for me. My parents continued to go out at night, and my mother would also go out during the days and at the weekends but she always cooked us a dinner. My father always put his belt on his chair in case one of us upset him. My sister and I always started to giggle which seemed to put my father in a rage. At least one of us would get the belt from him and it would often be one of my brothers. It used to make me feel so nervous at meal times.

My Career As A Nurse

I was getting restless so I decided to apply to St. Asaph hospital to do some kind of nursing. A friend wrote the letter of application for me. Eventually I received a letter from the Matron for an interview. My mother came with me although she was not pleased with me as she thought I was making the wrong choice. We arrived at Matron's office on time. The Matron did not seem to be pleased to see us and I thought she looked stern, in fact, I felt a bit scared at her appearance. She was a very tall, big lady, very round in figure. The Matron and my mother made decisions together about me. After a while Matron spoke to me and to my surprise accepted me on a pre-training course which made me feel very excited. People I spoke to could not believe the Matron had accepted me and many thought that I was making a big mistake. Then I gave my notice to Mr Clarke who looked very worried and told me I was making a mistake. I was determined to fight for my decision.

I went to a dance at the Ritz Ballroom in Rhyl. I met a boy that I knew at school called Kenneth. He asked my name and when I told him he remembered me. He asked me what kind of work that I was doing. He looked surprised when I told him but he said 'Well Louie, you were either in hospital, or going to hospital, or coming out of hospital'. He was the only person to give me a bit of encouragement. I was not going to give up! After waiting for some time, I received a letter from the Matron to start for duty at 1:00pm on 18th February 1954. I felt so excited, but I also felt very nervous.

LOUIE AT ST. ASAPH HOSPITAL

When I arrived at my room in the Nurses' home I found my uniform on the bed. I changed into my uniform but I had no idea how to make up the cap. I tried after a fashion, I looked in the mirror and I thought it was acceptable. I made my way to the dining room where all the Nurses were having dinner. As I sat at the table I could feel my cap moving around my head and then it fell over my eyes. The Nurse nearest to me took my cap off, then the Home Sister who always served our meals said to the nurse next to me, 'Nurse Evans, show Nurse Baker how to make up a cap.' The Nurse was Megan Evans; she became a very good friend during the following years. All the Nurses lived in the Nurses' Home. They were all single. After lunch the Sister told me that I would be working on the Maternity ward. The Matron could not have made a worse choice as I was very naïve about sex. As a young girl I had somehow got the idea into my head that a baby was made when a girl and boy were kissing each other and needless to say, this had caused a lot of problems. However, there was some good news as I discovered that Megan worked on the same ward. As we walked to the ward Megan told me about the Head Ward Sister, Hannah Owen, who was apparently the fear and dread of all of the Nurses because she was very stern and strict. When I reported to her in the office I was pleasantly surprised as I thought she was beautiful. I could not take my eyes off her. Her hair was grey with a blue rinse in the front and she had big brown eyes. She was tall and had a full figure. I soon came down to earth when she said, 'Nurse, are you listening to me?' I replied, 'Yes, Sister.' Then she told me to go to the nursery where all the babies were and put them on the trolley. I made my way to the babies' nursery only to hear all the babies crying. I started to change the babies' nappies while Megan was telling me what to do. I decided that instead of using the trolley I would gather as many babies in my arms as I could and carry them to the mothers. As I was doing this I met Sister Owen in the corridor who sternly asked me 'Nurse, what do you think you are doing? Go back and put the babies on the trolley!' By this time all the babies were screaming loudly but I did as she had asked. At the end of our shift we went to the dining room for our supper and the food was awful. Megan informed me that I was in Sister Owen bad books and it seemed as though I could not do anything right.

When I arrived at my room at St. Asaph hospital, I folded the bed clothes back and found to my absolute horror, three big cockroaches! I shouted for Megan, who came into my room but only laughed and said, 'It's only the girls playing a joke on you'. But I could not laugh at this joke as I would now feel very uncomfortable having to sleep in this bed.

The food at the hospital was atrocious! Not only was the hospital overrun with cockroaches, we also had mice. One day the Home Sister was serving out our soup at lunch time when a dead mouse came up with the soup ladle that she was using to serve. Sister just said 'It's alright, girls, its extra protein for you' so we just carried on with our soup!

Worse was to come later on! When I returned to my room three girls were waiting for me and they told me that I was to be baptised! The ritual was that all new girls were undressed and put under water in the bath. I could not do much about it because the girls grabbed hold of me. I thought that I would just have to go through with it. I heard Megan say to them, 'Don't be too rough with her, she's delicate'. They got that wrong because they didn't know me!

After my ordeal in the bath, I got dressed and then Megan came to my room and asked me to go for a drink in the town. So a group of us went to the pub. Megan told me to be careful what I drank as I may not be used to it. I was sure I would be alright as I was brought up with so much alcohol around. As the night wore on I noticed one of the girls had a bit too much to drink, in fact she was almost drunk. We had to go back to the hospital in a taxi. In those days Nurses had to have a late pass if they wanted to stay out late but only once a week. It was very hard for the Nurses to accept this rule. When we arrived at the hospital all the doors were locked and none of us had a late pass. One of the girls would usually leave their bedroom window, a downstairs window. The only trouble was that we had to beware of the Home Sister who was very stern; I had never seen her smile. I called her 'the panther' because she was like a cat prowling about to catch its prey. We went out nearly every night.

I was very happy on the ward. I worked hard and got along well with the patients and the staff, apart from Sister Owen. I did not seem to do anything right in her eyes which concerned me. We had to do a lot of cleaning on the ward but my cleaning never seemed to satisfy Sister Owen although I did try hard to please her. When I was working, I would get upset when women started in labour as most of them would scream so loudly. At home I told my mother about this and she said "They are all big babies." With that thought in my mind I tried hard not to let their screams and cries affect me.

One day I had to clean the rubber sheets and that was hard work in the sluice. The sister wasn't satisfied with my work and I had to clean those awful sheets all over again. I was nearly crying over them and then I had the awful job of cleaning bed pans. If the Sister was in a bad mood then it was difficult for any poor Nurse who was on duty with her! All the other sisters seemed to be very nice and I got on well with all of them. There were trained Midwives, Sister Hands, Sister Coward and Sister Nickson Jones, who was Welsh.

One day a lady was in the labour ward crying out with pain when Sister Owen called me to change a bulb in the labour ward. It was a light bulb over the sterilizers. Sister brought the step ladder and told me to support the steps while she was on the top step. I decided to go up the ladder as well but the steps would not hold the two of us and they collapsed. We both fell on the floor to the amazement of the labour ward Sister who was very concerned.

When the lady who was in labour saw what had happened to us she became very sensible. Sister was very concerned about me but I assured her I was alright and that I had not hurt myself. I was more concerned in case she saw the ladders in my black stockings, which had been there for weeks as I had not had the money to buy new ones. I told Sister an untruth that the accident had caused the ladders in my stockings and so Sister said she would make sure I would have new stockings. The lady who had her baby told me she could not stop laughing at the incident as all she saw was a big pair of black bloomers on the sister. After that incident Sister Owen seemed to be a lot nicer to me and she seemed more satisfied with my work. Unfortunately, the other girls started to tease me, calling me 'blue eyes' but I did not mind as I admired Sister Owen.

When I got home for my day off after the incident in the labour ward, to my amazement, Sister Owen was standing in our living room and my mother was looking anxious. I felt scared as I thought it was something to do with the Superintendent. Sister was in a long conversation with my mother and I felt very worried. But Sister was very pleasant towards me and said that she was going to take me to Rhyl to buy me new stockings as mine were laddered in the accident. I nearly died with fright because I was terrified in case we met someone from the hospital and I would never live it down.

My mother would tell me when we were alone together that I never should have gone into nursing and she kept saying to me that my sister should have been a Nurse and not me. I took no notice of her.

The mothers were usually kept in hospital for between ten days to three weeks. In those days babies were kept separate from their mothers except for feeding times. One day while I was on duty with Sister Hands, I was taking some of the babies to their mothers on the ward. Unfortunately, some of the babies had got mixed up. The mothers like me and they made light of this event. One mother said, 'Yesterday I had a little boy, today I have a little girl!' Another mother said, 'Yesterday I had a little girl, today I have a little boy!' All of the mothers sorted them out and all of the babies were united with their own mothers in the end. Sister was not pleased with me especially as I was not reading the babies notes correctly. After a good telling-off she ended by telling me that the patients liked me but she warned me to be more careful. She also said that she thought I would make a good Nurse.

The fathers of new born babies were kept separate and were only allowed to view the babies through special windows fitted in the nursery. One night, without realising it, I was showing the wrong baby to a father. The baby had a mop of black hair and the father said, 'I wonder where all his hair has come from?', and so I said, 'Maybe from the past from a relative.' The following night while I was off duty the father came back to see his baby. He said to the Nurse on duty as she was showing him the right baby, 'Where has all his hair gone?' The Nurse replied to the Father by saying that he had not had any hair. The father was unable to believe what he was hearing but the Nurse eventually convinced him that the baby with no hair really was his child.

When the women were in labour they were just given jelly to eat and then they would also have to have an enema before giving birth. I used to feel quite sorry for them.

One day the Sister in charge sent me to the kitchen to collect the jellies for the patients. The only trouble was that the Head Cook didn't seem to like the Nurses and consequently the Nurses did not like going to the kitchens. So, on this occasion when I went to collect the jellies Cook Jones appeared to be very cross and told me off for coming so late. I watched her walk into the fridge and then I slammed the fridge door, locking her in! I could hear her shouting but I took no notice. Then one of the porters came in to the kitchen. He used to tease the Nurses! He asked me what all the noise was about and then asked me 'Where's cook?' Then he looked at the fridge and he was laughing as he asked me, 'What have you done?' He opened the door of the fridge and out came Cook Jones glaring at me with a furious look! The porter explained that it had been the wind that had slammed the door shut. Cook Jones did not believe that and said so and told me that she was going to report me to Matron. When I arrived back on the labour ward the Sister was also cross with me and said, "You took your time!" But word soon got out that I had locked Cook Jones in the fridge. No one could believe what I had done!

After some one of my days off as I arrived back on duty on the ward, Sister Owen called me to help with a delivery in the labour ward. I could hear the poor woman screaming and I felt very afraid. I went in to help and Sister instructed me to hold the woman's leg up.

I did not have a clue about sex or about how babies were born. I did not know how babies came out of their mothers! Sister just stared at me and then said, 'Nurse, this is hardly the time to tell me how naïve you are!'

When the baby was born the mother immediately calmed down and became very sensible. The Sister told the mother the sex of the baby but I was more interested in the baby's mouth and exclaimed 'The mouth is normal!'

Afterwards, when it was my duty to clean up in the labour ward I said to the Sister, 'I will never have a baby'. Sister's reply was, 'One day you will change your mind'.

After having a day off I was back on duty in the nursery. I went into the kitchen to see if there was a baby there who may need to be fed by the bottle. There was one bottle left in the fridge so I took the feed and went to get the baby out of the cot but when I went to pick the baby up I noticed he was very blue in the face so I held him upside down and held him by his ankle, then I gave him a hard slap between the shoulder blades. Then the obstruction came up by vomiting, although prior to this I had not realised that there had been an obstruction. The Sister and Staff Nurse had already gone to ring the Doctor and get the resuscitation trolley ready for the Doctor. During this time I had started to feed the baby who had gone a normal pink colour. Just then the Doctor and Sister came rushing in to treat the baby only to find him on my knee feeding very well. Sister looked at me in disbelief and started to shout at me but the Doctor said, 'Sister, the baby looks very well and well done, Nurse', and walked off. Sister was not at all pleased with me and asked me what I had done. So I told her. Her reply was, 'Next time, Nurse, you wait for the Doctor'. So I said, 'Yes, Sister'.

Another day, the Sister in charge told me to take a patient to theatre as the patient was having a caesarean section. I felt a bit nervous, but became interested in the whole operation. A boy was born and he was quite normal. During this time I was getting on well with my work and Sister Owen appeared to be pleased with what I had done.

One day a Nursing Superintendent started to examine Nurses on the theory of Nursing. I was very afraid! I knew I would get nowhere and I was right! I had to hide the fact that I couldn't write and that anything that I knew about nursing I had learned from imitating others, from my own experience and by committing things to my memory. The Superintendent Sister was not pleased at my reaction towards her but, I seemed to get away with it; (thank the Lord)!

One evening, one of the Nurses that I was on duty with called me over and said, 'Listen, Sister Owen and the Superintendent were having a row about you'. We went as near to the office as we dared to and I heard the Superintendent telling Sister Owen that I was very uncooperative. Sister Owen, in my defence, told her that I had the makings of a good Nurse. The Super was having none of it and told Sister Owen that she was going to have a word with Matron. Sister Owen and the Superintendent argued about me for a long time. I was concerned about this and I expected to be dismissed from the hospital so I started to work even harder, however, I did not hear any more about it or hear anything from the Matron. I became increasingly popular with the other women. The Lord had overruled on my behalf as he had other ideas.

At home, my sister told me that my father's friend was on a medical ward in the hospital. I knew who he was so I thought that I would be kind and go to visit him. I went to see him and took him a bar of chocolate. He seemed pleased to see me and asked me how I was getting on in nursing. When my father's friend told him that I had been to see him, my father went into a rage and informed me that he did not want me to go near his friends.

Time Off From Nursing Duties

One of the girls I was friends with at the hospital invited me to her home. We both had the same day off so we went to her home. When we arrived it seemed that all of her family were there and Rosamond introduced me to them all. Then she ran across the room and said, 'This is my daddy, my lovely dad!' I just stared at him and then I burst into tears. I could not stop crying. Rosamond and her mother took me into the bedroom because I had no control over my crying. It was because I had seen Rosamond sit on her father's knee with their arms around each other.

Rosamond's mother was asking 'Shall I send for a doctor?' because I was so upset but Rosamond said 'No.' Rosamond kept asking me who had upset me on the ward as she thought it might have been the Sister but I said 'No one has upset me.' Rosamond asked me about each one of the Sisters and again I said 'No one.' I could not stop crying and I was deeply moved by what I had seen. I had to face these people again the following day which was difficult for me as I felt so embarrassed but they were all very kind towards me.

When we arrived back at the hospital, Rosamond assured me that she would not say anything to the other girls about what had happened at her home. She was a very kind and considerate girl.

Once a month, the Matron allowed the girls and their boyfriends to have a dance in the Nurses' sitting room. Matron always attended these dances. I suppose that this was to ensure that none of the Nurses sneaked off upstairs with their boyfriends!

During one of these dances Megan and I wanted a cup of coffee so I went into the kitchen to make the drink and I saw a mouse in the gas stove. I managed to get hold of it by the tail and so I ran into the sitting room shouting, 'Look what I found in the kitchen'. I held the mouse to show everybody. Suddenly one of the girls ran out of the room and left the poor man on the floor. I can tell you that I was not very popular that night!

Louie at St Asaph Hospital

During this time Megan was still teaching me to dance. One night we went to a dance hall and a young man approached me who I had met previously when he had asked me to dance with him. He told me that I had improved because I wasn't treading on his toes! Between dances we sat at one of the tables to have a drink and John said 'Wait for me here while I go outside for a smoke'. After I had waited for quite some time I decided to go to look for him. To my surprise, I found him outside with a pretty blonde girl and they were kissing each other!

As I stood in amazement he turned his head towards me and shouted at me to go back inside. So I went back inside to get a drink. When he came back to me he took me outside and started to tell me he wanted to go out with me seriously as he knew that I was to be trusted. My answer to him was 'No' as I had caught him kissing the other girl. His answer was, 'I don't trust her, and she belongs to everybody!' I told him I was interested in nursing, not in boys but he was not very pleased about this as I think he wanted to have things his own way.

After our arrival back at the hospital Megan came to my room to tell me I was making a big mistake because many girls wanted John. But I did not think that I was making a mistake. When I went home for my day off I told my mother all about John. However, I did not get the help from my mother that I was hoping for as she threatened me instead by saying "If anything goes wrong your father will break every bone in your body."

The girls and I would often go out in the evenings and we would mix with so many different boys. Megan would often warn me about particular boys such as those whose hands would feel all over the girls' bodies. I became increasingly aggressive towards males.

One day one of the girls wanted to make a foursome. She told me I would be alright as the boy was very nice and quiet. I felt uneasy as they all decided that after going to the pub they would drive in their car up Prestatyn hillside. I became increasingly uncomfortable as I realised that it was going to be very dark up in the hills. When we arrived it was so dark you couldn't see anything in front of you. To my horror the boy tried to kiss me so I attacked him like a wild cat. He was furious with me and said to me, 'If you think I have come up here for nothing, you are mistaken'. He started to take his belt off and I realised that he was going to hit me. I became very afraid and aggressive. I bit his nose and scratched his face and somehow I managed to get out of the car.

I took my high-heeled red shoes off and I ran down through the woods with the boy running after me. I was terrified! I kept saying, 'God help me.' The Lord did have mercy on me and I managed to get away from the boy who was chasing me. I arrived at my home where I found that my parents were out which gave me some time to calm down. Thankfully it was my day off the following day. When I saw the girl that I had been with in the car she was not very pleased with me as I had left her alone in the car and she did not understand why I was so fussy about boys. She also informed me that I had a nickname. Apparently they called me 'Spitfire'. She also told me that she had a good time with her boy and that they did not understand me.

One evening some of the Nurses had a late pass which was only until 10:00pm but generally none of the Nurses took any notice of the time limit on their late passes and we all usually stayed out after midnight. One evening I had a late pass so Megan asked me to go with the girls to a dance in Henllan. A crowd of us decided to go. We all got into a car [there were no laws relating to seat belts in those days!] At the dance, I sat at a table with Christine and we all had drinks. I was hoping that the girls wouldn't be too late going back to the hospital as I was feeling very tired and I felt more like going to bed. Then Christine said, 'Someone is coming towards us'. I turned my head round and firstly I noticed a pair of black shoes walking towards me. As I looked up I saw that they were worn by a tall young man with dark hair. He asked me if I would dance with him but I said, 'No, I can't dance'. He said to me, 'You will never learn sat there! On your feet!'

He took my arm and led me on the dance floor although I was not feeling very happy and to make matters worse, I trod all over his feet during the dance. 'You are right! You can't dance!' he exclaimed. Then he asked my name. I hated strangers asking me my name so I didn't answer. Then he said, 'Lift up your head, you've got nothing to be ashamed of and stop treading on my toes!'

Even worse was to come! The band did a spot prize and it fell on John and me! What a shock! I thought I was going to collapse with fright! John said, 'Go to the stage and get your prize'. The only trouble was some of the couples started to boo us. John said, 'I will sort them out!' So I said, 'No don't. I know who they are'. I thought the night would never end but eventually we all piled into a car and returned to the hospital.

John asked Megan to teach me to do the waltz and the foxtrot. Then he said to me, 'The next time I see you I will expect you to dance with me without treading on my feet'. I said to him, 'I think you are very bossy!' and we laughed.

Louie at St Asaph Hospital

So Megan taught me to do the dance steps with the old records in the Nurses' sitting room. The next week we went to Denbigh dance hall. We all went out most nights and when we arrived back at the hospital we had to climb through an open window. It was usually me who was lifted up because I was small.

One night when I was lifted up to get into the home, I thought someone had put a soft carpet down on the floor but when I put the light on, to my horror, the whole floor was covered with cockroaches.

After yet another night out we had all arrived back late as usual. I was the first through the window but the next girl, Rosamond who followed me got stuck in the window! Poor girl, she was half way through and the boys outside were trying to push her through, while some of the girls were trying to pull her through from the inside of the room. Then, to our horror, we could see a light coming along the passage. I knew it was the Home Sister so I put on one of the girl's dressing gowns and ran a wet cloth over my face to try and remove my make-up, then I went into the corridor, yawning my head off , pretending I had just got out of bed. Sister did not look pleased and said she had heard noises inside and outside so I said, 'No, Sister, I didn't hear a thing'.

But we still had a problem getting poor Rosamond out of the window so together we decided that two of the boys would come into the home while the others tried to get her into the room from the outside.

We were not allowed to bring males into the home and if anyone was ever caught bringing a male in then they would be given the sack. Anyway, eventually we managed to get her into the room but it was a very difficult ordeal! Poor Rosamond was very upset!

My friend Megan decided she wanted some male pen friends in the RAF and I thought it was a good idea. When I received my letter the young man appeared to be nice. Megan always helped me with the letter and what I should write as I did not have a clue! This went on for a few months then one day I received a letter to tell me that he was due for leave and that he was coming to Rhyl. He wanted to meet me and he also wanted a photo of me as he had sent me a photo of himself. He also said he wanted to know what the taste of my lips was like. I nearly died with shock! I told Megan I would no longer be writing letters to any man or boy I did not know. Megan read the letter and then asked me what was wrong with my mouth. I told her that I had an accident when I was a young child and Megan accepted it. I never told anyone the real truth because I was afraid that I would be dismissed from the hospital. But the trouble was that he didn't stop writing so I chose to ignore his letters. So that was the end of pen friends for me. Megan wasn't very pleased about it and said it was good for me to have a pen friend. I told her that I did not want to get involved with any boy and that I wanted to be a Nurse like Sister Owen. Megan looked a bit shocked and told me that the girls thought that because of the way that I reacted to boys that I was a bit queer! I did not take any notice. I now know that it was the Lord's way of protecting me during all of that time.

I was still going to the dance halls with the girls till the early hours of the morning. One night we went to a dance and I did not bother much about the way I dressed. This particular night I just had on a dress and ankle socks with red high heel shoes. After a dance with John, during the break I had a drink and then I went to the ladies' cloakroom. While I was in the toilet cubicle, I could hear two girls talking about me (I could not help but hear them). They were discussing the appearance of the girls on the dance floor.

Then one of the girls that I was listening to said "What do you think about Louie Baker?" The other girl answered "I think she has pretty lovely eyes but her mouth and her speech spoil her." After they had left, I just crept away but I felt very upset and anxious. I knew my speech was not very good although it did improve after a month of speech therapy. I tried my best to keep my mouth shut. But I felt furious about these two girls so I decided to go to Browns in Chester and I bought a very pretty bottle green dress. It had a short and flared skirt fitted tight into the waist, with narrow straps at the top. Everybody liked the dress when I went to the next dance. I wasn't off the dance floor once and John told me that I looked lovely. The only trouble was that all of the boys asked me for the last dance and I said 'Yes' to all of them which caused a lot of fights. We were drinking a lot and they called me a little fairy. Afterwards about eight of us all collapsed into an old car. I usually had to sit on someone's knee because I was one of the smaller ones.

On this particular occasion one of the girls had too much to drink and she was making a lot of noise. We were all a bit concerned as we knew that somehow we would have to try to sneak in through the window in the Nurses' home because none of us had obtained a late pass. When the car stopped at the hospital we all tumbled out of the car. We all felt very stiff as we had all been squashed in together. It was a miracle that we got home alive as there were no seat belts and the car was overcrowded, as always.

Eventually we got in through a window which was in the Nurses' sitting room. We had all had too much to drink. The girl who had drunk far too much just collapsed on the floor so we had to carry her to her bedroom. The only trouble was that she kept shouting so I put a cushion over her face to quieten her. Then as we carried her along the corridor, to our horror the Panther Sister was coming towards us. We had no escape! Sister was very angry with us and told us all that we were to report to Matron's office the next morning! The problem was that whenever I had a few drinks I usually said exactly what I thought and this occasion was no exception! I told the Home Sister that she was jealous because we had a good time and she had not! Sister was furious with me and said 'Get to your rooms and I will speak to you in the morning'. The other girls could not believe that I had spoken to her in that manner.

In the morning we all had to go Matron's office who was very displeased with us all. We had to go in to her office separately. I apologised to Matron who told me that she always had good reports about me but any more bad behaviour and I would be dismissed. The girls were amazed because I was always so quiet and they kept saying that butter wouldn't melt in my mouth even when I had almost had a row with Matron over the food which was atrocious.

All the Nurses arranged to have a meeting with Matron over different things that we thought were unfair. Everyone had decided what they were going to say. Eventually the Matron appeared in the Nurses' sitting room but all the girls seemed to clam up at the sight of her as she did look quite fearsome! Only one other Nurse, Mary and I stood up to her and spoke our minds. Matron was furious! She told us how ungrateful we were. When Matron ended the meeting all the girls surrounded Mary and I. They could not believe how we had stood up to Matron but it was a long time before I lived that episode down!

During this time, I was still attending Broadgreen hospital in Liverpool for my own treatment and my mother always went with me. I did not mind attending there as I was hoping to have a palatal obturator. This is designed to cover a cleft palate and it is made to fit the roof of the mouth. It can be quite uncomfortable until a patient becomes used to it.

After our visit to the hospital we went to visit my Aunty who was my mother's eldest sister. She was a music teacher and had played on the radio during the war. Aunty lived in West Kirby, near Liverpool and she was also involved with Spiritualism, although she was a Catholic. The sad thing was that my mother also got involved with Spiritualism and tarot cards. The conversation was about fortune telling which at this time I enjoyed.

There used to be a good fortune teller in Sussex Street, Rhyl and I went to see her a lot of times but she never told me what I wanted to hear particularly about passing exams. I also began to read the cards myself and I had lucky charms. I used to wear one around my neck. My mother also went to a séance. I never felt secure though. It all comes from Satan and I think that it is very deceitful.

My Mother often told me about the ghosts that she had seen and how she would hear from her stepfather when she attended the Spiritualist Church. What a terrible mess that all was; a mess which, unfortunately I became involved in for many years.

On one of my days off from the hospital, my mother and I went to the infants' school at Caradoc Road, Prestatyn to collect my youngest brother at the end of the school day. Whilst we were walking to the school, I told my mother how I was in awe of her and of how much I admired her. My mother was alarmed at this and was not able to accept what I had said. She told me that I was 'backward.' She said, 'You should have had these feelings when you were younger, like for a school teacher'. I knew what my feelings were for school teachers, so there was no way that I was going to have feelings of admiration for them!

On one of my days off from the hospital, I was at home having a cigarette. My mother caught me and gave me a good hiding with a coat hanger. It was very painful! On another of my days off, I went to the pictures with a boy. He did not know it but I had made a private decision to leave my job at the hospital. I felt then that it was time for a move. Just as I was thinking about this a big ship sailed past on the picture screen and it had the name of 'Bristol' written on the side of it. It caused me to have a change of mind and I decided that I would go to Bristol. My mother was not pleased about it when I told her and neither was the Matron when I handed my notice in. The Matron almost begged me to stay.

Bristol Hospital

With the help of a friend I applied to a hospital in Bristol and to my surprise I was accepted. Megan and the girls couldn't believe that I was leaving. When I went to see Sister Owen in her office she told me how sorry she was that I was leaving and told me that I would make a good Nurse. I told her that I wanted to write to her and she appeared pleased and replied "Yes, I do want to know how you get on in your future." My mother was not pleased that I was going away and seemed very concerned about me. I assured her that I would be alright. I left Prestatyn with my Grandmother's blessing.

I knew then that the Holy Spirit had started to move in my life.

After a terrible night's sleep the day arrived for me to start at the hospital in Bristol. What a shock was waiting for me! As I entered the Nurses' home it looked so depressing. I sat on my bed and lit up a cigarette. I sat quietly on my bed for a time and thought that I had made a terrible mistake by coming to this hospital. Just as my thoughts were far away I was brought back to reality by a knock on my door. I opened the door to see a Staff nurse who said, "Nurse Baker, come with me please." I followed her down a dingy corridor with low lights. The nurse informed me that her name was Maureen. She was walking very quickly and I was trying to keep up with her. We turned a corner into an even more depressing corridor. Then to my bewilderment the Staff Nurse started talking about Jesus. I was amazed at what I was hearing but to be honest I was not in the mood to hear about Jesus at that moment. Little did I know what was going to happen during the next few years. Eventually we arrived at a women's medical ward where I was taken into the Sister's office. I thought that Sister looked at me as if to say "I'm not impressed by you." I felt very unhappy. Sister called another Nurse to instruct me what to do and I followed her into the kitchen to prepare special drinks. While we were there I could hear the Sister going around the patients and to my amazement, she prayed aloud for them. While Sister was in the ward praying for the patients, I decided to have a cigarette. I was standing by the sink smoking and thinking what on earth had I done by moving to Bristol. I missed St. Asaph so much and I felt like an alien in my new surroundings.

Everyone's accent was so different that I found it difficult sometimes to even understand what they were saying. Sister came storming into the kitchen straight up to me and said, "How dare you smoke in my ward!"

Sister was very strict and was not going to stand for any nonsense from wayward nurses like me! After that Sister sent me to the sluice to carry out the uninspiring job of scrubbing mackintoshes and bed pans. From that point on the Sister kept a close watch on me. I think she thought that I might light up a cigarette again while I should have been doing my duties! I had already decided that I would go back to St Asaph.

Sister came to examine my scrubbing and she was not satisfied with what I had already done and insisted that I should do it all again. I felt fed up and depressed. When I eventually got off duty I sat on my bed and the flood gates opened. I cried. I lit another cigarette and decided that I would get in touch with my mother. Then there was a knock at my door. One of the Nurses came into my room and asked me why I was so upset. I responded "I am leaving! I hate this hospital!" The Nurse's name was June and in time she became a good friend. June encouraged me to give it a chance as I had only just arrived. I asked her if she would help me to telephone my mother.

My parents did not have a landline telephone at home but my mother's friend who lived next door did have one so that was a way that I could speak with my mother. I told her that I hated the hospital and wanted to come back to St Asaph. My mother was very angry and she told me straight "You are not coming home; your father will not allow you to come home! You have made your bed, now you lie in it!" and she put the 'phone down. I felt broken hearted. June consoled me and said, 'Come on, just give it time'. Today I thank the Lord for June and that I stayed there because He had a plan.

Eventually I started to settle down. I got on well with the patients and staff. I also took an interest and learned about different illnesses and diseases.

Another problem was emerging as I was having terrible nightmares. They had started early in my childhood but now if I woke up after a bad dream my new friend June, who was in the room next door to me, would very graciously let me get into her bed. It was a bit of a squeeze in June's bed though as it was only a single bed. June did not seem to mind at all and she would say to me "You might as well come to me early at night so that you don't wake me up. " She was very kind to me.

Eventually it was time for me to visit Matron's office to sign on.

I realised that I had let myself in for training for two years State Enrolled Nurse (SEN). But by this time I was beginning to settle down in my new hospital surroundings.

I was filled with fear and dread as I arrived in the classroom although the Tutor seemed to be nice and approachable. The Tutor Sister did not realise that I had some serious problems. I still had a cleft palate and so I had been very careful with my speech because I did not want anyone to know. If they did know, no one had said anything. I was getting on well on the hospital ward and I had been giving my all for the benefit of the patients. I genuinely loved the work and I was interested in all that was going on.

One day I did something to upset the ward Sister. I was in the sluice cleaning bedpans and sputum mugs which was a horrible job. There were no disposable items in those days. Sister came in to tell me off because I had left a bed untidy and the wheels were not facing the correct way after making the bed. Sister told me I was very slapdash and did not concentrate on my work. As Sister walked towards me I thought she was going to hit me. I quickly lifted my arm up across my face. Sister looked alarmed and said, "Good gracious girl, I'm not going to hit you." I felt so nervous. I think she thought I was behaving like a frightened rabbit. After that Sister seemed a bit more tolerant towards me.

As time went on I became more settled working on the ward. I got on well with patients and with the staff. One night we went out to a dance and I met a young man called Colin. We got on well and went out together for a time. I was very concerned about him kissing me though because I still thought that a baby was made through kissing, even then! One night we had an argument when he tried to kiss me. I told him that I didn't want to have a baby. He answered "I do not plan to go that far!" He also said that he thought I needed some kind of help. After that our relationship did not last long.

The time came when I had to join the other girls in the class for lectures which I found difficult. The Sister Tutor was quite nice. The other nurses were taking notes while I just scribbled in a notebook feeling very apprehensive. The time soon came when we had to complete test papers, which I dreaded.

Much to my surprise, I had been learning much more than I realised and I had remembered almost everything that the Sister Tutor had taught us in the classes. I was also accomplishing the all the requirements of the practical training. I did not find the test too difficult and the Sister Tutor appeared to be very pleased with the way I was progressing. After she had examined my bandaging techniques she told me that I would go far and even commented that it was perfect! However, I was finding it increasingly difficult to hide the fact that I could not write.

One day after several excuses for why I was not writing the Sister Tutor became a bit suspicious of me. She was noticing that I had an excuse every week and whenever we had a test Sister noticed that I was not starting to write. On one particular day when the other girls were writing answers to the questions Sister came to me and asked, 'Why haven't you started to answer the questions on the paper?'

I told Sister that I did not need to write because I already knew the questions. Sister replied, "Well nurse, I don't know that you know the answers to the questions. I need to see your answers on the paper." The problem was that I did not know how to write the answers down. I felt Sister watching me and then she sent for another Sister to come into the classroom and take care of the other girls while she asked me to go with her to her office. I went into Sister's office feeling very concerned. Just as Sister Tutor had sat down and as I was standing in front of her with my hands behind my back, (thinking I am not leaving) - the phone rang. Then Sister Tutor said to me, "Go to your room, I will get back to you." I went to my room in the nurses' home and sat on my bed feeling very anxious about what was going to happen to me. I lit up a cigarette and thought again "I am not leaving." At that time I was feeling very determined. Then there was a knock at my door and I panicked, as I thought that it was the Sister Tutor. I opened the door but to my surprise it was a nurse in my class called Dorothy. I let her come into my room and she said, "I want to talk to you about your performance and excuses in the class. You can write, can't you?" So I replied "Yes, I can!" Dorothy said, "No, you cannot and I want to help you." I replied, "I do not need any help!" Then Dorothy said, "You won't last long here unless you get help. My parents have got a friend who is a retired policeman and teaches backward children." Then Dorothy said she was going to arrange for me to meet the policeman.

The day came for me to go to the policeman's house to meet him as arranged. As I reached the door I felt very nervous. Quite a big man opened the door but he was very friendly towards me. We had a long chat and we talked about my difficulties. Then he started to teach me how to write. As I wrote, he remarked "I don't know how you have got away with it!" I found learning to write very hard but he persevered with me.

Sometime afterwards the Sister Tutor told me that I had to complete the test paper. She said that I was a good Nurse and that I must try a lot harder with the theory. I decided to start to fight for this aspect of my career and so I started to work hard. With the help of the policeman my writing improved considerably. I also learned how to spell medical words which was also very difficult for me. Then my marks for completed test papers started to go up and I always came top in the practical tests.

Sister Tutor seemed to be quite pleased with my progress.

During all this time I was still involved with the occult. I had lucky charms around my neck and I was reading the stars in the paper. I also read books about predicting the future and I tried to find a good fortune teller. At this time I had another friend and we used to go for picnics in the country in her boyfriend's car. Sometimes we didn't have enough food for the four of us. On one occasion, one of the girls decided to go for a long walk and left me in charge of the food. I felt so hungry that I started to eat and ended up eating it all! There was no food left for the other three. I was not very popular that day!

One day while we were on duty the Ward Sister informed all of the nursing staff on her ward that we would be required to attend an early morning service in the Church of England. I was not looking forward to going to the church and the idea of it seemed quite bizarre! I was also finding that the thought of it jolted some painful memories. The night before our scheduled church visit I went to the pictures and then I went to bed very late. The consequence was that I overslept the following morning and I did not hear the night nurse banging on my door. When my friend came to my room expecting me to be ready for church I was still asleep in bed! We had to put on clean uniforms and I was in a rush to get dressed. I felt horrible and certainly not ready to attend church!

When I was eventually ready we met up with the other staff at the main entrance. The Sister said to me, "You are late, a bad start to the day." I felt awful. We had a long walk to the church and it was very cold inside the church. I had not had anything to eat or drink and no sooner had we stood up to sing the first hymn than I fell flat on my face in the aisle. When I came back to my senses a man was trying to give me a drink of water. Sister was not pleased with me at all and told me to 'pull myself together.' She asked me what was wrong with me. I did not know what the trouble with me was. Sister said that I had let the nursing profession down and no one spoke to me for some time. On the way back to the hospital I felt dreadful. I asked my friend, "What happened to me?" June informed me that I had fainted. I still felt dreadful and I was sent to my room on our return to the hospital. Then a doctor came in with Home Sister, who just glared at me whilst the doctor asked me some questions. Although my answers were not very intelligent the doctor told Sister that I was fit to go back on duty.

At this time I made friends with a nurse called Marta. She was a German girl who was engaged to an English boy. Sometimes four of us went out to have picnics. I did not want to get involved with any boy because my only interest at that time was nursing. Then one day Marta asked me to be her bridesmaid. My answer to her was "No!" Marta seemed disappointed and wanted to know why I had refused her request so I told her that I did not like weddings. Marta was a bit surprised but she left it at that and never asked me again.

Christmas was approaching once again but I was not looking forward to it. At that time in my life I did not understand the true meaning of the celebration although we did have a lot of fun once all of the decorations were up. On Christmas Day and Boxing Day we did not have any time off. We had to do all the essential work of the ward, such as dressings and treatments. Only when the ward work was finished were we allowed time to enjoy ourselves. All the Nurses on the ward had to subscribe for a present for Sister and we had to buy presents for each other which were put into a tub. We went into the kitchen to distribute our presents to each other. Sister appeared to be in a good mood. We also helped some of the patients to open their presents. When all the work was done to Sister's satisfaction we were allowed to go to visit the other wards.

I usually went to see what alcohol was available on the other wards and we usually had a quite lot to drink, but I always put the patients first. Some of the staff had too much to drink but I was fortunate that I was able to 'hold' my drink.

At this time I was on the men's ward which I enjoyed because they were quite good fun. The men's Christmas dinner was the best part of the day. There was turkey and pudding and plenty of beer. All the Doctors used to come on the ward and usually the Senior Surgeon would carve the turkey. The visitors came after lunch bringing presents and strewing the ward with paper and string. During Christmas time some of the Nurses visited the theatre for the pantomime and I went along but I did not enjoy it, especially when the clowns came on. Their faces reminded me of the burnt faces I had seen in hospital.

Also when I went to the circus, I had to leave. The memories of when I had to be shown how to apply make-up on my face when I was fifteen years old was too painful for me. I had to watch the make-up lady apply make-up on two patients in a room and they reminded me of clowns. They used Max Factor make-up and even to this day I do not like that name.

After that Christmas there was a different kind of crisis called the Asian flu. Many patients died and a lot of the Nursing staff were off sick. It was fortunate that I didn't get the flu. Eventually the epidemic came to an end and our lives returned to normal again.

One day to my surprise I received a letter from Sister Owen from St. Asaph hospital. I also had one from Stoke Mandeville hospital for an appointment for the outpatient's clinic. I felt so excited! The thought of going back to the hospital that I loved! I had to make an appointment to see Matron and I felt a bit concerned as I anticipated what her response might be. However, I need not have worried because Matron appeared to be understanding about it.

It was quite a long journey from Bristol. I attended my appointment at Stoke Mandeville Hospital during the afternoon.

Stoke Mandeville Hospital

The hospital was built in 1940. It was converted Nissen huts. In 1944 Stoke Mandeville spinal injuries unit was opened to receive British D Day casualties. It was Ludwig Gutmann, a German Jewish refugee who revolutionised the treatment of the spinally injured.

While waiting in the outpatients department a Nurse called me in to see the consultant, a Professor Kilner. I was surprised that a new Surgeon was seeing me. I started to feel excited as I thought that there might be another chance for my palate to be repaired. He examined my mouth and then he asked me if I had got any problems so I immediately asked him if he could repair my palate. I told him that I couldn't be a good Nurse with a cleft palate. He appeared to be a kind man and he smiled at me. He was a lot different from my last Plastic Surgeon, Emlyn Lewis. At that moment one of the Surgeons amongst his entourage stood up and said, "She has been told over and over again that her palate cannot be repaired." I recognised him from Broadgreen Hospital in Liverpool. The Professor did not even look at him but just said, "Sit down, Mr. Osbourne." Again he looked at me and smiled and told me to go outside with the Nurse while he discussed my case notes. While I was waiting in the corridor I turned my thoughts to God, the highest authority of all. I asked God to make the Doctors say that they would attempt to repair my palate.

Eventually I was called back in to the room. Mr Kilner smiled again at me and told me to sit down. I felt very nervous indeed! He then explained to me what he was going to attempt to do for my palate. They were going to take a tube graft from my side and try to repair it using this. I thanked him and I left the hospital feeling very excited. I made my way back to Bristol feeling very elated. I eagerly awaited the letter informing me that I was to be admitted to the hospital.

I returned to my duties on the ward in a very happy mood and I tried to please the patients as much as I can.

The ward Sister appeared to be stricter towards the staff about ward hygiene and was always chasing us around and harassing us. We also had to watch out for the ward cleaners as they could make your life a misery, especially if you walked on their recently mopped floors! Sometimes if you were in a mad hurry to get through your work load you would forget but the cleaner would soon remind you with a hard slap across your legs with a wet floor cloth, which was quite painful!

One of the Doctors asked one of my friends, Pat if she would baby-sit for him and his wife. One day Pat asked me if I would go with her. I said "Yes!" because I thought I could do some studying while I was there. (Sister Tutor had informed me that she could not make any sense of what I had written in the last test paper).

Pat and I arrived at the doctor's house to meet his wife and baby who was a six month old pretty little baby girl. Much to my annoyance the baby would not settle down to sleep. Pat took her out of the cot, changed her, gave her a bottle and made a fuss of her. I did not approve of this and told Pat to put the baby back in the cot. Pat did so but the baby kept crying so that meant that we did not get any studying done at all that evening!

After a few weeks of us babysitting Pat was not able to attend so the Doctor asked me if I would babysit. I replied "Yes" but I was not going to put up with a crying baby! So I arrived at the Doctor's house with my books ready to study during the evening.

As usual the baby would not settle down to sleep so I changed her and gave her a drink in the cot and told her 'You are not coming out of the cot'. I also told her that if she had my father no way would she come out. The baby started to cry and scream so after a bit I'd had more than enough and I decided to look for some whisky. I did not have to look far! I found the drinks cabinet and I thought the doctor must be an old boozer! I then remembered that my grandma used to give her children whisky when they were teething so I poured 1 part whisky and 2 ounces of orange into a glass. The baby didn't like it but I made her drink it. After 15 minutes there was silence at last. I looked at her in the cot and she was flat out! When the Doctors came home they seemed pleased that the baby was asleep.

The next day when the Doctor was doing his ward round with Sister he called me over and said, 'Nurse I want to speak to you. Whatever did you do to our baby?' A sudden thought came to me that the baby might be dead. Sister was looking at me in a very disapproving way because in those days Doctors did not speak to junior Nurses in front of the Ward Sister. Then the Doctor said, "It was the first night's sleep we have had since the baby was born."

After the ward round the Sister asked me how I knew the Doctor so I told her it was through babysitting while they went out. Sister gave a funny sort of laugh! When I told Pat all about it she could not believe what I had done and asked me "You do not like babies, do you?" I had to think about that for some time as I was not sure.

Back to Hospital Again

I received a letter to inform me that I had been given an appointment at Stoke Mandeville Hospital. I was so excited that during my coffee break, which was just half an hour, I changed my apron and went to Matron's office to show her the letter. After discussing it with her Matron gave her permission for me to attend the appointment.

Eventually the day came and I was admitted onto ward 6 of Stoke Mandeville Hospital which was a converted Nissen hut. On my arrival the Nurse showed me to my bed. My excitement at being admitted for my operation did not last long as I met the girl in the bed next to mine. Her name was Ruth and she had horrific injuries and disfigurements due to burns. There were rumours on the ward that her parents had disowned her because of her injuries.

Sadly, when we were asked to sit at the table at tea time there were even more horrific sights as two of the patients there did not have noses! Ruth appeared to be friendly towards me and we became friends. In between operations we became a bit of a trial to the Nurses on duty because we wanted to go walk-about and we also went to the pictures. Ruth was so brave in the way that she faced people who did not understand her disfigurements and eventually I got used to it all.

One day the doctor came to see me. He examined me and said that I was going to theatre the next morning to have an abdominal rise for a pedicle flap. The trouble was that I didn't realise the extent of the surgery. I thought it would only be a skin graft. I still felt excited because I was thinking it would all be over soon. Little did I know what was to come!

When I came round from the anaesthetic the first thing I did was to put my tongue to the top of my mouth. Oh dear, what a shock I got! I still had a cleft palate and I felt so upset. Then I realised my side was very sore and I could not turn over. The nurse came to examine my side and the hundreds of stitches that I'd had. I had to stay flat on my back for a few days. When I was allowed up I felt very weak but it soon passed.

We all used to go down to the restaurant or to the pictures in one of the huts and we all seemed to be so happy. (I think that we were as happy as we possibly could have been under the circumstances).

Eventually I was given the 'all-clear' by the Medical staff for me to be discharged from hospital. I went home to Prestatyn, which was not a very good idea! My father ignored me and I did not get on very well with my mother who continually told me that I should not be in nursing.

I had to lie flat on my side for five months. Eventually the day came for me to return to work at Bristol hospital to continue my training. On my return Matron was quite kind to me. I was asked to work on a women's ward. When I arrived at Sister's office to report for duty she asked "Matron tells me that you have been in hospital. What did you have done?" I explained to the Sister that I had an abdominal rise for a pedicle flap. Sister looked surprised and her reply to me was, "Say that in English, Nurse!" Then Sister gave me the job of blanket bathing with another nurse who informed me that this ward is christened 'Harvey ward' because one of the women patients was very dominant and her name was Mrs Harvey.

I was soon to discover just how much when it was her turn to have a bath! I sensed that she took an instant dislike to me. Apparently one of her favourite Nurses, called Rose, had left the hospital, and there was no way that I would be able to live up to 'Rose'!

Mrs. Harvey found fault with everything that I did. I thought to myself "Why did I have to replace a Nurse who could do no wrong?"

To make matters even worse for me, Mrs. Harvey had a lovely ornament which had been given to her by Rose. On my first day back at work I felt a bit insecure and nervous as I did not know the patients and unfortunately whilst turning Mrs Harvey, my elbow knocked the precious ornament onto the floor and it broke into pieces. Sister came running in as Mrs. Harvey started to scream loudly. Sister wanted to know exactly what was going on. Although Mrs. Harvey was hysterical she was only too quick to inform Sister of what had happened to her precious ornament. By this time I had gone brilliant red in my face. Sister asked me "O Nurse, why are you so careless?" I felt terrible as Sister tried to comfort Mrs. Harvey who was not willing to be consoled.

I did offer to pay for the ornament or even to buy a new one but that seemed to make Mrs. Harvey even more hysterical as he continued to scream and glare at me!

Eventually when the drama had ended we had to give her some treatment, which took up most of the morning. Sister was not very pleased but I did apologise and I tried to appease Mrs. Harvey but she never forgave me.

I wondered if anything else could possibly go wrong. I soon found out that it could! The Nurse who I was working with told me not to worry as it was an accident and told me nobody liked Mrs Harvey. This same Nurse also said that she felt sorry for me. After that the Sister sent me to the sluice to test the diabetic urines for sugar. The only trouble was that I made a mistake with the amount of spirit I used in the Bunsen burner. The next thing that happened was that there were flames coming out of the test tube! It frightened the life out of me! Another Nurse quickly came to my rescue and exclaimed "Oh dear, Nurse Baker, what are we going to do with you?" Together, we managed to get the mess sorted out before Sister found out about my carelessness but by this time my confidence had gone completely. It was such a terrible start to my first day on the ward. When my shift finally ended, I returned to my room exhausted but I still had to administer my own treatment on my pedicle graft.

On a day soon after I had to attend the dreaded classroom. On that particular day we were having lessons on how to bandage. We were taught how to do the figure of eight bandage and the spiral bandage on arms and legs. I got top marks for the practical test and Sister Tutor appeared to be very pleased with how quickly I learned the practical side. She told me that I was making good progress in nursing but said that I need to work harder with the theory but I had decided that I would carry on regardless.

I made huge a mistake because I showed my friend Pat, the surgery that I had received myself. When I showed her my pedicle graft she could not believe what she saw but assured me that it would be kept confidential. I later found out that the information had been passed all around the hospital. However, I was not too concerned as I thought that others would learn about plastic surgery.

Some of the staff thought that I should be off work on sick leave. But the thought of being at home for any length of time did not appeal to me at all! One day whilst I was on duty a very disturbed patient grabbed my side and was holding me and pulling me so I had to push myself into her body and shout for help until someone came to rescue me.

During this period of time in my life I was still involved with lucky charms and reading the stars in the papers and magazines and I was still having nightmares.

I went to the pictures when I was off duty. One night one of the Nurses with whom I was friends asked me to go to a dance with her. It was the last thing I wanted to do especially with the graft on my side. I was worried that it might get damaged. I was also worried that we might meet some boys. Anyway my friend said that it would do me good to have a change so I decided to go with her. We were going to meet her boyfriend at the dance. As usual I wore my green dance dress. I felt scared because of my pedicle graft but fortunately no one asked me to dance. After a while my friend was dancing the night away and so I decided to go outside for a cigarette. I was sitting down on a seat when a young man came and sat by me. We started to have a conversation but I was not in the mood for talking because I felt very weary and told him so. He appeared to be kind and went to get me a drink, a gin and orange which seemed to revive me. At last the time arrived to go back to the Nurses' home. I felt absolutely exhausted. When we arrived back in our rooms we decided to make a cup of coffee but then I discovered that we had run out of sugar. I told Pat that I had seen the light still on in one of the Nurse's rooms so I would go and ask her for some sugar. Pat replied "No, you cannot ask her; because it is the 'Holy Joes' having a prayer meeting!" That did not bother me because I just wanted some sugar and so I walked down the dimly lit corridor. I knocked at the door and it was opened by Maureen, the very first Nurse that I had met in the Nurses' home when I arrived. Maureen gently pulled me into the room and said jokingly to the other three girls, "A fairy has come into my room and she keeps on twirling me around." I asked Maureen if I could please have some sugar.

Christians!

It was the first time in my life that I had come into contact with Christians. I did not like them because I thought they were strange. When I got back to my room with the sugar Pat said, 'You have got a nerve!' Another thing that had been happening on a regular basis around that time was that someone was leaving me a drink and a cake every night. Then one night I caught the person who was leaving the things. To my amazement, it was the Sister Tutor. She looked embarrassed but she didn't say anything and neither did I.

Considering I went to bed so late at night I was able to wake up early. I had the job of getting some nurses up because they were not able to get up after Sister had called them. I would often put a lump of ice down their backs then I would make sure that I would be standing by the door to make a quick getaway as they were not very pleased to have ice put down their backs!

One day I received a letter from Westminster hospital, London for an out patient's appointment to have my pedicle examined. I felt quite excited but also nervous wondering if I had looked after it well enough. When I arrived at the hospital, I was waiting to see the surgeon when I noticed a girl coming out of the doctor's room crying. Then another girl went into see the doctor and she came out crying too. I thought to myself 'What is going on here?' I began to get worried, especially when one girl showed me her pedicle and it had died. It had gone black and blue.

When eventually I was called in to see the doctor they were very pleased and said my pedicle was beautiful. They rang another doctor to come and have a look and they all seemed delighted with my progress and told me what the next stage would be: my right arm would be attached to one end of the pedicle for three to four weeks. I would be admitted back to Stoke Mandeville hospital in a few weeks' time. I did feel genuinely sorry for the other two girls but very excited for myself. When I arrived back at Bristol hospital I told

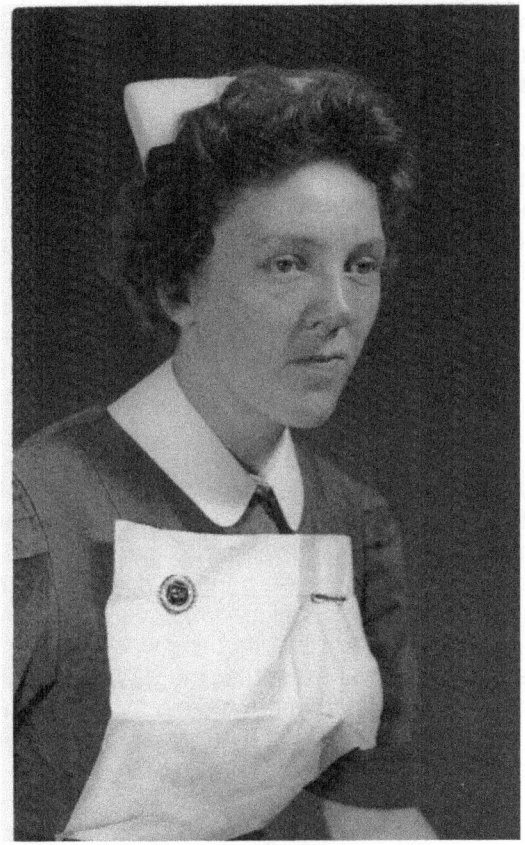

Louie Baker at Bristol Hospital

Pat my news. She said, 'I do not know how you can be so happy about it when you have all that surgery ahead of you. I would be

terrified'. I did not feel worried about it at all.

The day came when I received a letter to be admitted to the hospital. At work, I went through the same process and once again I changed my apron in my coffee break and took the letter to Matron, feeling very nervous because during training the Matron had the right to say what she thought was best for her nursing staff. As it turned out Matron appeared to be very kind towards me and gave me permission and special leave to go.

So the day arrived when I took myself off to Aylesbury, Buckinghamshire on the steam train via London and the underground. When I arrived at Stoke Mandeville I walked up the usual corridor to ward 6 and as I walked past the theatres I felt very excited but I also began to feel some apprehension as I considered what was ahead of me. I was determined to co-operate with the medical staff. As I approached the ward Sister Clarke was by the main door to the ward. When she saw me she said, 'Come along, Louie, we are waiting for you.' I went into the office to be admitted and then I was taken to my bed.

Oh dear, what a shock I got! I noticed the other patients and it was not a pretty sight! One girl had her arm up to her forehead; another had a raw red flap from the lower part of her face holding her head down. Another girl had a pedicle hanging down from her arm to the lower part of her of her leg which looked very uncomfortable. I felt very sorry for them but the amazing thing was that they all appeared to be cheerful. That is, all except for me as I was beginning to feel very nervous. We all sat around the table for our tea, which I could hardly eat because I was put off by a strong smell of antiseptic that was about.

Eventually I settled down with the other patients. The next day all the doctors were doing their ward rounds and they seemed very pleased with my pedicle and told me that I have good healing flesh. I was told that I was going to have one end of the pedicle attached to my arm just above the inside of my elbow for three to four weeks and that I was due to go in to the theatre the following morning. I had the usual tests that all patients go through. The doctor came at night to examine my chest and gave me the all-clear. I was feeling increasingly nervous wondering how I would cope with it all.

The next morning I was taken to the theatre and wheeled into the anaesthetic room. The anaesthetist came to me with a syringe, put the needle into my veins and told me to count to five. I didn't make it and the next thing I knew I was back in bed being very sick.

Then I was given an injection and knew nothing until the following morning. The night nurse gave me a cup of tea at 6:00am and I forgot that my arm was attached to my right side and it hurt when I tried to move it. I shouted out and the nurse said, 'You will get used to it and you will learn how to deal with it'. So as the days wore on I became stronger and I was allowed to get up although I found it very difficult only using one arm to do certain things like washing myself or using the toilet. But somehow I found a way round the difficulties. The Sister took me to the dressing room to examine my side and clean the pedicle I looked at it and there seemed to be a lot of stitches around my arm which caused me to lose my appetite and I just did not feel like eating anything.

One evening one of the patients asked me to go to the pictures which were shown in one of the Nissen huts. I thought that I would really like to go with her but of course we had to have permission first from the Staff nurse who was in charge of the ward that evening. She said 'No1' firmly that I could not leave the ward and I felt very disappointed.

On another night some of the patients went to the Social Club and again I was not allowed to go with them. I was feeling a bit fed up! One evening a nurse was in charge of the ward and she was a nice soft nurse and we managed to win her around and she allowed me to go to the pictures. The nurse was concerned about it though and said that I could only go if I was in a wheelchair and instructed us to come back to the ward as soon as the film ended. I felt much better after getting away from the ward for a few hours and I enjoyed the films.

The day came when I was to have my stitches taken out and Sister was very pleased with my progress and pleased with the fact that I had no infection in my pedicle. I remember one occasion when a poor little girl was very upset because apparently she had an infection in her graft and it had died which meant that she would have to go through all of those operations again.

I was getting stronger every day and I was able to dress myself in some sort of way, but that is not easy when you have a pedicle between your side and your arm but I did manage quite well, considering my circumstances! I was given permission to leave the ward on occasions and we usually went to the canteen to have a chat with some of the patients from other wards or we would go to the Nissen hut for the pictures.

Towards the end of the four week stay the Sister told me it was nearly time to have my pedicle raised up to the inside of my mouth. I felt very uneasy about this news. One morning the surgeon came round the ward with his entourage. He examined me and he told me, 'You are nearly ready for the next stage, the raising of the pedicle. You know what to expect, don't you?' I just nodded my head but I quietly thought to myself 'God, help me!'

The next day I had to go to the Dental department to have caps fitted on my own teeth. The dentist was called Mr Hamilton and was a tall, dark-haired man. He was quite good looking and I had an infatuation for him, poor man! I think he would have run a mile or maybe he would have just laughed if he had known! I found it difficult to eat with caps on my teeth as they were quite big and uncomfortable. The following day a doctor came to measure me for a helmet made of Plaster of Paris which had steel rods sprouting from it and were screwed into the plaster. He told me what the procedure would be which I thought was quite nerve racking!

Sister told me that if I was sick after the operation then the pedicle would be damaged. I replied 'Sister I am always sick after having anaesthetic.' To which Sister replied 'Oh well, we will have to give you something to calm you.'

On my return to the ward the patients laughed at me! They said that I looked like something out of space! I replied to them, 'Yes I feel like an alien!', but I felt very nervous. During the afternoon Sister told me that I was on the list for theatre the following morning. I did not feel like eating any tea or supper in the evening so the nurse said, 'You must eat as it will be a long time before you eat again'.

During the evening we heard a scream from the dressing room. Then one patient said, 'Oh dear, they have shown her a mirror.' I remembered that some patients did not like what had been done for them and were very upset when they saw themselves in the mirror.

The night nurse gave me a sleeping tablet and I slept until 6:00am when the night nurse brought me a cup of tea and a round of toast which I could not eat. Then the nurse prepared me for theatre. My bed was then moved to the front of the ward by Sister's office. Then I had my pre-med which was Omnopon and Scopolamine. As I was lying quietly waiting for the theatre trolley I started to have second thoughts about my arm being raised up and when the trolley arrived and I climbed onto it myself then I lay down but I began to feel very sick. The staff nurse said, 'Relax, take a deep breath' but it did not work. My mouth was bone dry and I was nervous at the thought of what it was going to be like afterwards when I came round from the anaesthetic. The nurses calmed me by their words. They told me that I was doing well and that it would soon be over.

The anaesthetist came and took my arm and said 'Count to five' but again I did not make it to the number five. They told me later that when I came round from recovery I had been asleep for 24 hours. Later on however, it felt like I could not move at all. I tried to move my head but I could not. I tried to talk but I could not.

I felt very uncomfortable. A nurse started to give me a drink with a rubber tube attached to a feeder. Everything was very difficult and uncomfortable when I tried to do things. When the day came that I was taken out of bed I felt very top-heavy and I thought I was going to fall over. The Physiotherapist helped me to take a few steps around my bed. Going to the bathroom and toilet was a bit of a nightmare. But eventually I got my balance and could cope with the situation that I was in.

When Sister did a ward round, which was usually in the morning, I would ask her 'Can I be moved up in the ward?' The answer to that question was always a firm 'No!' I did not feel very keen at being just under the office window and I wanted to be near my friends.

One day I saw Mr Osborne in the office. I used to see him in Broadgreen Hospital in Liverpool. He had been against my palate being repaired and had told me that it could not be done. As he walked towards me I felt nervous as I wondered what he was going to say. But he was kind to me. He looked at my pedicle and the inside of my mouth and he put his hand on my shoulder and said, 'You are doing very well, Louie'.

When new patients came on the ward they just stared at me until they got used to the sight of me. One day two girls came and sat by my bed and they massaged my arm and shoulder because it was always aching until the night nurse told them to go back to their beds and said, 'Louie is alright'. I felt disappointed as it was the first time in my life that I had been spoilt like that.

All the visitors used to stare at me but I got used to it. One day I asked Sister if I could go to the pictures. When I saw the expression on her face I knew that her answer was going to be 'No.' One of the awful things was the food stuff they gave me at mealtimes as it tasted horrible and I would enter into a battle over it with the staff.

Sometimes I would give the food to the plants which all died! The staff could not understand why the plants had died! Then one day a nurse caught me just as I was doing it and I got into trouble. She told me she was going to stand over me until I had finished it all.

One morning Sister informed me that I was to go to the dentist for a check-up on the caps around my teeth. Sister brought a wheelchair, which I refused, telling Sister that I could walk.

Sister and I walked down the corridor and three workmen were coming towards us. They were all talking together and laughing until they saw me and the expressions on their faces changed completely. They all looked quite shocked!

When I arrived at the dentist I sat on a chair opposite a boy who looked horrified at me and said, 'Mum' and pushed his face into his mother. These people had come from outside to see the dentist and they just sat and stared at me. Then the dental nurse came out and called me and Sister took me in to see Mr. Hamilton who seemed pleased to see me.

Since my arm was raised he came twice a day to give me treatment which was not very pleasant when I was lying on the dressing room trolley. I just lay quiet and let him get on with Sister and staff nurse. I think they were expecting me to make a fuss but I did not. He even used to come to see me on Sundays.

One of the patients said, 'We don't hear you cry out. You are very brave'. They told me that some patients make a fuss. The only reason that I did not react badly was because I liked Mr Hamilton so much!

During the mornings Matron always conducted her ward round with the ward Sister. I was usually the first patient Matron saw because I was so near to the office. Matron had a word with Sister about my progress and then asked me, 'How are you?' I thought to myself, should I answer her by saying that 'My head is driving me nuts with the continual itching' or I thought maybe my answer should be 'My shoulder is aching most of the time' or maybe I should just tell her how hungry I am! Instead of all these options I just tried to nod quietly and politely. Matron just smiled and walked off to see the next patient.

One morning Sister came to me and said, 'Come, we are going to the photograph department. As we were walking down the corridor I was given the usual stares by everyone who saw mw. It was a bit of a nightmare having the photo session. I had to look in different ways, up, down and sideways. When I got back on the ward I realised that I hadn't seen myself in the mirror so I got my mirror out. Oh dear, what a shock! I knew that I looked a bit freakish by the way people stared at me but I realised then that I looked frightful!

I just stared at myself in the mirror and then I started to cry and I could not stop. Then a nurse came to me and she said 'You must stop crying or you will damage your graft', so I tried to stop crying which was difficult for me to do.

I was still receiving treatment from Mr Hamilton, the dentist and during the treatment Sister and Staff nurse would join him. Staff was holding my loose arm and Sister stood by my legs. Mr Hamilton stood behind my head with his machine giving me the treatment whilst my head was tipped right back. I tried to keep still as much as possible which was not easy at all. When Mr Hamilton had left Sister and Staff began to tease me about why I had kept so still and

115

said, 'You must like him'. I nodded my head and thought quietly 'Yes, I do.'

As I entered the third week of my stay I was moved up the ward some distance away from the office and Sister's gaze.

One day I received a letter from my mother and also a parcel of sweets and chocolate. I do not think that my mother had much idea of what I was going through. I also received a letter from Sister Owen who, I think must have obtained my address from my Mother.

I could not read her writing so I asked one of the girls who was a teacher to read the letter but I decided not to tell her of how much I hated school teachers. Then I thought of Hannah and thought if only she could see me now she would have a shock. I started to cry again because I knew that I was not able to write to her and I liked her so much. On the ward I tried to help the other patients and the nursing staff by carrying cups of tea but Sister came out of the office and caught me. Sister was not pleased with this and she would not allow me to do anything. I remember sitting down and feeling a bit weak because I was not eating. Deep down inside me I was feeling as though I had had enough of it all. Then came some news which cheered me up a bit, my friend Ruth was coming back for more skin grafts. Once a week the head Plastic Surgeons did a ward round with Sister and when they arrived at my bed Sister complained to the doctor that I was not eating or taking the fluid that was sent for me. I tried to tell the entourage that the stuff they were giving me was atrocious but the doctor just smiled at me and told me that it would not be long now for the next stage of my graft and that all was well. Then all of the doctors went to examine patient next to me.

I was full of dread about the next operation. Ruth arrived back on the ward and as usual appeared to be confident. I felt envious of here because in the evening she and some others were going to the pictures, which were held in one of the Nissen huts and I was not allowed to go. One day I was walking about the ward feeling fed up and hungry. Ruth was in theatre having her next skin graft and a big discussion was going on amongst the patients about the Suez Canal crisis. This was 1956 and the Prime Minister was Anthony Eden. Nasser had nationalised the Suez Canal Company of Egypt and the invasion by British troops almost started the 3rd World War.

Everybody was very worried as the invasion was illegal. Eventually the crisis passed after a lot of trouble and anxiety for our government.

The day came when the Surgeon and his entourage came to examine me ready for the next stage of my graft. It had been decided that I was going to theatre next day so I was feeling very nervous about the result of my pedicle and palate. The following day I went through the usual performance of getting ready for theatre, the trolley arrived Sister came with me to the Anaesthetic room.

Whilst I was waiting there, I fell asleep and began to dream.

I dreamt that I was in a garden full of flowers and Sister was in the garden with me. Eventually the Anaesthetist came to put me to sleep.

When I came round after the operation Sister was standing by my bed. I asked her where my arm was. Sister touched my arm and I nearly screamed because I was in such agony. I couldn't bear to touch my arm as it felt like a ton weight. The next day the Physiotherapist came to give me exercise but I tried to stop her because it was so painful. She was very nice but also very firm. I kept asking her not to touch my arm but her answer was that I must co-operate with her and that I must do exercises with her or I would lose the use of my arm! So I began to do what I was told to do which was not easy as it was all very painful. When the day came to get me out of bed I nearly fell flat on my face. I could not believe the weight of my arm as it was so heavy! The two physiotherapists had to hold me up. Some of the patients told me I was quite good as one of the patients kept screaming when she had her arm done but I do not think that I had enough energy to scream like that! At first my fingers would not work but after about two weeks my arm started to feel normal again although it remained weak for some time. Eventually I started to walk and get stronger and get dressed. Ruth was also up and about. My appetite was not very good and it was decided that I should have a 'jaw 1 diet' which meant fluids only which was not very nice for me. I thought that the dinners were horrible and that they were like slop, but I liked the blancmange and jelly that they served me.

Another patient who was admitted to the ward was a girl called Ann. She had an extensive birthmark covering a large area of her face. Sister allowed us to leave the ward together so we went down to the canteen. As we passed the Spinal wards we became inquisitive to know what the wards were like but we did not get very far because Sister stepped in our way. However, we did know that the patients were in wheelchairs as we had seen them in the corridors and in the grounds. We used to have a good time in the canteen seeing other people from different wards. When we arrived back on our ward I felt very weary as it was nearly bedtime and I soon fell asleep.

The next day I had to go to the dental department to have the caps removed from my teeth. When I went into the dental room Mr Hamilton was with another dentist. When He saw me he said, 'Here is Louie, my star patient'. One morning the head Plastic Surgeon did a round with his entourage. I was told that my next operation was due and that during the operation I would have one side of my pedicle attached to my palate.

So once again it was the same routine, I was dressed in the usual cap, gown, long white socks and the usual pre-med. As soon as the nurse appeared with the syringe containing the pre-med injection I began to feel sick at the thought of it. I felt very apprehensive and, as usual, the nurse told me to take deep breaths but it did not help. The theatre trolley arrived and I was taken to the anaesthetic room where I was still feeling unwell. Once in there all of my feelings soon ended as I was put to sleep. Later on when I came round I found that I had been returned to the ward. Once again my bed was placed by the Sister's office but, as the days went by, I was moved further up the ward. I felt very weak. Ann had her operation but she was not very pleased with the result. Part of the problem was that when people have plastic surgery they expect to look normal very soon afterwards but it does not usually happen that way and more often than not it takes a long time to heal.

We began visiting the pictures as soon as Sister allowed us to.

Then one night Ruth fell out with me over a boy. Ruth arrived at the entrance to the ward with a boy and she looked very pleased with herself. After the boy had gone Ruth came up to my bed where I was sitting up and she asked me if I liked him. I answered her, 'No, I don't like him.' Ruth was upset about that so Ann took her aside and they would not speak to me after that. I was not in the right mood for a boyfriend. I did not mind speaking to boys but I did not want to get involved.

Soon after this Ruth and Ann were planning to go out of the ward without me. So, I apologised to Ruth and she accepted it and that evening we went to the pictures in the Nissen hut. On another afternoon while we were having our tea at a long table in the centre of the ward I noticed a new patient unpacking her case by her bed. I thought how nice she looked. Then the nurse brought her over to the table and said, 'This is Miss Campbell' and we all just smiled. Little did I know what was to come later on!

There was also another new patient who did not have a nose but just had two holes in her face, which was due to burns. When we had finished our tea some of us went to the social Nissen hut.

The next day the new patients had their operations. In the evening we left the ward but when we returned the night nurse told us off for coming back late. Just as I was collecting my night clothes to get ready for bed I heard someone call my name. All the lights were out so I had a bit of a job finding who was calling because my bed was now at the top of the ward. Then as I was walking down towards the bathroom I realised it was one of the new patients. Her bed was by the office and as I was walking past I heard, 'Louie'. It was 'Miss Campbell' so I asked her what she wanted and to my amazement she asked me to read a passage from her Bible. I was shocked by this and I found what she had asked me to do unusual and difficult. I immediately answered her by saying 'No!' But she would not take no for an answer. I explained to her told her that I could not read very well but Miss Campbell said, 'Come, now, this is a very easy verse from the Psalms'. I started to feel infuriated and I told her that I did not like Bibles and suggested to her that she should ask the night nurse to read to her. Then the night nurse came and told me off for not being in bed. The next morning Miss Campbell called me over and again asked me to read a passage from the Bible.

Again I made all of the excuses that I could think of as to why I could not read for her. Later on I told Ruth what had happened and Ruth informed me that 'Miss Campbell' was 'religious' so the next time that 'Miss Campbell' called me I told her straight that I did not like religious people and she just laughed when I told her I was going off to the pictures. That was not the end of the matter as 'Miss Campbell' was a determined lady!

On one of the following says, after the Doctors had finished their rounds and we were all having our tea a nurse called me over to my bed as the Doctor wanted to examine my chest. I should have known this Doctor by now as he was the anaesthetist. He told me that I was going to theatre in the morning. At this stage I was feeling a bit fed up with having operations but I knew that I had to go through with them. Also Ruth had been discharged and sent home for a short time but had returned for more surgery. Poor Ruth, she was so brave facing up to so many operations! I did not know it then but I would never see Ruth again.

The next day arrived and began in the usual way with tea and toast early in the morning. I was beginning to feel nervous as I wondered if the operation would be successful. 'Oh dear', I thought as the nurse came towards me with my pre-med. I took one look at her coming towards me and then I immediately began to feel sick again. Once again she advised me to 'take deep breaths' but this technique never did seem to work at all until the anaesthetist would put a stop to it by putting me to sleep. When I came around from the anaesthetic I felt as though I had a huge lump at the top of my mouth. Then I fell asleep and when I woke up again Ena Campbell was sitting by my bed. I thought 'Oh no, this is all I need!' I could not speak to her because I was so tired from the anaesthetic. Ena Campbell was a Christian from Armagh, Belfast. We thought she always dressed quite smartly and was quite nice looking. She was a tall girl and we thought that she looked and behaved like a typical 'Brethren' as she was very strict in her views but silently and deep down I liked her. I admired her because she was always neat and orderly. Ena was born with a single cleft lip and palate but even so her speech was very good. Ena did not approve of me going to the Pictures or of my other worldly ways. When I got out of bed after my operation I felt as though the floor was coming up to meet me.

I gradually got better and stronger and one evening I went out to the pictures in the Nissen hut with some of the other patients. When I arrived back on the ward Ena asked me where I had been and when I told her we had an argument about why I should not go to the pictures. I thought, 'What a cheek!' as I did not appreciate being told what to do by Ena! I did not understand Ena at all until about three years later.

One day while I was in bed on the ward I had the giggles and I could not stop laughing. A patient called out, 'Keep your mouths shut, the dentist is coming; he is in Sister's office!' Mr. Hamilton, the dentist came into the ward and when he arrived at my bed I stood up but when he asked me to open my mouth I started to giggle and I could not open my mouth. Mr Hamilton looked a bit amused and said, 'Come along now', but I just could not stop laughing. I don't think Sister was very pleased with this situation and so he moved on to another patient. On another morning Sister told me that I was going to a Speech Therapist so off I went for my visit but I felt a bit nervous.

I walked down the long corridor feeling even more anxious as I remembered the Speech Therapist from St. Lawrence Hospital, Chepstow who seemed to be very cruel to me and even locked me in a room until I had done some writing, which I was unable to do.

As I approached the door which marked 'Speech Therapist' I was feeling very apprehensive and I knocked at the door gently. A pleasant voice called out 'Come in!' As I entered the room I was greeted by a lady who smiled at me and asked me to sit down. I sat down on the chair next to her desk. The lady began by asking me some questions and then instructed me to repeat some words after she had spoken them, which I did. I was not used to a Speech Therapist being nice to me and smiling at me! She told me that I had a slight amount of air escaping from my nose, but apart from that all was well and at that I was all finished with the Speech Therapist.

On my return to the ward I became aware of a patient who did not have a nose and who was upset. Her pedicle graft had died and she was very upset as she would have to go through the procedure all over again. I put my tongue to my graft in my mouth and although it felt like a huge lump I thought that I would not complain as I realised how fortunate I was that my operations had been successful. Sister had reassured me that the lump would go down eventually.

I did not like visiting times as I never had any visitors although some people, who would usually be there visiting other patients, were nice to me and they would come over and talk to me. During visiting times I would usually just take myself off for a walk along the corridor to the canteen and sometimes I would take a patient who was in a wheel chair as I thought that it would be a pleasant change for them.

One day when the doctors conducted their ward round they told me that I was to be discharged before my final operation. I eventually left the ward to go back to my home in Prestatyn, North Wales. When I said 'Goodbye' to the patients Ena replied, 'I will see you again, Louie', I thought 'maybe' and then she gave me her address which was in North London. I felt sad about leaving the ward and I was certainly not looking forward to going home except that I would see my Grandma again. I began my journey from Aylesbury to Prestatyn and as I came into London to get the Holyhead train I thought of Ena.

Much later as the train approached Prestatyn I began to feel apprehensive about going home but I also felt some excitement. When I got off the train I made my own way up to Bryn Rhosyn Estate which consisted of council houses. I think my mother had a shock to see me as she did not know that I was coming home from hospital and she did not appear to be overjoyed to see me. My father just ignored me completely! My younger sister was very pleased to see me but my brothers just seemed to be indifferent. My mother remarked that I looked very thin. Whilst I was in the hospital a patient had asked me, 'Does your Mother know how thin you are?' to which I had replied, 'I haven't seen my Mother for months'. Well now I had seen her so now she did know. I visited my Grandma who seemed surprised to see me and said, 'I haven't seen you for a long time!' I told her that I had been in hospital but I did not talk to her about my experiences there. We talked about other things.

I found it very difficult to settle down in Prestatyn or at home and I was feeling very restless and resentful. I visited my aunties. One evening I went to a dance in Rhyl with my sister but I hated every minute of it. My sister was on the dance floor dancing with a young man but no-one asked me to dance. I most probably looked like a right misery! I went to my sister and told her that I wanted to go home. She was not pleased about this and said that I would have to wait for her and she went to get me a drink. I just sat quietly and remembered my happy days at St Asaph hospital.

During the nights, I was still having nightmares. The days were also difficult for me. On one occasion, I had a row with my mother and I was shouting at her saying, 'You should have let me die when I was a baby. Unfortunately for me my mother was washing up and she turned round and hit me hard across my face with a wet dish cloth and it really hurt. I did not feel able to talk about my medical care with anyone. My mother wanted me to get in touch with my old friends and with Sister Owen but I could not bear to do that.

One day I took myself off to the amusement arcades to find some cards in the machines that used to claim they could tell someone their future and the machines would also issue lucky charms that I would hang around my neck. Then one day my mother told me to go to see a clairvoyant who she said was very good. Her name was Margaret smith and she was situated in the Market at Sussex Street in Rhyl. My mother had given me some money to pay her so I went to visit the clairvoyant.

However, I felt a little disappointed because she only told me what I already knew. It was also around this time that my mother asked her sister, who was a music teacher, to read the tea leaves in my cup.

I could never understand this aunty as she was an intelligent and clever woman but had become involved with psychic spirits. None of these women would tell me what I wanted to hear which was whether I would be successful in nursing or not. My mother continually told me of the reasons why I should not be a Nurse but I took no notice. I also found out that my sister was involved with fortune telling and sometimes my mother would go to Liverpool to meet with the psychics there. It was around this time that my sister joined the W.R.A.F. This sister, who was born after me, was clever and she did very well for herself.

My father was not happy about me being at home. He wanted money from me and I was only receiving a small amount from sickness benefit pay. For most of the time I stayed with my Grandma who also voiced her doubts about me training to become a Nurse and she advised me to 'listen to my mother.' But I had no intention of listening to anyone and by now I had started to hate everybody in Prestatyn and Rhyl and I just could not wait to leave my home.

I received a letter from Stoke Mandeville Hospital for a further operation. I felt very excited as I could not wait to leave home again.

I was not looking forward to another operation although I was looking forward to seeing my friends again. My mother, my little sister and my brother saw me off at the railway station in Prestatyn. I travelled by steam train to Aylesbury in Buckinghamshire.

As I entered the hospital I had mixed feelings of apprehension and excitement as I wondered what was ahead for me. As I was walked along the corridor towards the ward I entered Sister's office and she greeted me warmly by saying, 'Come on, Louie, I have been waiting for you.' She asked 'How are you?' Then I asked Sister about the patients that I knew when I was in before. But she told me what I did not want to hear, that Ena Campbell was on the ward. I thought to myself 'Oh no, I do not want to see her!' A nurse took me to my bed and I unpacked my suitcase. Then, as I looked around the ward, I saw Ena talking with a patient. I thought 'Good!' as I was glad that she was occupied as I did not want to talk to her!

Then I noticed another patient that I remembered who had no nose. She was still in hospital having operations, poor girl! Later on we all sat together at the table for our tea. After tea I asked about the pictures. I had become friendly with a girl called June who was in the next bed to me. She was in hospital for a skin graft.

The next day as the doctors were conducting their rounds the Surgeon examined my mouth. He appeared to be very pleased with it and told me that I was now ready for the next stage of my graft. I had to go to the Photo department and also to the Dental department. It was so nice to see Mr. Hamilton again. He remembered me and he gave me plenty of smiles which made my day! However, that moment was short lived as when I arrived back on the ward the Anaesthetist was there waiting for me. He examined my chest and told me that I was to go to theatre in the morning. Then we all helped the Nurses move our beds to the entrance of the ward.

The following morning began with the usual routine of tea and toast. I was given the pre-med and then taken to theatre. I was feeling very anxious as I wondered again if the operation would be successful. The trolley moved noisily along the corridor with me on it and the 'bang, bang, bang' of the trolley echoed the thump, thump, thump of my heart! Once again the arrival of the Anaesthetist in the theatre put a stop to it all as he sent me to sleep. The next thing I knew I was back in the ward with Sister standing by my bed telling me to wake up! As I awoke I immediately felt the top of my mouth. It felt different and huge but I knew that it was all 'joined up.' It seemed strange that there was not a cleft palate any longer or even a big hole inside my mouth.

I was in bed for two days then I was able to get up. As usual I went to the Pictures with whoever was allowed to leave the ward and we would go on walkabouts and for visits to the canteen. I remember feeling quite happy! Then one day my bed was moved up the ward. I was lying on my bed when Ena came and sat by my bed and asked me if I would write to her when I went home from hospital. I told her that I would not because I could not write letters but the real truth was I did not want to write to her. Ena said, 'When I asked you to read a few verses from the Bible you told me that you could not read and now you are telling me that you cannot write either.

Ena asked me "What work do you do?" I told her that I was training to be a Nurse. Ena said "How on earth do you manage that?" I replied "You would be surprised!" and Ena said "I would be very surprised!" By the expression on her face I got the feeling that she was laughing at me.

I got into trouble because I went into Aylesbury without permission. When I arrived back on the ward Sister wasn't very pleased with me and told me off. I apologised to her and then I went on the ward with my new clothes which was a dress which was far too big for me. Ena altered the dress for me. The colour was plain green.

When the surgeon and his entourage came to do their rounds we all had to sit by our beds. When they arrived at me I stood up and they were very pleased with the results of the pedicle graft. After that I had to go to the speech therapy and dental departments and they were also pleased with my progress.

Two weeks later I was discharged. I had mixed feelings. I was put off sick for two weeks so I had to go back to Prestatyn. I was not very happy about that or about leaving my friends. I arrived back home in Prestatyn and as usual my father ignored me and he was not at all happy that I was back home. My mother told me that I looked terrible and I suppose that I did because I was so thin and underweight. In those days if you had surgery on your mouth you were only allowed fluids so the consequence of that was weight loss.

My mother sent me to the Hairdresser to get my hair cut. Again I found it hard to settle down and I just did not want to mix with anyone. The only people I wanted to be with were Grandma and my father's sisters.

My sister had joined the RAF and was doing very well. I decided to see the clairvoyant in the Rhyl market once again. My mother thought that she might be able to help me as she didn't think that I should be nursing. I didn't realise the danger that I was putting myself in and she didn't tell me what I wanted to know. I was completely ignorant of the danger of going into Satan's kingdom. I felt very restless and didn't know what to do. A young man who worked in a paper shop wanted me to go out with him so I said I would only if we went to the Pictures.

That just made me feel worse as I started to think about the Nissen picture hut. I was getting stronger in my body so I tried to smoke a cigarette but I couldn't cope with it as the inside of my mouth felt lumpy. One night my parents went out and when they arrived home my mother attacked me. I went to Dr Macleod's after two weeks and he signed me off so that I could go back to Bristol.

I got in touch with the Matron at Bristol Hospital and she gave me a date to start back to continue my training. My mother came with me to the station and she apologised to me for attacking me. I took no notice because I knew that she would attack me again either physically or verbally. And she did!

I travelled on the steam train which had coaches, not like today's trains. I was sitting in the carriage with four other people and a young sailor to keep me company. The trouble was that the sailor was a bit of a nuisance and kept asking me questions and telling me that I was pretty (which I did not believe)! Then, to my annoyance, he asked me if I would write to him. He was getting off the train at Bristol too but the other people got off earlier. One lady looked at me and said, 'You will be going through the Severn tunnel, which is a long one'. Then I felt a bit nervous and I thought, 'Please, God, don't let him touch me' and he didn't. As the train came into Bristol Temple Meads I started to feel apprehensive. I came out of the station, made my way to the bus station and on to the hospital. The Home Sister remembered me and took me to my old room and told me that I was going to be on the Women's Medical Ward.

I had a shock to find that my friend June had left and my other friend Pat had been dismissed from the hospital. I tried to reach her by going to her room but she would not have anything to do with me. Despite all this disappointment I was very happy to be back at work but I found it strange being back in uniform which was now too big for me as I had lost a lot of weight. My role had changed from being a patient for so many months to being a Nurse once again. As I made my way onto the ward I was feeling very nervous and had no confidence.

When I reported to the Sister's office she smiled at me and appeared quite pleasant and put me at ease and the staff remembered me.

As the day progressed I settled down into the routine and I enjoyed the work without any mishaps, for a change! When I went back to the classroom, although Sister Tutor was pleased with my practical progress, she was not so pleased with my paper test work. As usual, I am bottom in the written test and top in the practical.

One day Sister Tutor went through the procedure of laying out a patient after death. She told us about their teeth and that if they have false teeth to always make sure they are in place. One day, soon after, we had a death on the ward so the ward Sister told me and another Nurse to lay the body out. Firstly the doctor had examined the body and then Nurse and I got to work. After we had finished I remembered what we had been taught about the teeth. As this lady had no teeth in her gums I thought she must false teeth so I looked in her locker but there were no teeth there. Then I found a set of false teeth on the window sill so with some difficulty I managed to attach them to the gums and I felt quite pleased with myself. When we have finished with the deceased I went with the porter to take the body to the mortuary and after I had signed the mortuary book I went back to the ward. Whilst I was washing my hands I heard a patient calling 'Nurse' so I went to see what she wanted. She said, 'I can't find my teeth, Nurse' so I said, 'don't worry, I will help you look for them'. I did not realise that I had put her teeth into the mouth of the deceased! Meanwhile a lady, who was the daughter of the deceased woman, was in Sister's office as she had been to see her mother in the mortuary. She said to Sister, 'Well, I am a bit puzzled because Mother hasn't had teeth for a few years so how is it that she has teeth now she has passed away?' Sister realised what I had done and she was furious with me and sent me back to the mortuary to remove the teeth. The problem was that rigor mortis had set in and it was very difficult to remove the teeth! The porter who helped me was not too pleased with what I had done and didn't waste any time in telling me what he thought about me. Anyway we succeeded in removing the teeth and when I arrived back on the ward I scrubbed the teeth and gave them back to the rightful owner who was very pleased to get them back. I heard her tell another patient what a sweet little nurse I was! Anyway I didn't tell her about my mistake and when she asked me where they were found I told her they were higher along the window sill and she seemed to be quite content about it.

One day two trained Nurses came on our ward to teach the pupil nurses about practical nursing. One of them looked pleasant but the other one looked very firm and strict. My colleagues were hoping that they would be with the pleasant Nurse and they were but guess who ended up being trained by the strict Nurse McNamara. Yes, it was me! She called me and said, 'Come along, Nurse Baker, you are with me!' 'Oh dear', I quietly thought to myself. But she was a very good teacher and did not let me get away with anything. I quite enjoyed working with her as she always seemed to be pleased with my work. I was sure that it was due to her that I got top marks in my practical tests. Then, one day while we were in the linen cupboard Nurse McNamara asked me, 'Who did your repair?' but I could not bring myself to answer her as I did not want to talk about it so I just turned away from her. She went on to say 'well, whoever did your repair did a very good job'. When I came off duty I just sat on my bed and cried. During this time I was still having nightmares. Also because I had not done much walking for so many months my legs were quite weak. Some of the nurses noticed that I was not eating properly as I was only picking at my meals. I had no appetite for food. One day, after a busy time on the ward my legs were aching badly. I reported to the person in charge that I was going off duty and as I walked away through the main door of the ward I overheard a patient saying 'Please, God, make some Nurse give me a bed pan'. I knew the night nurse was in the office receiving the day's report so I turned back to give the patient a bed pan. The Nurses who were just coming on duty asked me what I was doing there. When I told them the junior nurse said, 'I will finish, you go off duty.'

I arrived back in my room and changed out of my uniform. Just then there was a knock at the door. When I opened it a Nurse came into my room and asked me to go to a dance with her because she did not have anyone else to go with. I could hardly believe what she was asking. She said that she remembered how I used to like dancing. But I did not any more as all I wanted to do was to have a bath and go to bed. But she was very insistent and eventually I gave in and dressed up in my old green dance dress. I was very tired and the last thing I felt like doing was dancing. As we walked we passed some Nurses who were going in to one of the Nurses rooms. I thought she was religious and I wondered what they were doing.

On arrival at the dance I felt very tired but after a few drinks I started to feel better on my feet having nearly crippled one young man who made sure that he did not ask me to dance again. We sat down after the dance he bought me a drink and then he left me which I did not blame him for as I had almost forgotten how to dance. After a while I started to remember the dances that I had learnt when I was in St Asaph. I was happy then but it all seemed so long ago.

I started to think about Ena Campbell and I wondered what she would say if she could see me now. I knew that she would not approve of the way I was. I watched my friend dancing the night away. At last we went back to the hospital in someone else's car. Back at the hospital, we found an open window, climbed in and after drinking coffee we went to bed. I could not sleep and I was on duty the next morning. Needless to say when I arrived on duty I looked and felt terrible. I do not know how I got through the next day because it was so difficult.

Out of the blue one day I received a letter that was unkind and full of hatred towards me. I presumed that it was from someone in the hospital. I showed the letter to Dorothy as we were still friends as I wanted to ask her opinion about it. Dorothy was shocked by the letter and commented that I had an enemy in the hospital and that I should show the letter to Matron. I made the decision not to tell Matron because whoever had written this anonymous, hate-filled letter would be only too pleased to know that it had upset me. I remembered the clairvoyant telling me that in my work or in my life I would have an enemy but I did not think I would find out so soon. I decided to tear the letter up and throw it away.

However, that was not my only problem! One of the Sisters, who was also a Tutor in the class and also the Home Sister, did not think that I should be nursing as she thought that I would not be able to cope with the training. I was furious about that. It was only because I looked delicate and I was behind in theory in class. 'They have got a fight on their hands.' I thought quietly to myself because I was determined not to leave the hospital! It was winter time and it had snowed. It was very cold. I sat in my room one morning during coffee break and I saw the Sister who wanted me out of nursing. She was walking towards the Nurses' home so I quickly got a bowl of very cold water, opened the window and as she came just under the window I threw the cold water all over her head.

Sister was absolutely furious! I was on the top floor so I ran away as fast as I could back to my room. Shortly afterwards I calmly showed up for duty on the ward.

Christmas came and we followed the usual routine of preparing decorations and presents. I quite Liked Christmas on the ward because we had more freedom as we were allowed to walk about other wards and also we were allowed to drink alcohol but I always put the patients first. I also went to a dance which was a terrible mistake. I was persuaded to go with some of the girls. As usual my friend was dancing the night away and I was sat at a table with a gin and orange feeling not in a very social mood. I started to go into a day dream. I stared at people's faces on the dance floor and I imagined them with no nose and also thinking about my old friends at Stoke Mandeville.

Then a young man took my arm and said, 'Come and dance with me'. I knew he had drunk too much and was what we called 'four ways to the wind' or 'tight.' I thought to myself "You are going to regret this after we have broken each other's toes!" The young man went to get some drinks from the bar and when he came back he was even more unsteady on his feet. After we had finished our drinks, to my horror he started to try to kiss me and he told me that he thought I was pretty. I was furious as I was very protective over my mouth. I pushed him away which was not very difficult because he was so unsteady. I said to him, "It is the drink that is talking! Tomorrow you will be very sorry!" He became angry as he retorted "There is something wrong with you and you need help!"

At last we arrived back at the hospital. As I lay in my bed I thought about the young man and that I had not meant to be unkind to him at the dance. I had snapped at him because I was afraid of any harm coming to my graft. I had another problem. All the nurses had to have a B.C.G. which was an injection used as a means of protecting Nurses who were at risk of tuberculosis infection. A positive reaction was evidence that the individual already possessed a degree of immunity to T.B. but a negative reaction meant that the individual was more susceptible to the infection. Guess who had a negative reaction? Yes, it was me! This meant that I would have to have three more attempts of BCG and in the end I had to have immunisation.

Of course, as a result of all this performance, the Home Sister decided that I was not physically fit for nursing. Well, she had reason to think it even more the next day because I received a letter from Stoke Mandeville Hospital about my previous operation. I was under the impression that I would have to have three more operations. Once again I went to see Matron with the letter and she gave me permission to go. Matron told me that she was very pleased with my ward reports from the ward Sisters. Matron also told me that the Sister Tutor was pleased with my progress in practical work but she could not say the same about my test papers as I had not had a very good report about my theory work. I could feel my heart stop with fright because I thought Matron was going to sack me but I was very relieved when Matron just told me to work harder with my theory. After that I did try to make more effort with my work.

There was an assistant auxiliary Nurse working on the ward who I liked a lot. She was twenty years older than me but she invited me to her house for tea. We got along together very well.

A few days later I woke up feeling unwell but I went on duty anyway. I began to feel more unwell as the morning wore on but I did not report to the Home Sister because I did not trust her. Later on I decided to go to the auxiliary Nurse's own home. I found that the pantry window was open so I climbed in through a very tiny space. Once inside her home I found an easy chair and fell asleep. When my friend arrived home she was surprised at what she saw and was puzzled as to how I had got into her home. She was amazed when I told her but became concerned as I explained that I was ill. She insisted that I should inform Home Sister but I told her that I had not done so because I do not trust her. The Auxiliary then said to me "Nurse Baker, I am not your mother!" I immediately started to cry as I blurted "I will go now. I am very sorry." But my friend answered "You are not going! I will make you a cup of tea and a meal and my husband will take you back to the hospital later." Later on back at the Nurses' home I felt a lot better so I decided not to report that I was sick.

Sometime later on my arrival back at Stoke Mandeville Hospital I found that the same Sister and the same Staff nurse were still there and they remembered me. The nurse took me to my bed.

As I unpacked my case I looked round to see if I knew anybody but I was a bit disappointed as I did not know any of the patients. I noticed a young girl in the next bed to me who was in a wheel chair. She told me that her name was Louise and I thought, "How nice." When I told her that my name was Louie I do not think she quite believed me as she remarked "Oh, how unusual!" We went to the table for our tea and whilst we were eating I had a shock to see a patient lying on her bed with her arm raised with a pedicle flap.

I thought, "I was in that position a few months ago." I felt a bit restless so I asked Louise if she would like to go walkabouts but she replied to my request by saying "I cannot walk." So, I cheerily said "That is no problem. I will push you in a wheelchair." I managed to persuade the Nurse in charge to let us go although she was reluctant to let us leave the ward. Off we went along the corridors.

I showed Louise the Spinal wards and the Theatres and we both shivered! When we arrived back on our ward the nurse was not very pleased with us for being away from the ward for so long but that did not matter to us as Louise and I were very happy about it!

Later on, I lay on my bed unable to sleep as I thought about my old friends wondering where they all might be. I thought especially about Ena Campbell. The next morning all of the doctors conducted their ward round with Sister who was behaving like a cat on hot bricks insisting that everything was so tidy with nothing out of place. The usual performance was that we sat on a chair by our beds and those who could, stood up when the surgeon and his entourage approached. It would always be a bit nerve wracking as everyone would wonder about what they were going to say. As it happened the surgeon appeared to be pleased with his handiwork and told Sister that I was ready for the next stage.

I was informed that I would have to visit Mr. Hamilton in the Dental department. When I saw him he was as gorgeous as ever! He seemed pleased to see me but after examining my teeth told me that I may have to have some of my front teeth removed. The caps that had been fitted on my teeth when I had my pedicle raised up to my palate had made my teeth very loose and they had become crooked. I was not very pleased to hear that news.

I returned to the ward and after we had eaten our dinner I took Louise to the canteen which was full of staff and patients. I took our drinks to the table and while we are sat talking together Louise told me how much she liked me.

Louise also told me how she thought that I was pretty, which I did not believe! After our conversation we decided that we would go around to the general side of the hospital which was all Nissen huts. When we arrived back on the ward we went to the table for our tea and I was just enjoying a jam sandwich when I noticed the Anaesthetist in Sister's office. I felt a lump come in my throat and my heart started to go like a race horse. A Nurse called me over to my bed and the doctor examined me and told me that I was going to have my operation the following morning. The only thing that cheered me up was that I thought that it would be the last visit to theatre. That night when the lights went out I could not sleep because I felt terrible and I could hear one of the other patients moaning. Then I saw Night Sister come into the ward with her big torch to do a ward round with another nervous looking Nurse. Sister always shone the torch which had such a strong light that it usually woke the patient up. The poor Nurse got the blame for that!

I pretended to be asleep.

At last the morning arrived and I got early tea and toast which I could barely swallow. I felt terrible which was due to nerves. We went through the usual routine of moving my bed down the ward so that it was by the main door and office, which I did not like! I was given my pre-med and after a while the theatre trolley arrived. I was taken off to see the Anaesthetist who once again put an end to my terrible feelings with the anaesthetic! The next thing I knew was back in the ward and feeling very queasy.

Sometime later on I was allowed out of bed but I felt as weak as a kitten and my mouth was very sore inside. I was back on 'Jaw 1 diet' for about one week.

I gradually progressed onto the 'Jaw 2 diet' which included mince and eventually I was allowed a normal diet. Louise and I were allowed to go out again which was good fun.

I did not like weekends because it was visiting times and I never had any visitors. One day Louise asked me what I was doing and I said that I was going to the canteen. Then Louise said, "I want to come with you." I reminded her that her Mum and Dad would be coming to see her. Sure enough all of the visitors entered the ward including Louise's parents who immediately made a fuss of her. Louise soon forgot about me.

I just sighed, turned away and wandered off down the corridor. I walked to the canteen but as it was very noisy, filled with patients and visitors, I left there and walked around the hospital grounds. Eventually when I thought it was around tea time I made my way back to the ward. I was very thankful that the visitors were leaving the ward just as I arrived there. I joined the other patients as we all sat at the table for our tea. Louise told me about the things that her parents had brought for her and then asked me why I did not have any visitors. I made up an explanation that the hospital was too far away for the people who know me. Later that evening we were allowed up to go to the pictures which cheered me up a bit. Two days after this while all of the doctors conducted their ward rounds, they discharged Louise and she was sent home.

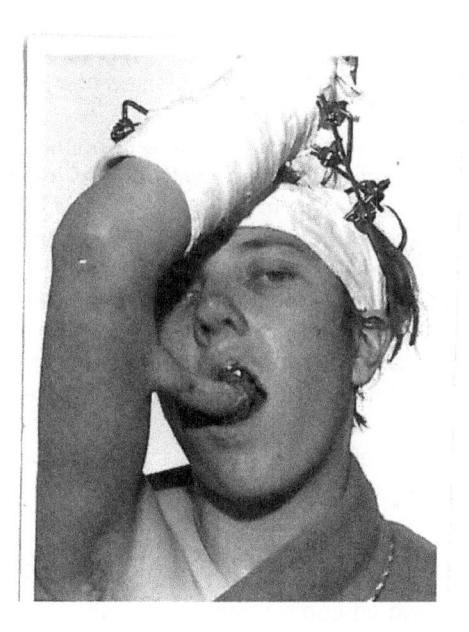

I had to go to the Dental department. Oh, what fun! The dentist told me that I was to have a brace fitted to try and straighten my front teeth. I did have a brace fitted but it was very uncomfortable in my mouth. I had to wear it for a long time. It also had screws which had to be tightened every so often but eventually I got used to it.

About two weeks later, I was discharged. As the Doctor had examined my mouth, he had put all of my medical notes including photos of my treatment out on the table to show me. He gave me a photo with my arm raised up.

The doctor told me that all the operations for my graft were finished but said that there was no guarantee that it would last and I could still lose the pedicle graft. He cheered me up no end! I said to the doctor, "Oh please don't tell me that." He gave me two weeks off work so the next day I left there, feeling a bit sad and made my way back to my parent's home in Prestatyn.

I was looking forward to seeing my Grandma and my sisters but I did not show my Grandma the photo. However, I did show the photo to my Mother. She was startled by it and a bit taken aback but said that she hoped it was successful for me. My Father completely ignored me. He was not even a bit pleased to see me.

My Mother said she thought that I looked ill and encouraged me to go to a clairvoyant she had been to see with one of her sisters. My Mother wanted me to pay a visit to the clairvoyant in Rhyl as she would not accept the fact that I wanted to be a Nurse and would not give me any encouragement to pursue Nursing as a career. She thought that the clairvoyant would direct me towards some other type of work. So once again I went to Sussex Street in Rhyl to visit the clairvoyant in the market. She remembered me but she did not mention nursing but just told me about things which I already knew.

During this period of time at home I visited some relatives and also Grandma who was always pleased to see me. I had noticed that Grandma never kissed her grandchildren but I gave her a kiss anyway. I saw my old friends Margaret and Shirley who lived in the same road. My parents continued to go out for drinks and leave me in charge. My mother would come back home 'tight' and she would usually attack me and continue to do so until she would finally fall asleep. After one of these episodes, the next day, she said that she was sorry and gave me some money to go to the pictures.

Around this time, I was still having the same nightmares. I missed being in the hospital terribly. As I was gradually growing stronger, I went out with my sister and brother. I felt very sad and I did not want to talk about my hospital experiences. I found it very difficult to cope with the people in Prestatyn.

Back To Bristol

I went to visit Dr McLeod to ask him if he would sign me off from work on sick leave. I was very pleased as he gave me permission to go back to Bristol.

Soon I was back in Bristol hospital working on a women's ward and I was on duty with my old friend Marta, a German girl, who I thought was a fine example for the German race.

One day as we approached the ward there was a terrible smell coming from the ward. I asked Marta, "What on earth is that terrible smell?" Marta replied "You will soon find out!" We routinely reported 'on duty' at Sister's office where Sister asked us to do the patients' dressings. I went to lay out the trolley and then we went to the patients together. I had such a terrible shock as we arrived at the patient where the smell was coming from. She was suffering from secondary open breast cancer. What I saw was horrific. It took us over half an hour to do her dressing. In those days there was no cancer awareness. Later on I would see many more patients on that ward who had cancer. Usually the patients did not know that they had cancer as the Nurses were not allowed to tell them because it was considered to be like a 'death sentence' for them. Most of the patients died without knowing. During my time there I witnessed some very sad cases. Later that evening after we had finished our duty we went out for a drink. Marta told me that she was getting married to an Englishman. Everybody was smoking in the pub but by this time I had given up cigarettes as I was afraid that it would damage my pedicle graft.

One day I was told by Sister Tutor that I was going to the Frenchay Hospital in Bristol to work on the children's plastic surgery ward. I could hardly take it in and I felt a bit nervous but also quite excited.

When the day finally came I felt very apprehensive. As I approached the children's ward I reported to the ward Sister and she told me what to do and which Nurse would be working with me. As Sister was telling us what to do and what not to do she told us that one of the rules was that Nurses were not allowed to make a fuss of the children. I considered this to be quite hard. While Sister was giving us this lecture I could hear them crying in their cots. At last we went onto the ward to start our routine. We had to bath the children and try to meet their needs.

Some of the babies on that ward had cleft palates and some had cleft lip and palate and in those days it was not easy to feed them. I felt a bit overcome with emotion and I was relieved when it was coffee time and I met the other nurses. I was told that the Sister on my ward was a battle-axe which made me think, "Oh that is all that I need!" I was soon to find out just how strict Sister was! Some of the children were burn cases and it was difficult to hear them crying especially when it was time for their dressings to be done. Sometimes in those days the children would have to be held down to receive some of their treatments.

One day when I came on duty a baby boy was screaming loudly and when I reported it to Sister's office she was furious with me. Sister came into the ward with me and said, "Just look at that child, Nurse Baker." It was Michael who was making all the fuss and according to Sister it was my entire fault because the baby had taken a shine to me. This baby was standing up in his cot with his arms stretching towards me. Sister told me that he was refusing his food or any actions from the other Nurses and told me that I was not to go anywhere near him again. I felt very upset about it. Anyway one morning while we were bathing the babies one of the Nurses brought Michael in to bathe him so I asked her, "Please let me have Michael" but the nurse replied, "You will be in trouble." I said to her that Sister would know. Anyway after I had cuddled and hugged and kissed him I said to the Nurse "Sister will not find out." But the Nurse I was with said "Oh, yes she will, Michael has lipstick marks on his face!" Which meant another face wash for poor baby Michael! He was born with a cleft lip and palate. Two days later he was discharged and when he went home I missed him a lot.

There are some children that I will never forget, especially one little girl who was four years old. She was a burns case and her moans and cries were horrific. She had fallen into one of the old tin bath tubs full of boiling water (It was the old tin bath tubs in those days). When her father came to see her he just sat with his head in his hands. The staff and the doctors did everything they could for her. One day she was very restless and died. Soon after this, the cleaner on the ward was leaning on her mop and was looking threateningly at me in case I walked on her newly mopped wet floor. She just kept on saying, "There ain't no God, there ain't no God'. I was so surprised to hear myself say "Yes, there is a God!"

I thought of Ena Campbell who had a strong faith. Then one child told me, "Yesterday I was a boy and today I am a girl!" The child had been born neither a boy, nor a girl so the surgeons turned her into a girl!

The children only had visitors at weekends and when the parents went home again there were lots of tears and it would take the children a long time to settle down again. One of our duties was to accompany the children to the theatre. Some children would struggle against the anaesthetic, especially if the Anaesthetist used a mask. On these occasions we would have to hold the child down. It was a bit of a nightmare especially as I remembered how it felt so well from my younger days so I knew what they were going through.

Another thing that I found hard was giving the children injections. They would start to scream before you even began to give the injection because they would recognise the kidney-shaped dish. But, fortunately, I was quite quick at giving injections and before they realised what was happening it would all be over.

I remember that there was a twelve year old boy patient in the ward who was a perfect nuisance and such a 'know-it-all'! He was in the hospital for a long time and he became very cheeky and he was always making fun of my names. When it was tea time he would shout at me and say, 'Baker, baker, bake us some nice cakes!' He always wanted to know the nurses' Christian names and then, one morning, whilst making the beds one of the Nurses told him my first name was Louie. He fell about laughing and said, 'Louie 14th, King of France'. I thought to myself that I would get my own back and it was not too long in coming. One day the Staff Nurse told me to bathe him. He was quite a big boy and he tried to pull me into the bath with him. By the time he had finished I was soaking wet, including my cap just at that point the Staff Nurse came into the bathroom and asked "Whatever is going on here?" Do something about yourself!" The other Nurses said that he was teasing me. Then, one day, I had to bath the little horror again and he tried to get me wet. By this time I had had enough of him. I told him "I am going to give you a good hiding!" He just laughed and cheekily asked "You give me a hiding?" And I slapped him hard across his legs but he just laughed and said that it did not hurt. The rules were so very different in those days!

Because I was cross and fed up with him I told him that he was going to theatre next day which meant that we would have a few hours peace. At that point he became very serious and said "I want you to come with me to theatre." I told him that I could not because Sister had already arranged who was going with him and that it was a very nice, pretty nurse who would accompany him. He started to make a fuss and said, "No, I want you." So I asked him "Why?" and he replied, "Because you have had operations." I asked him who had been talking to him but he said, "No-one, I know because you have scars." I said, "Oh, thank you very much!" and I also told him that I had to do what Sister said in my work, not what I wanted to do. Next day when I asked Sister she relented and allowed me to go to the theatre with the boy. When the theatre porter came with the theatre trolley I said to him, "Boy, when the Anaesthetist puts you to sleep, if you start thrashing about, I will go to your school and tell all your classmates what a big baby you are and that you had to be held down while you had anaesthetic." I knew I was getting my own back on him but I did not relish the thought of trying to hold him down. Any way he went to sleep peacefully and looked like a little angel! After his operation I did not have any more trouble with him. He would constantly ask me if I would go to his home for tea. Of course, I did not go.

Sister would not let us relax for one minute. Before you had finished doing one job, Sister would be telling you to do another! It was hard work keeping up with her demands and I was always so tired when I went off duty.

One day I was informed that I would be going on the men's ward and I was very pleased at that news! Then one day Matron sent for me. I was feeling very nervous wondering what it was all about. When I arrived at Matron's office I found out that it was just to tell me that she had received a very good report from Frenchay Hospital about me. That was good news!

I began working on the men's ward which was for heavy geriatric patients. At first I felt nervous and after coming out of the office after hearing the night report I felt even more nervous and my confidence had sunk. I think that this was also due to the way I was coping with the change of wards.

While I was feeling down I noticed a young Nurse who looked very summery and appeared to have a happy disposition as she was always singing. I still remember her favourite song, "I've got a handful of songs to sing to you of happiness, no more or less." It was jazzy but it cheered me up and my nerves went back into place. The ward Sister wrote my name down to work with a male Nurse to do the patient's dressings. I was in for a terrible shock as I had never seen such terrible bed sores in all my life. The male Nurse poured methylated spirits into their bed sores and the patients screamed with pain. I could not comprehend what I was seeing and I asked the Nurse what he thought he was doing because it was too cruel. His answer was, "You will be surprised at how quickly the wounds heal up." I did not feel very happy about that treatment but I had to get used to it. The Nurse told me that I was too soft and that I would have to get harder. However, I saw such improvement in their horrific bed sores. One morning when I went into the office to hear the night report, to my amazement, there was a black Nurse. It was the first time in my life that I had seen a black person. This was a time when more people from other countries were coming to the United Kingdom. I could not take my eyes off her because I thought she was so beautiful! We also got along very well in our work. I tried to help her in any way I could although she was a bit puzzled by me.

On one of my days off I went out with two Nurses but I got very badly sunburnt on my face, back, arms and legs. It was very painful. In those days we never used sun cream and because my skin was very fair the sun burnt me badly. I had to report to Home Sister who was furious with me. When I went back on duty the black Nurse was amazed at what the sun had done that to me and I think the Home Sister thought that I had got burnt on purpose. There was no sympathy from the Home Sister at all!

One of the patients called Ted told the other Nurses how much he loved me, which made me think he was mad and I told him so. The trouble was that he refused all treatment and attention from other staff which did not please Sister and I was told off for all the fuss he was making! As usual, it was always my fault so I decided not to take any notice and just get on with my work. There was also a patient from the mental hospital who was very disturbed and used to become very violent, especially when it was time for ant treatment or medication.

One day I thought he was quiet so some of the staff went off for their lunch break and a young nurse was left on the ward with me. I was just giving out some medicines and I came to give Darky [that was his name] his medicine when he attacked me and put his hands around my neck. I couldn't loosen his hands and he was hurting me and I was having a job to breathe. Then just as I thought was dying a male nurse came and rescued me. The nurse had come to collect a book which he had left in the office and saw me in difficulty. He told me that I would have been strangled if he had not come back to the ward. We had to report this incident and my neck was very sore but it didn't put me off nursing this patient. When he got better physically he was transferred back to the mental hospital, to everybody's relief!

I then had to go back to the classroom which was another headache!

Sister Tutor was pleased with my practical work but not with my theory.

She took me into her office and informed me that if my theory work did not improve I would fail. She said that there were so many mistakes in my writing that she could not make out what my answers were to the questions. I thought I was going to die with fright! I apologised to Sister but I could tell by the way she looked at me that she was puzzled about me. When I went for my lunch I felt very frustrated after my interview with the Sister Tutor and by the time I arrived in the dining room my appetite had gone and the food just stuck in my throat. Then two nurses came to me and asked me if I would help them with their practical work. I said yes but I felt a bit annoyed because I felt I could help them with their practical work but no-one could help me with my writing. I realised that no-one can do it for you and I felt very alone with my huge problem. However, I was determined that I was not going to give it up so I decided to put more effort into studying and learning how to spell which was very hard because of the medical terms. I did try very hard to achieve a pass in my exams. I prayed to God to help me! After a while Sister Tutor began to notice an improvement in my paper work. I think she looked a bit pleased and just said to me, "About time, Nurse." So I pressed on and tried to work hard.

Then, on top of all this, I had another problem with a male patient on the ward who insisted that he was in love with me and kept telling me that he thought I was beautiful and had a figure like a doll.

Of course, I did not appreciate that kind of talk or him telling me that I was his favourite nurse! I thought this man was a nuisance and an annoyance to me because he was up and about and he was also 6ft tall. One day as another nurse and I were making his bed we ran out of draw sheets so I went to the linen cupboard to fetch more. As I was reaching up for the sheets I sensed someone behind me. When I turned round Bill was in front of me and tried to kiss me (to my horror!). I shouted at him to part his legs because he was very tall and I was only 5ft. As he parted his legs I was able to run out between his legs into the ward. The nurse who was making beds with me wanted to know what had happened to me but I said, 'Don't ask' When Bill was back in bed I told him that I did not appreciate his attentions and if he didn't back off I would report him. After my warning he lost interest! Anyway, I couldn't think what he saw in me! I was still very naïve in my thinking.

After all the bother with certain patients I loved the work and I did all I could for the patients but it was quite hard as we had to do so much cleaning. The worst job was cleaning the sputum mugs which were stainless steel and hard to clean. None of the nurses likes this job but one just got on with it and if the ward Sister wasn't satisfied you had to do it all over again until your face shone in the drums, bedpans and mugs.

One day I went for my coffee break and called in the nurses' home to change my apron, as was usual daily procedure, the home Sister handed me two letters. One was from Sister Hannah Owen. I couldn't read her writing, as she had really nice adult writing, so my friend, Dorothy read the letter. It said that Sister Owen was leaving St Asaph Hospital and had got a job in Mayday Hospital, Croydon, near London. I decided in my mind that if I passed my written exam I was going to go to Croydon General Hospital so I would see Sister Owen because I liked her so much. To my surprise I received a letter from Westminster Hospital, London to see a Plastic Surgeon called Mr. Reidy. The day arrived when I was to go to London to the Outpatient's Clinic. Mr. Reidy seemed to be a very kind man and was very pleased with me and told me that if I had any problems I was to get in touch with that hospital. Whilst I was in the clinic I looked at the other people to see if I knew anyone but I didn't know anybody and felt quite disappointed so I took myself off to a café and then back to Bristol.

I also started to think about Ena Campbell in London and wondered where she was and in time I did find out.

When I arrived back at the hospital we had to prepare for our exams. The brace under my front teeth was driving me nuts when the dentist tightened the screws and it made all my teeth ache. When I told the dentist he said it was too soon to take the brace out so I had to put up with the discomfort. During this I was trying to put more effort into the theory which I found so hard. I did know the answers and all the medical terms but putting them down on paper was a nightmare. I knew that I could do the practical with my eyes shut but I started to have doubts about the written exam. Oh, God, help me! All the class started to study and one of the girls started to study with me. The day before the practical exam the Staff nurse on my ward called me into Sister's office and told me that she thought I was very nervous and gave me a small, white tablet to take when I woke up the following morning. She also told me not to tell anybody and that I was a good nurse and I must pass. The tablet was a drug called Phenobarbitone and it seemed to work [whatever it was!] The next day we had the practical exam with two examiners. We had to lay up trolleys for different things. The examiner kept asking me questions and when I gave my answers she smiled and said 'yes, nurse'. The other examiner was stern and appeared to be quite strict and there were no smiles there! Anyway, I did my best. When it was all over none of us thought that we had done well. I dreaded the written exam when, at last, the ay came. The Staff Nurse gave me another tablet which calmed my nerves but I was slow writing and a girl at the side of me had written a page before I had written my name! So I said, 'Oh, God, help me', and I tried to do my best. When it was all over, of course no-one thought they had done well and I certainly didn't think I had passed. Some of the girls went out for a drink but I felt absolutely drained mentally and physically however when I went out I started to feel better after I had a few drinks. We used to read our horoscopes in any magazines or papers. I was Aries, the lamb and I still had my lucky charms and still kept in touch with clairvoyance whenever I could.

The day came when we received our exam results. I was very pleased because I had passed and I had very high marks for the practical but as for the written, I probably passed by the skin of my teeth!

Sister Tutor was very pleased and told me that had done very well. I think it was due to Nurse McNamara who was a good practical teacher. When I went for an interview with Matron she told me that I had done well and decided to award me the silver medal because I had the highest marks. I didn't think that I deserved the medal as I thought the other nurses deserved it more. When I said this to Matron I had a telling-off because she did not appreciate me telling her how to do her job! When the day came for the prize-giving I had to go through with it and I also received a book about Albert Schweitzer who was a German man. He was a doctor of medicine and also a doctor of Music and Theology and gave his life to the African people. I chose this book because I had heard about him on the radio and I became interested in him. It was the Chairman's prize for the highest marks in the Hospital examinations. My friends told me that I must have more confidence in myself. The problem was that I didn't have any confidence as it was down to nil after all the apprehension I endured.

My First Exam Success

One day, sometime later I received a letter from the General Nursing council which told me that I was a State Enrolled Nurse. I was very pleased about that although I did find it hard to believe! I felt freer now that I did not have to study. One night one of the girls asked me to go out to a dance with her so once again I wore my old green dress. I had not thought to buy a new dress as I had not really felt like going dancing. When we arrived there in someone's car the dance hall was full of smoke. I made for the bar, bought a drink and carried it to a table and started to dream about Stoke Mandeville Hospital and Miss Campbell. I wondered what she might say if she saw me now. I thought that she was like the 'Holy Joes' in the hospital. Then a young man came across to me and asked me to dance with him. I stood up reluctantly as I felt a bit annoyed with him because he had interrupted my dreaming. After a while dancing I trod all over his feet and he got the message that I could not dance. I did not want to remember how to dance so we went back to the table and had more drinks. He started to tell me that I was pretty and I had a nice speaking voice and to my surprise asked me which college I went to. So I laughed and "Cambridge." (I thought he was either mad or drunk).

I started to feel restless with my life and also I was searching the horoscopes for some direction for my life and which way to go in my work. For, although I loved nursing I didn't feel content. Then I was told that I had two weeks holiday so I had to go back home to Prestatyn as I had no money or anywhere else to go and we were not allowed to stay in the nurses' homes. Anyway I was looking forward to seeing my Grandma and my aunts. When I arrived home my mother told me that she had been to Liverpool to see a clairvoyant who was supposed to be very good. So once again I visited the clairvoyant in Rhyl. What a mistake that was! I got a terrible shock!

I told my mother that I was going to see the clairvoyant in Rhyl and she agreed with me but for some reason I didn't feel very happy about it and I couldn't think why. As I went into Sussex Street and into the market and as I climbed the stairs I felt very apprehensive. I didn't understand the way I felt because usually I looked forward to seeing the clairvoyant. Anyway, she remembered me and we had some conversation and then she took my hand to read my palm. She then looked into a ball that she had on the table. Suddenly she looked very angry and she pushed my hand away and said, 'What are you doing here? You are coming into a strong kind of faith'. She frightened me because she looked so angry! I gave her my money and left. I did not know that it was the last time I would see her. When I arrived home I told my mother what the clairvoyant had said about a faith and my mother was not at all pleased. During this time I felt very confused and I also thought to myself that I was not going to be a religious person like some of the nurses at the hospital so I decided to find another clairvoyant.

My holiday was soon over and I was more than glad to get back to Bristol because I did not have an easy time at home. My mother continued to tell me why I shouldn't be a nurse and also my father could not stand me in his sight so it was always a difficult time. Back in Bristol I was on the women's ward which I was pleased about as the Sister and Staff nurse were both easier going. I also had a new friend called Jean who sometimes went out with me. The only drawback was that Jean had a boyfriend which I thought was a nuisance because she wanted to go out as a foursome. When I went out with a boy I didn't know how to cope with him especially when Jean told me to watch his hands as they were everywhere and I didn't know what she was on about! After a few drinks I was able to relax in their company but no way would I let any boy touch me.

One night one young man wouldn't take 'no' for an answer so I bit his nose and he was just furious with me and called me a wild cat. I was glad when we arrived back the hospital. Jean wasn't pleased with me and she couldn't understand my behaviour towards young men. My problem was that I kept remembering my mother saying, 'If anything goes wrong your father will break every bone in your body'. That was why I was afraid to let any male touch me as I didn't know what my mother meant and I was afraid to ask her and I was also afraid of her reaction to my ignorance. After this I decided in my mind that I wanted a friend who did not have a boyfriend. My wish wasn't long in coming! One of the nurses was off sick with flu so I went to her bedroom to see if she wanted anything. She looked ill but she smiled at me and then we had some conversation. Then I asked her if she had a boyfriend and her answer was "No."

I was very pleased about that. Her name was Ruth and I thought that was a good name, one that you could trust! Ruth asked me if I had finished with operations and I answered "As far as I know."

I did not want to talk to anyone about my mouth or my operations or Stoke Mandeville Hospital or about any of the awful injuries I had seen; the result of which was that I suffered horrific nightmares. So I gave her a kiss on her cheek and left. How I never caught the flu from her I will never know! When I reported back on duty the ward Sister told me that she was off duty so that meant that I was in charge. My heart dropped because it meant that I would have to write the day report for the night staff so I decided to start writing as soon as Sister went off duty. Sister also told me not to get behind with the ward work. I said, 'Yes, Sister' but I was thinking the other staff could get on with the ward work so that I could start the day report! As I was writing the day report Sister returned for a book that she had left behind. When she saw me at the desk trying to write she asked "Nurse Baker, what are you doing?"

I answered "Writing the report, Sister." She laughed and said "Good heavens, girl, it's only 1pm. I know I told you not to get behind with your work but this is going too far. Anything could happen between 1pm and 9pm!"

That wasn't my only problem; the cleaner on the ward had a psychotic mental illness and the staff had a difficult time with her. We never knew from one day to the next how she was going to be in her mental state. One day when I came on duty I went in the kitchen and she was there with a broken cup in her hand. She started screaming so I went up to her and I slapped her hard across her face. She looked very stunned but she went quiet. Then, another day, I found her in the bathroom attempting to drink from a bottle of disinfectant. I noticed that she always played up when Sister was off duty so we decided to report her to Sister as we thought she might be a danger to other patients. Apparently Sister already knew all about her so soon afterwards she was taken away and I never saw her again.

I was getting on well with my new friend Ruth whom I thought was wonderful. As usual I went over the top in my admiration of her. I did not want her to be friends with anyone else and I became very possessive of her. But Ruth wasn't having any of that behaviour.

One night Ruth went out with another friend without me so I was very upset over it and I told her how I felt. But Ruth was not putting up with my possessiveness and told me that I was a friend and nothing more than that. She also said that I was very insecure. I didn't know what she meant by her reaction towards me. Ruth was eight years older than me and I thought that she was too old for boyfriends but I thought wrong. Ruth did have a man friend and eventually got married. I was very surprised and disappointed.

Moving To Croydon

I found someone to help me apply for a job at Croydon Hospital, London and we filled in the application form. Much to my surprise, I was offered a job a state enrolled nurse. Then I had difficulty writing out my notice for Matron. It was the usual routine: in coffee break I changed my apron and tried to tidy up my hair which was usually a nuisance (I was told off twice for having untidy hair. I was told by matron to either get my hair cut or tie it back as we were not allowed to have our hair on our collars). When I thought I looked respectable I made my way to Matron's office feeling very apprehensive. As usual, I was not the only nurse waiting to see Matron. Others were there looking rather nervous.

As I entered Matron's office I felt as though I was going to pass out with nerves. Matron looked surprised to see me. I stood meekly in front of her desk and I expected that when Matron saw my letter she would think it was from Stoke Mandeville again. I passed the letter to her and said "Please, Matron, I wish to give in a month's notice." Matron accepted my notice and after that I worked the four weeks' notice. Some of the staff told me that I would be missed but I felt that I was due for a change.

At last I was on my way to Croydon wondering if I had done the right thing. One thing that encouraged me was that I would be seeing Hannah Owen. When I arrived at the hospital, I reported to the Home Sister in the Nurses' home. She took me to my room and told me that I was to report to the Women's Medical ward. After I had finished unpacking I made my way to the Nurses' dining room for my tea. I was enjoying a jam sandwich when a young Nurse came and sat opposite me and said "You look forlorn." I just smiled. She continued "My name is Muriel. You are new, aren't you?" Muriel was a bubbly type of girl. Later on I went back to the dining room for supper but I didn't feel very hungry, even less so when I saw what the supper was! So I went back to my room and as I was about to get into bed there was a knock at the door and Muriel appeared with her friend Shirley who asked me which ward I was on. I told them 'Women's' Medical.' Muriel told me what to watch out for especially the ward Sister. By the time Muriel had told me all about the ward I felt as though I was in for a stormy ride. When the girls left my room after a night cap I decided that they were nice girls but I felt wary of getting too close to anyone after all my upset with Ruth at Bristol.

I could not sleep and started to wonder whether I had made a mistake leaving Bristol. When I was on the train as it pulled out of Bristol Temple Meads I felt very sad as I knew it was the end of an era. I have since realised that the Lord led me to Croydon and I praise Him that He did.

The next thing that I heard was a bang on my door and night Sister shouting, "It's 7:00 a.m. Nurse!" I woke out of my sleep feeling like awful. My body felt like lead as I as I got washed and dressed. I did not think that I looked too bad in my new dark green uniform although it felt strange. I made my way to the dining room with the other Nurses heading the same way. Then I discovered that I had lost my appetite and could not eat my cornflakes. The dining room was very noisy with the Nurses' chatter but that soon stopped with the appearance of the Night Sister who looked very stern. In fact, I had never seen a person look so stern before. I was afraid that she really discouraged me as she shouted "Nurse Baker, go to the Women's Medical Ward," which I already knew. As I approached the ward I felt very apprehensive. I noticed the Night Nurses who looked very tired. They were rushing about because they had not finished their work. The Ward Sister was in the office and so was the other Nurses who were going to be working with me. I reported to Sister and the two Night Nurses came into the office looking very haggard. Apparently they had two emergences during the night. After hearing the night report Sister told me and another Nurse to do bed baths which I liked because you got to know the patients more. Then before I knew it, it was coffee break. We had the routine coffee break and then changed our aprons. Time off duty during the day was either 3 hours in the morning, afternoon or evening or half day and day off. My off duty on the first day was in the afternoon. As I was making my way to the dining room for my dinner I saw what we were having and I didn't think I should have bothered. The food was not at all appetising. Soon the dining room had filled up with Nurses either coming off duty or going on duty but no one spoke to me. I started to wonder if the staff would like me and I thought in my mind "Probably not!" During my off duty I decided to go into Croydon and I went into a coffee shop for something to eat but no one noticed me so I walked out without paying. When I arrived back on duty the Staff Nurse told me to give out the drugs. I felt a bit scared in case I made a mistake and killed someone! But, fortunately for the patients, I got through OK.

I was always good at remembering patient's names and, as usual, I discovered that the patients liked me.

One day I had a shock because I gave a patient a bed pan and I said to her, 'You have got lovely hair'. As usual, my hair was out of control as it seemed to go everywhere but under my cap, where it should have been! When I went back to collect the bed pan the patient was dead. It was a shock to me. I went to get Sister and she called the doctor who certified that the patient was deceased. Sister told another nurse and me to lay her out and I took her to the mortuary. It was my first death in Croydon and it was sad because the patient was young. But in the midst of life there is death.

When I was alone in my room I started to miss Bristol and my old friends and again I was thinking that I may have made a mistake. But, praise the Lord, I hadn't. One day, Muriel came to my room and asked me if I would go for a ride on her motorbike. I was a bit surprised but anyway I said yes and I found it very exciting. In those days people didn't wear helmets. I was wearing just a dress and a cardigan but I thought it was great fun. I was going to have a lot of bike rides with Muriel.

Back on the ward I soon discovered that the patients liked me. They thought that I was a sweet little nurse! Well at least I didn't have the classroom or theory to worry about! I did try to help the patients as much as I could. There were quite a few deaths on the ward which I found a bit upsetting. I also had a new friend. She was a quiet girl and we went out a few times to the pictures. I got on well with the staff on the ward and then one day a new nurse came on the ward. Her name was Margaret and she appeared to be a very nice girl but she was religious. I thought she was like the Nurses I knew at Bristol. I had settled in well at the hospital and got on well with the staff but during this time I started to think about getting in touch with Hannah Owen at the Mayday Hospital

So one day I made my way to the hospital Maternity Ward where she worked. The Staff told me that she was off duty so I decided to wait in the staff dining room. Eventually Hannah turned up and looked very surprised to see me. We went to her room and had some conversation about how pleased she was that I had done well in training.

During the week we met in town for coffee. I didn't tell her that I went in restaurants and didn't pay my bills for the meals I had to eat! I had a feeling that Hannah had not settled down in Croydon because she was very Welsh. I think she was missing St. Asaph in North Wales.

Back in my hospital I picked up magazines to find out my horoscope and also planned to find a good clairvoyant. I was enjoying the work on the ward. I was working with Margaret who I now know was a Christian. She was a lovely girl but I always felt a bit disturbed and I didn't know why.

I met Hannah again in town and I enjoyed her company but I didn't know that it would be the last time I would see her in my life. Later I was told that she had left the hospital. I was a bit upset at this news but in time I got over it.

During all this time I still had the brace under my top front teeth and also I had to go to a new dentist to have the screws tightened to try to straighten my four front teeth. This was a bit uncomfortable and usually made my other teeth ache. This was not the only problem that I was going to have. One day I noticed that I had a strange sensation in the upper part of my nose where I had the bone grafts done in St Lawrence Hospital, Chepstow, and South Wales. The operation had been done by Mr. Emlyn Lewis who took a bone from my ribs to straighten my nose. The sensation in my nose gradually got stronger and then started to hurt. I could hardly bear to touch my nose and other people started to notice that something was wrong. When I looked in the mirror I could see that the bones had moved and were protruding out and it was becoming very painful. I couldn't believe that this was happening. I had just started a new job and knew that I would have to go back to Stoke Mandeville Hospital and I felt very upset. I reported to the home Sister who took me to the nurses' doctor. I showed the doctor the outpatient's card that I had for Westminster Hospital, London.

Once again I was trudging up the corridor to ward 6 in Stoke Mandeville Hospital. I was still in disbelief as I entered the ward and went into Sister's office. After a chat Sister took me to my bed which was near the office. I could see Mr Osborne in with Sister then he approached my bed. I felt very nervous because I did not want him to touch my nose as it was so painful. When he did I nearly screamed. Then he said, 'I will take a bone from your hip' and smiled at me. Mr Osborne was the Plastic Surgeon in the clinic when I first saw Professor Kilner with his entourage. I don't think at that time he wanted me to have my palate repaired but on this occasion he seemed quite kind. I also felt that all this was a nuisance. I was sitting in a chair by my bed feeling very sorry for myself and I was just about to start crying when someone came on the ward and a voice said, 'Louie'. As I looked into her poor face it put an end to my self-pity. She was a burns case called Val and I knew that she would never look normal. We had a friendly chat and then, with permission, went for a walk. It seemed strange to me being back on ward six and wandering around the corridors again. I cheered up a bit but I couldn't help wondering what was going to happen to my nose. We followed the usual routine of lights out at ten but I couldn't sleep. I didn't bother to get in touch with my mother and that was another thing I had to worry about later when I was discharged. The next day I had to go to the photo department which I usually hated. After that I just stayed in the ward and got to know the other patients. During our dinner time I couldn't eat anything because my appetite had gone down to nil and then Sister came to tell us who was going down to theatre next day and I was one of them. Then some of the patients went to the picture hut but I was not allowed to go. I was glad in a way because I was not in the mood for pictures so I just had a bath and chatted to the patients who were not allowed up. Then in the evening the Anaesthetist came to examine my chest.

The next day, which I dreaded, was the usual routine of early morning tea and toast, which I couldn't eat. Then it was time for me to put on my glamorous attire, cap, gown and long white socks. Then it was time for my pre-med which is a drug called Omnopon and Scopolamine which didn't seem to do me much good. I was as nervous as a kitten and one would think I would be used to all this by now. Oh, no! Then the theatre trolley arrived! On my way to the theatre I hoped that Mr Osborne would do the same repair a Mr Emlyn Lewis. Then the Anaesthetist soon put a stop to all my worries. The next thing I was coming round in the ward. I tried to lift my hand, which felt like lead, to feel my nose. Then I heard a voice saying don't touch your nose. Then the next voice that I heard was Val who was sat by my bed saying, 'I love you, flower'. I opened my eyes. I wanted to laugh but it hurt too much. I was in bed for a few days but when I eventually went to the bathroom I didn't like what I saw; more stitches and suturing. I sat on the edge of the bath and started to cry and Val came in and comforted me. After five days I had the stitches out and after a few more days it all looked normal when Mr Osborne came to do award round. He was quite pleased with what he had done. I still had a problem with the brace in behind my front teeth. When I visited the dental department the dentist told me that the brace was not working and that he was going to remove three of my front teeth and he would send for me in two days' time. On the way back to ward six I wasn't feeling very happy about it all so I kicked the side of the corridor. I was feeling very sorry for myself and when I told Val she said, 'It's only your teeth, not your head', and made me laugh. Then we had our tea and went to the pictures.

The next day, while we were having our dinner, Sister told me that I had to go to the dental department. I nearly choked! As I made my way to the dentist I started to feel very nervous because I missed Mr Hamilton and I didn't really know this dentist. As I sat in the waiting room a lady called my name and I approached the chair. When I was sitting down two ladies came in and one held my arms down and the other stood at my feet. I felt a bit alarmed so I said to the dentist, 'I don't need to be held down'. The lady who was holding my arms said, 'It's only to steady you'. Then the dentist removed by three front teeth by injections. After, when it was all finished, I made my way back to the ward, my face and nose hurting very much. I looked in the mirror and I looked a mess, especially my mouth. I found it hard to eat and drink for a few days. I didn't leave the ward because my mouth felt so strange. At last the day came for me to have my new teeth which I found very uncomfortable. The dentist told me I would have to get used to it so I persevered. Val had another operation on her face and she still said she loved me only I was wary of getting too close as I was still licking my wounds over Ruth in Bristol. I did say to Val 'I love you', but there was not much feeling in it!

Eventually the day came that I was discharged from hospital after the doctor's ward round. On the day I was going home I was in the bathroom getting myself ready and whilst looking in the mirror at my new nose I suddenly thought about my mother. I thought I couldn't take the risk of living at home with my mother so I decided to go to Rhyl and get in touch with one of my aunties who was my father's younger sister. My Aunty Lucy worked in a furniture shop called Hutchinson's in Queen Street, Rhyl. As I left ward six after saying goodbye to the patients I felt very sad and apprehensive about going home. When the train arrived in Rhyl station I made my way with my suitcase to see my Aunty and as I entered the shop my Aunty saw me and said, 'Louie' and looked very surprised to see me. I explained my reason without saying too much about my mother. My Aunty told me that I looked ill and too thin. After a while my Uncle came to take my Aunty and me back to their home in Prestatyn. My Grandma is also living with my Aunty. They were surprised when I told them I had just come out of hospital. The next day I went to see my mother who lived on the Bryn Rhosyn estate. She wasn't pleased with me because she didn't know I was in hospital and wanted to know why I hadn't told her. I told her that I didn't realise that I would be so long in hospital. I mother didn't mention the reason why I was sleeping at my Auntie's home so I got out of the predicament with my mother. I was off sick for two weeks and I saw a lot of my Grandma as she was living with my Aunty and always seemed pleased to see me. Towards the end of my time off work I started to get fed up after seeing people from Prestatyn who I felt I didn't like or I resented. I decided to go to Doctor McLeod to be signed off sick leave. Then I was on my way back to Croydon which I was only too happy about but I also felt very apprehensive and also sad to be saying 'goodbye' to Grandma.

Little did I know what was going to happen back in Croydon! I decided to find a good clairvoyant as I wasn't going to the one in Rhyl although I was still going through horoscopes in magazines and newspapers. When I arrived back in the nurses' home I was told that I was back on the same ward, the women's medical ward. It seemed strange going back into uniform after being a patient myself but, oh, it felt good! It was a bit nerve-racking as I approached Sister's office but she seemed quite pleased to see me. Then we heard the nurse's night report which was a bit depressing as there had been two deaths.

It was quite a busy ward. Then, one day, while I was on duty, I was working with a very nice nurse who was a Christian. Her name was Margaret and I had seen her before. I felt quite happy in the work routine and I got on well with the patients. Whilst on duty one day I started to think about the Bible. I kept trying to shake it off my mind but was unsuccessful. As time went by I had a few weeks holiday. During this time my sister, who as in the RAF, was also at home in Prestatyn.

I feel sad when I write this because she was also involved in clairvoyance.

One day I told my sister that I wanted a Bible and my sister couldn't believe her ears! She said, 'You hated religious people and you were terrible in Sunday school!' In the end, my sister bought me a black King James Bible. I didn't tell my mother about what was going on as I didn't think she would appreciate me telling her that I had an interest in the Bible. When I arrived back in the hospital I sat on my bed trying to read my Bible and I discovered that I couldn't understand it. I tried to read the Old Testament and that was even more difficult to read! I tried to read the Bible early morning before I went on duty. Then I became discouraged so I threw the Bible away in the waste paper basket in my bedroom. However I didn't feel very happy about that so the next day I started to try and read it again but, once again, I could not understand it so I started to get a bit frustrated with trying to do the impossible. So I gave it up as too difficult to attempt. I usually got up at six am to try to read the Bible. One day, while on duty and having our coffee break in the dining room, we started to say what time we got up in the morning. I said that I got up at six am so Margaret asked me why I was getting up so early so I replied "Mind your own business!" The next day there was a knock on my bedroom door and when I opened it there was Margaret who said, 'I want to talk to you', and so I invited her to come in. Then she said, 'You are reading the Bible, aren't you?' so I said, 'Yes, I was trying to read it'. Then Margaret said, 'Give me the Bible'. She sat on my bed and I sat next to her. Then she opened the Bible in the New Testament at St John's Gospel chapter 1. We read for a time and then Margaret left my room. What a good friend she turned out to be! She didn't tell me to go to a church which was very wise of her. I couldn't believe that this was happening! Not only had I started to think about Miss Campbell and at the same time I was thinking about finding a good clairvoyant but I didn't tell Margaret about my plans.

Then one day Matron sent for me to go to her office about my holiday.

So afterwards I decided to get in touch with Miss Campbell who lived in North London. I found her address in some of my papers which I didn't think that I still had, and a friend helped me to write a letter. To my surprise, I received a letter back from her asking me to come through London on my way home to North Wales and to stop a weekend with her. So that's what I arranged with her.

At the beginning of my holiday I visited her and she met me at Euston Station in London. Then we went to her flat. To my surprise Ena had a photograph of Professor Kilner, who was the head of plastic surgery and we had a long chat. The next day was Sunday and we went to her church which was open Brethren. We also went again in the evening and I heard the gospel message for the first time in my life and I responded to the gospel message which was: 'He that believeth on the Son hath everlasting life and he that believeth not the Son shall not see life but the wrath of God abideth on him', St John 3: 36. So I accepted the Lord Jesus into my life and that was in 1959. There was no counselling at that time when I was young. I just told Ena when we arrived back at her flat. The next day I made my way back to Prestatyn in North Wales.

When I arrived home all hell was let loose as I decided to tell my parents what I had done about Jesus. My father went into a rage and brought his fist down on the table and shouted at me and said,

'I am as good as the next man!' As for my mother, she didn't appreciate me telling her about Jesus but when I visited my Grandma and I told her what happened to me accepting Jesus as my own personal Saviour , to my amazement, Grandma accepted Jesus and found her old Bible. When I arrived home I told my mother about Grandma and how she had decided to accept the Lord Jesus. My mother wasn't pleased about that news and said, 'Grandma is an old lady but you are too young to be religious'. I took no notice of what my Mother said because I just wanted Jesus in my life.

Soon I was pleased to be back in Croydon. I was on the same ward and I told Margaret about what had happened on my holiday and Margaret was pleased at this good news. Then one Sunday I had a day off so in my mind I decided to look for a church. I was looking for a Brethren church but couldn't find one and then I came across a big looking church which was Baptist. I bless the Lord that He led me to the right church. At that time the Rev and Mrs Geoffrey King were the Minister and his wife. I went wandering into the Baptist church and after the service a lady came towards me and said she was Mrs King and wanted to know who I was and where I came from. I was a bit surprised as the church was full of people but I told her, 'I am from the hospital'. Then Mrs King asked me if it was my day off and when I told her it was she invited me to her home for dinner and tea. What a difference from the hospital cooking! I ate all of my dinner up, the first time for years! My appetite had always been so poor. Mrs King was very kind towards me and I did not want to return to the hospital. Mr and Mrs King lived in a big house called 'the Manse'. They had three children, two sons and a daughter called Christine who, at that time, was a teenager. The sons were younger. Mrs. King was quite strict with her children and a few times with me too! I didn't tell the Kings about my background or about Stoke Mandeville Hospital or about being involved with the occult. At that time I was still being plagued with terrible nightmares.

One morning, back at the hospital during breakfast I was eating my cornflakes when the night Sister came into the dining room and announced that nurse Baker, was to go on to night duty and to stay on day duty till 1pm and another nurse also was to go on nights. We just looked at each other and I felt sick and couldn't finish my cornflakes! When I came off duty at 1pm after being on nights, I would go to my room and go to bed but I would find it impossible to sleep as there would be so much noise in the corridor outside my room. I would try to read but found that I was unable to concentrate. Eventually there would be a loud bang on my door and a voice calling out "It is 7 o'clock, Nurse!" I would drag my body out of bed and get ready to face what was coming to me. I would look in the mirror to do my hair and I would usually look more ghostly than human! Then I would wearily make my way to the dining room only to be faced with a breakfast which I could not eat! Usually the Sister would arrive to tell us which wards we would all be working on and on one occasion I remember that I was very pleased to know that I would be working on the same ward as I had been during the day because it helped that I already knew the patients. As Sister turned towards the door I noticed that she was glaring at me. Then I noticed that the other nurses were staring at me but, of course I had not registered what I was supposed to do. Later I realised that as I was sitting at the end of the table it was expected that I should open the door for Sister. In those days etiquette was very important.

Eventually the penny dropped and I stood up to open the door. Of course Sister was all smiles and joking but night Sister looked very sternly at me. The Night Sisters were everybody's dread and after that episode it soon became apparent that I was not in the Night Sister's good books. While we were leaving the dining room a Nurse who would be with me through the night called to me and I cheered up as I knew her and we got along very well together. As soon as we entered the ward we realised that it was going to be a busy night particularly as the Day Nurses had not finished their work. We entered the office to receive the day's report from the Staff Nurse, who looked haggard, and informed us that two patients were dying and that two more emergences had come in. Then, I quietly decided in my own mind, to tell these patients about Jesus. When we came out of the office onto the ward the Day Nurses went off duty and they looked exhausted. We started our usual ward routine of settling the patients down and giving out drinks. As I was giving out bed pans to those who needed them, I met the two patients who were dying. While the other nurses were giving out drugs to other patients who were able to swallow them and while Nurse was busy in the office I went to tell the dying patients that Jesus loves them and He died for them and informed them that they should repent. Whenever I told patients about Jesus they always seemed to respond in some way. I went into the ward kitchen and whilst I was concentrating on my work and trying to figure out which patient had which specific things in their fluids and which ones had specific things in their food alongside washing up I turned round and suddenly came face to face with Night Sister. I nearly dropped a jug with fright! Sister just said, "Carry on, nurse." Later on when the ward lights were switched off all except for one night light, my body began to tell me that it was not time to work but that it felt more like bed time and I began to feel unwell. The Nurse in charge sent me for a break for half an hour so that I could have a meal but when I reached the dining room I felt even worse. Then, to my disappointment, I discovered that dinner was salad with cold meat! I took my miserable-looking salad to the table but I felt too tired to eat it so I lay my head on my arms on the table. As I did so I noticed a caterpillar crawling inside my limp lettuce. I thought about stabbing it with my fork but decided against killing the little creature. I dragged myself up to get a hot cup of coffee, only to find that it was cold. The pudding that night was unrecognisable so eventually I gave up!

When I arrived back on the ward I could see that the other Nurses looked as bad as I felt. The Nurse in charge was going off for her break next but before she went she warned me to watch out for Night Sister and the two patients who were dying and then she smiled at me and told me not to look so worried. Needless to say I felt terrified, but not of death as I had dealt with death before at Bristol. As far as I remember, during my time as a Nurse, Night Sisters wore noiseless shoes and no one ever heard them approaching! They reminded me of the way that a cat would creep about ready to pounce on a mouse! After I had answered numerous patients' calls and given them all their bedpans and cups of tea I started to feel very cold. The staff on duty would usually have our cup of tea on the ward after Night Sister had finished her rounds which seemed to be, more often than not, just as a patient was expected to die which used to seem unfortunate for me!

We would be expected to stand up when a Sister entered the ward but at that time, because I felt so tired, stiff and cold and we were all having our cups of tea, and I was just trying to eat my Marmite sandwich, Sister appeared, standing directly in front of me, shining her torch straight into my face. I nearly choked! Sister was glaring at me and I had not responded quickly enough to her. If looks could kill

I would have certainly died that night! To make matters worse, I had cramp in my leg and I could hardly move!

Sister pointed out to me that one of the patients needed attention. I managed to drag myself to the patient who told me that something had woken her up. I thought that it could have only been the Night Sister shining a torch into her face while she was asleep!

Eventually it was time to start our early morning routine. Whilst Nurse was writing the night report I prepared the tea trolley ready for the patients early morning cup of tea along with a cup of coffee for me and the Nurse I had been working with. During the night I had checked on the two dying patients and the following morning, much to my surprise, they were still alive! I made tea for them and also made tea for their relatives who were sitting with them. All the while I was still keeping a watch out for Sister who kept paying us random and frequent visits! Once we were off duty we went to the dining room but the food was appalling and I could not eat anything.

As I approached my bedroom the corridor was so noisy with cleaners and staff, I was concerned about how I would ever be able to get to sleep. At that moment the Home Sister came along and informed me that I was to move to the night staff corridor which was on the top floor of the Nurses' home. By the time I had carried all of my belongings to my new room I felt absolutely exhausted. Eventually, I got into bed and, to my annoyance, I was unable to sleep. As I was feeling a bit hungry, I decided to get up, dress and go into town to a café to get something to eat. Then I checked my money situation which was very low so, in my mind, I began to devise a plan to get away from the café without paying for my meal. I suddenly realised what I was doing and rebuked myself inwardly "What are you thinking of? You are a Christian now and Christians do not steal or travel on trains without paying." So I repented of all those thoughts and plans and I have never looked back since.

Then Muriel came and took me on her motorbike to her home for a meal. She gave me a telling off because I got over excited on the bike, waving at the other cars on the road and shouting at Muriel to go faster. Muriel asked me if I was trying to get us killed. I answered "No!" as well as that Muriel was horrified as when her Mother made us a dinner and put it onto the table, I put my dinner on the floor for the dog, which immediately wolfed it all down! Muriel's Mother was not very pleased about my behaviour and neither was Muriel! When we arrived back at the hospital I went to my room and tried to sleep but I found it impossible. I tried to read but I could not so I just gave up trying altogether. However, I must have dozed off because I was awoken by a banging on my door and a shout of, "It is 7 o'clock, Nurse!" Once again, I dragged myself up out of my bed and on that occasion I had a quick bath. Once again as I was doing my hair and looking in the mirror I thought that I looked more dead than alive. I made my way to the dining room with the other night Nurses and this time I made sure that I was not sitting at the end of a table by the door as I did not relish the thought of having to open the door for Night Sister as I was convinced by then that she did not like me. When Night Sister did arrive in the dining room, I was just about to swallow a mouthful of cornflakes and as everyone was expected to stand up immediately, I nearly choked on my cornflakes!

Then Sister informed us that we would be on the same wards again. She slammed her books together and walked towards the door.

The poor Nurse at the end of the table nearest the door silently opened the door for Night Sister. We all breathed a sigh of relief as Sister swept away through the door. We all finished our breakfast and then departed to our respective wards.

As I approached the ward Sister's office I was experiencing a terrible headache and began to feel worse by the minute. I did not feel encouraged as I saw the day staff looking haggard and I realised that they had not finished their work. When I heard the day report it made me think that I would probably be on my feet for most of the night. We were informed about a young 17 year old girl who was dying of leukaemia. Quietly in my own mind I thought I must tell her about Jesus before she died. Then Sister told me to help the day staff finish their work. As I entered the ward I noticed the curtains around the beds of the dying patients and I realised that the young girl was too poorly and too far gone to hear what I had planned to say to her that Jesus loved her. Her visitors were still on the ward with her and much to my annoyance so was the Night Sister. The day staff went off duty and eventually the Night Sister and the Doctors left and we were on our own which made me feel pleased. We started our night routine of giving out drinks and bedpans and at 10pm, drugs. The young girl with Leukaemia was sinking very fast. The Senior Nurse sent me for my dinner which looked even more unappetizing than usual. I could not eat anything so I just had a cup of cold coffee. None of the other Night Nurses were eating much either. I noticed that no one felt like talking except to complain; usually about the day staff or some poor ward Sister or even more likely some poor Night Sister! The Nurses who were sitting with me looked how I was thinking and feeling myself that I would never last through the night. When I arrived back on the ward my Senior Nurse told me that the young girl with Leukaemia had died and the Doctor had come to certify her death. Then the Nurse was going off for her dinner but before she left the ward she told me to prepare for laying out the body. Unfortunately for me the Night Sister arrived and, as usual, woke half the patients up which meant that they wanted bedpans and cups of tea. It was then that I discovered that I was the only Night Nurse who would make a patient a cup of tea during the night. No wonder they liked me and the patients always told me that I made a good cup of tea! Well, that was due to my Mother, who hated weak tea. I was alone on the ward then as the Doctor and Nurse had left. The hospital was very old and was very eerie at night, especially that night as there was a strong gale-force wind blowing outside and it seemed to make strange noises in the ward. When Nurse arrived back from her break we laid out the deceased young girl. It made me feel sad as she was a pretty girl and even today I can still see her face, as I have never forgotten her. When the porter came to collect the body I accompanied him to the mortuary and, after signing her in, I went back to the ward in tears. Then I prepared to make our tea and sandwiches and after that it was time for the ward routine. Then the day staff arrived and Nurse gave the day report whist I was still clearing away in the sluice. Day Sister came and told me off for using too much tea during the night and told me that the ward was only allocated a certain amount of tea each week. I wanted to reply to her "The war is over!" but I felt too exhausted to reply to her. I tiredly walked to the dining room where I found that supper was as unappetizing as ever. Then Night Sister arrived and told me that I was due for three nights off. Oh the joy of that! Once again I went to my room and I tried to sleep but much to my annoyance I was not able to as there was so much noise such as banging and shouting in the corridors. So I got up, had a hot bath, and decided to go to the Pictures in town with my new friend, a young girl who was training to be a Nurse who had also been on night duty.

The next day was Sunday so I made my way to church. When I told Mrs King that I was off duty for three nights she invited me to her home. We had Sunday lunch and I had absolutely no problem eating it all up. I was hungrier than I realised but Mrs King was happy especially as she would not allow any food to be wasted. All too soon it was time for me to return to duty. When I arrived the Ward Sister appeared to be very busy. After I had received the day report I entered the ward and to my surprise all of the patients started clapping! This really cheered me up but realistically I suppose it was just because they had missed their cups of tea during the night.

One Sunday following this, while I was in church, Mr. King was talking about baptism. I did not know much about this so I did not take much notice. Later on, however, Mrs. King started to talk to me about baptism so, in the end, I decided that I would be baptised. The day arrived, 22nd November 1959. My friend, Margaret, gave me a book called 'The Pilgrim's Progress'.

On the day of my baptism, Mrs. King's daughter came to the hospital and then we went to the church together and I took along a change of clean clothes. I was not the only one to be baptised during that service. When it was my turn I said a few words as a testimony about what the Lord had done in my life and then Mr. King baptised me. I did not feel nervous as I had a good feeling about it all and I knew Jesus was with me in my life. After the end of the service I went back to the King's home and we had a chat and some supper together but I did not eat anything but I had a drink and then I went to bed. That night something awful happened. I fell asleep but I woke up to see a very dark shape standing at the side of my bed. Then the shape came up to the head of my bed and then fell behind the bed. I felt terrified and got out of bed and ran into the corridor. I was lost until Mrs. King found me. I did not tell her about what I had seen but said that I was looking for the toilet. Of course, the problem was that I had not been delivered or set free from my previous involvement with the occult and I did not understand then that I needed to be.

One night while I was taking my break for dinner from the ward one of the night Nurses told me that the ward that I was on was haunted by the ghost of a ginger-haired Nurse who had died on the ward and who always washed the patients early in the morning. So I answered them "Tonight I am going to leave a note on the bedpan cabinet to tell her that it is her turn to give out the bedpans and I will do the washing of the patients." The nurses just laughed.

Christmas came again which meant extra work on the wards but once I began the work I enjoyed it and I was seeing it in a different way than I had before. This time I knew the real meaning of Christmas. Night Sister came into the dining room before we went on duty for the night, and she told us that the night staff were to meet in the dining room for some kind of party. My heart dropped down to my big toe because I was terrified of Night Sister. Fortunately, on the day, which was Christmas day, I went to bed and slept solidly and I did not wake up until there was a bang on my door and a voice saying, "It is 7 o'clock, Nurse." I dragged myself out of bed and went to the dining room. When Night Sister arrived the first thing that she said was, "...And where was Nurse Baker this afternoon?" to which I replied "Sorry, Sister, but I did not wake up." This made all of the other Nurses laugh.

After Christmas, while we were having our breakfast before going on night duty, Night Sister arrived in the dining room and announced that there was going to be a change and that we were going on different wards. Then Sister said, 'Nurse Baker is to report to the men's medical ward'. I nearly choked on my limp looking toast. I felt very anxious as we went to our new wards. If I thought that the last Sister on the women's ward was bad enough, she was an angel compared to the Sister who was my superior on the men's ward. When I entered the office with my Senior Nurse to report for duty the Sister looked at me as if I was something nasty that the cat had dropped at her feet! We listened to the day report which was not very encouraging. The ward was a very busy one and a poor patient had died. Most of the patients were suffering from Emphysema, lung problems, cardiac chronic disease and were on oxygen. I did not feel that I had much confidence after hearing the day report and also as I did not know the patients. As I entered the ward and got into the ward routine I, as usual, got to know the patients' names and I tried to do all I could to help them. I got on well with the Nurse in charge and eventually we came off duty and went to the dining room for our disgusting looking supper which I could not eat. I took myself wearily off to bed and tried to sleep but was unable to do so. So I got up and decided that I would try to see a Doctor to get some sleeping tablets. I went to the Doctor's surgery in town. It was a lot easier to see a doctor in those days as you just waited and took your turn. After the Doctor had given me the sleeping tablets that I wanted I made my way back to the hospital. I did not tell the Home Sister as Nurses were supposed to be treated by a specific Doctor and I did not like that. Another reason was that Home Sister was always with him and I knew that I would be in trouble if Sister found out that I had gone to another Doctor outside of the hospital.

When I arrived back in my room I took one sleeping tablet and then got into bed. The only trouble was that I was still wide awake at 1pm so I took another sleeping tablet which was a terrible mistake. The next thing was that I woke up to a loud banging on my door and a voice saying, '7 o'clock, Nurse'. I wearily dragged my body out of bed and then the floor came up to meet me. I staggered to the bathroom and washed in cold water which did not help. As I made my way to the dining room I fell over a stack of chairs in the corridor. The other Nurses who were eating breakfast were staring at me. I sat opposite one Nurse and asked her, "Is your name Mary?"

We chatted a bit and Mary got up to get a cup of coffee for me.

By the time Night Sister arrived I could hardly stand up but fortunately for me she did not notice me. As we left the dining room my Senior Nurse with whom I am supposed to work with took hold of my arm and said, "Come along, Nurse Baker, tell me what you have taken." I told a lie because I replied, "Only coffee, Nurse" but I do not think that she believed me! When we arrived at the office to hear the day report I felt that I was swaying so I leaned on the desk, to the Sister's disgust! Sister shouted at me and asked "Nurse, are you listening to the report?" I weakly replied "Yes, Sister." She then retorted "Nurse, will you please stand up straight. Whatever is wrong with you?" I said, "I am sorry, Sister, I will still do my work" to which Sister answered, "I should hope so, Nurse. I will expect all of your work to be done by the time I come on duty in the morning!"

Oh dear, I did not receive any sympathy.

I entered the ward and the patients soon realised that there was something wrong with me. I heard them asking each other "Has she been taking drugs?" I staggered around the ward with the drinks. I also tried to feed one poor man but I kept missing his mouth and it went down his chin but he was kind towards me. He said, "Don't worry, Nurse," but all the patients were laughing at me. When the other Nurse and I had had settled the patients down for the night we went into the kitchen. My Senior Nurse said, "Sit down, Nurse Baker; I will make you a cup of strong coffee." She told me how awful I looked and told me to go and lie down in the store room. At first I refused but the Senior Nurse insisted so I made my way to the store room with a blanket. Then I lay down on the floor and I saw two big black cockroaches scuttling across the floor. I did not take much notice because I felt too worn out to bother. The next thing I heard was nurse saying to me, "Nurse Baker, come on, Night Sister's on the prowl!" So I got up, although I was feeling awful and I washed my face with cold water. Nurse sent me for my dinner break but I could not eat it. No one spoke to me because everyone was too tired. When I arrived back on the ward one of the patients had died. (This often happened during that period of time because the drugs that we have available today were not available then). The Doctor was also on the ward to certify the death so whilst Nurse went off for her break I prepared the trolley ready for when she came back.

I was so preoccupied with my work that I did not hear Night Sister come up behind me. When she spoke to me I nearly jumped out of my skin! She told me off as I had not been on the ward. After the porter and I had taken the deceased patient to the mortuary I was feeling better as I had the opportunity to have a breath of fresh air in the meantime. When we eventually arrived back on the ward it was so busy that I did not have time to think about how I felt.

At last the day duty staff arrived on time and went into the office to hear the night report. Then we were off duty and made our way to the dining room for our supper which, as usual, looked ghastly. After Night Sister had left us in her usual friendly manner I made my way to my room and, to my annoyance, no longer felt tired but I had made a decision not to take any more sleeping tablets so I threw the tablets away and I have never taken sleeping tablets since for the whole of my life.

Although I was still being plagued with nightmares whenever I fell asleep I woke one morning feeling very happy because I had three nights off and one of those nights was a Sunday. I went to church and afterwards the Kings took me to their home and I had a good time. After staying with the Kings and enjoying Mrs. King's lovely meals I arrived back at the hospital feeling a lot better and relaxed. However, that was to be short lived. As I was getting ready to go on duty I wondered what I would be confronted with during the night on duty. I was in for a shock as I arrived at the dining room for my breakfast at 7:30pm. The Night Sister breezed into the dining room and announced that I was to take charge of a young Nurse who was in training to go on the men's medical ward. I was trying to enjoy my cornflakes at that moment but my heart nearly stopped with fright! As we entered the ward it looked like a nightmare. My heart dropped as we heard the day report from the Nurse in charge as three patients were dying. Then Nurse put the keys into my hand and said "It's all yours, dear!" The day Nurses came into the office and my friend Muriel was one of them. She smiled at me and then went off duty. Nurse went off to give out the night drinks while I got ready to give out the drugs. I was wondering if any of the patients would be alive in the morning! I had no confidence and I prayed that Jesus would go before be. I also dreaded Night Sister paying a visit. The Doctors were still on the ward but they required to see only the drug charts of their patients.

Eventually the Doctors left and the Nurse and as we had the ward to ourselves it was up to us to do the ward routine. Nurse went off for her dinner break and I checked the patients who needed drugs and then I went to the office. As I sat down at the desk I realised with horror that I would have to write the report. I was just trying to get some paper work sorted out when I heard footsteps coming from the ward door to the office. I quickly stood up, thinking that it was Night Sister coming but when I went into the corridor there was no-one there, so I went into the ward expecting to see someone but no-one was there. At that time the ward was cold and eerie and when the Nurse returned I didn't tell her about the footsteps as I did not want to worry her. While Nurse and I were having our tea in the kitchen we heard the footsteps again. We rushed out into the corridor but no-one was there. Then the Night Sister arrived on the ward. I accompanied her on her usual ward round and to my horror we found that one of the patients had died. I thought Sister would give me a telling-off for not knowing the patient was going to die but Sister just told me to send for the Doctor on call whilst Nurse took the deceased to the mortuary.

I tried to settle down to write the night report but it was very difficult as my writing and my spelling were so poor. When Nurse arrived back on the ward we started the ward routine. I tried my best to tell the two patients who were dying that Jesus loved them. It was a difficult night and I had never been so glad to see daylight arrive and to see the day staff coming on duty. My feelings were to be short-lived as I arrived at the office and saw Sister glowering at my report and the Day Nurses standing around the desk with their hands behind their backs. I stood very fearfully next to Sister who instructed me to read out my report. To my horror I could not read what I had written! Then Sister said, "Come along, Nurse, we have not got all day! Read out what you have written!" I was inwardly and silently asking God for his help and said "Please, Lord, if I ever needed your help, I need it now!" I made a decision to tell the Sister the night report from my memory which did not please her. Sister asked me some questions and then said "Very well, Nurse, off you go!" Off duty." My feelings of relief were so great that I thought I was going to collapse in front of her! I made my way to my room where a letter had been put underneath my door and, to my surprise; it was from Miss Ena Campbell asking me to go to see her.

As usual, I did not sleep very well but I had nodded off when I was awoken by a loud banging on my door. I dragged my body out of bed and thought, "So this is the body I have to carry around all night!" I felt dreadful and when I looked in the mirror to try and do something respectable with my hair I thought, "Is that really me in the mirror?" I looked like a ghost!

As I made my way to the dining room for my breakfast I hoped and prayed that Sister was not on duty. After Night Sister had arrived in the dining room like a mother hen making sure her chicks were all ready to start duty we went to our various wards and when we entered the office I felt relieved to see that Sister wasn't there, just a pleasant looking Nurse who gave us the day report, which was not a very encouraging report. The two patients who were dying the previous night were just about still alive. Eventually the day staff went off duty and Nurse and I got into the ward routine. After we had settled the patients down and the lights were off I noticed that one of the patients was not in his bed so I went to the bathroom. There was no-one there so I went into the toilets and he was there sitting on the toilet, dead. What a shock! I rang for a doctor and a porter to come and help us get him back to his bed. After the Doctor left, the Nurse and I laid out the deceased and while Nurse took the deceased to the mortuary I checked the other two patients and discovered that we had another death. Then I had to get the Doctor back. The Night Sister was also on the ward and was pestering the life out of me to inform the relatives. Later, when I was alone on the ward, I tried to get the paper work sorted out but the office was in such a mess. I was tidying up when I heard footsteps again. I thought, "O no, Lord!" I went into the corridor but there was no-one there. I did not think it was a ghost although by that time the ward was once again eerie and I felt cold. Nurse arrived back from her dinner break and told me not to hurry to the dining room because the dinner was disgusting. I was soon to find out what she meant. I decided to have some coffee when I got back to the ward. When I got back to the ward Nurse was looking terrified so I asked her what was wrong. She said the ward was haunted. I tried to keep calm and told her that it was not haunted but I was determined to get the problem sorted out. I asked the Nurse to make us some coffee and toast while I stood in the corridor by the entrance to the ward. I wondered if one of the patients was playing tricks on us as some male patients would put whisky in the urine specimens!

However, I do not know where they obtained the whisky from! I went into the ward to check on the last patient who was dying and discovered that he had also died. As I came out of the ward I heard footsteps again but then, as I turned, I noticed a patient who was making a noise like the footsteps but he was fast asleep. Just as I was phoning the Doctor, Night Sister arrived in the office. Then I told her that we had another death and Sister asked me where my other Nurse was. I thought, "Oh, no, she is in the kitchen!" Sister was quicker than me and she went into the ward to check on the patients and just at that moment Nurse came out with coffee and toast and got a telling-off from Sister. I felt awful about it all and I told Sister it was my fault and then I got a telling-off for not being firm enough with the junior Nurses. It was not in my nature to be strict especially not after we had dealt with deceased patients.

I realised that I would have to write a report as time was getting on towards the morning. As I was trying to decide what to write, I thought I saw a Doctor on the ward but I did not take much notice as I thought if it was important he would come into the office, but he did not come in.

At last Nurse and I started the ward routine and I apologised to her for getting her into trouble with Night Sister and she answered, "I do not want to work with you any more, Nurse Baker" and she laughed. Then we went to the patient who made a noise like footsteps and we asked him about it and he told us that he grinds his teeth when he is asleep. He told us that when he was in a London hospital he frightened two Nurses. Then he apologised to us and we forgave him. I was in the sluice testing urine samples and I came out to fill in the urine charts and I noticed that the day Sister was talking to a patient. My heart dropped as I thought of the night report and the urine charts that I had only just finished. To my surprise Muriel came to me. I smiled at her but the smile left my face when she told me that Sister was waiting for me in the office and warned me that she was not in a good mood. As I approached the office I could feel that I was trembling all over as I could see that Sister was glowering at my report. The day staff were standing in front of her desk, with their backs straight and their hands behind their backs. I stood by the side of the desk with my hands behind my back and tried to look intelligent but probably failed. I was about to feel Sister's wrath as she asked me "Nurse, one of the patients has just told me that one of the Doctors came to visit him last night. Is that correct?"

I replied "Yes, Sister, I did notice a doctor on the ward."

Sister asked me "Why have you not reported it?" My answer was,

"I thought it was the doctor who came to certify one of the deceased." Sister shouted at me "That is no excuse!" I sheepishly said "I am sorry, Sister." Sister replied, "Being sorry is not good enough. It could have had a serious consequence for the patient!" I thought that the patient actually looked in far more robust health than I did. He was lively and he was up and about. Then Sister told me to read the night report which I did with great difficulty. Sister shouted at me again because I had not put the time down for one of the incidents. Then I saw Muriel looking pityingly at me. I tried to use what mental strength I had to control myself. Then Sister said that she wanted me to correct my report before I went off duty so I sat down to do it but when Sister left the office Muriel came to help me because I just did not know where to start! When Sister came back in the office Muriel went to do her ward work and Sister told me that she could never read my reports and it was not for the first time and that she would be reporting me to Matron. She then told me to finish my work before I went off duty. I had already finished my work but I went back into the sluice to make sure that I had not left anything undone. I did not want Sister to find any more faults with me. Then as I turned round to go I was surprised to see all of the patients that could walk standing before me in the doorway of the sluice. One of the patients said, "Nurse Baker, we are all on your side. If anything happens to you we will all go to see Matron."

I thought that they were only thinking of their cups of tea but I laughed and thanked them and assured them all that I would be alright. As I left the ward I saw my night Nurse waiting for me and she said to me, "I felt so sorry for you but do not take any notice of Sister." I thought that was all very well for her to say but I knew that I could possible get the sack from Matron. We went to the dining room but the supper looked disgusting and as usual I could not eat a thing. Then I went to my room and just collapsed on my bed. I did not even bother to get undressed in case Matron sent for me. I felt so exhausted that I was surprised that I was not in tears. I did know that Ward Sisters could make nurses cry. One thing cheered me up and that was that I was off for three nights. I started to wonder what I would say to Matron if she sent for me. I was still lying on my bed when Muriel came to my room in her coffee break. She was all smiles and said that I did not realise how popular I was with the patients and that Sister didn't stand a chance.

Muriel's visit and her good news had made me feel a lot better. I gave thanks to Jesus for his protection. I made a cup of coffee and then I had a hot bath. Later on I went into North London to meet Miss Ena Campbell by the underground station. Ena took me to her flat for a meal but I could not eat much. I did not tell Ena about the trouble I had been in with Sister. We talked about different things especially the Lord Jesus. We discussed Stoke Mandeville Hospital.

Ena gave me a book called, 'By Searching' which was an autobiography by Isobel Kuhn. It was the first Christian book I had ever read. I liked the opening of the first chapter:

On to the misty flats

To every man there openeth

A way and ways and a way

And the high soul climbs the high way.

And the low soul gropes the low

And in between on the misty flats

The rest drift to and fro

But to every man there openeth

A high way and a low

And every man decideth

The way his soul shall go.

John Oxenham

I spent a very happy afternoon with Ena. It was a change for me to feel so happy. I made my way back to Croydon. In the evening, whilst I was on the train I decided that I was going to get a job in North London to be near Ena as I now felt that I loved her as my friend.

I spent my last night off work with Mrs King but afterwards when I arrived back at the hospital I was in fear and trembling at the thought of going back on duty and having to face the day as the Ward Sister filled me with dread. I tried to sleep for two hours but it was impossible because of the noise that I could hear in the corridor. Once again there was someone banging on my door with a voice which shouted "It is 7 o'clock, Nurse!" I made my way to the dining room for my breakfast but I could not eat anything so I just had a cup of coffee. As I approached the ward, feeling awful I saw a Policeman in the ward and two Doctors.

It was a great relief to find that Staff Nurse was in charge and not Sister. When we heard the day report I soon realised why there was a Policeman on the ward it was because one poor patient had tried to commit suicide! He had swallowed weed killer. In those days it was a crime to attempt suicide. At that moment I did not know what that policeman would come to mean to me. Nurse and I started our ward routine and when I entered the ward the patients started clapping at the sight of me. It cheered me up no end and my nerves went back into place. When we reached the dying patient I thought in my mind that I must tell him about Jesus before he died. I did that but there was no response so I tried a bit harder but there was still no response. The Policeman looked a bit surprised but he did not say anything to me. When Nurse and I had settled the patients down and the ward lights were out; we cleared away and then I made some coffee and took a cup to the Policeman. He seemed very nice and he was quite young! At first I felt a bit nervous at the thought of a Policeman being on the ward but he soon put me at ease. When I went for my dinner break the food looked so unappetising that I felt I could not eat anything and the other Nurses were not eating much either. When I arrived back on the ward all appeared to be quiet until Night Sister arrived on the ward and did her best to wake the patients up with her torch. She complained to me about something very trivial but, of course, I took it personally as I just thought that Sister did not like me. By that time many of the patients had woken up and wanted cups of tea and were asking for bottles so that they could pass urine (urinals).

When all had settled down again and the patients were asleep we were able to have our tea break which we had on the ward. The junior Nurse would usually prepare the tea and sometimes a few sandwiches too or even coffee to try to keep us awake! Most of the night we felt very tired. I commented to the Nurse that I did not like sandwiches so she made me some toast instead. We did have to watch out for Night Sister who would visit more frequently because there was a Policeman on the ward. The Nurse took some sandwiches and a cup of coffee to the Policeman. After we had finished our tea I realised that I had not started the night report which I was dreading. I silently prayed "Please, God, help me."

As I sat at the desk trying to write down what I knew about the patients during the night, Night Sister appeared behind me and I nearly jumped out of my skin! I immediately stood up.

Sister did not want to do a ward round, but just wanted to check up on the suicide patient. Sister must have thought that I looked like a scared rabbit which was not far from the truth because I felt so nervous I could hardly answer her questions. After Sister had left the ward I settled down again and began to write the report but I had great difficulty writing my thoughts down on paper. I left it for a short time and went into the ward again where all seemed quiet. I checked all of the patients. When I reached the Policeman I thought it must be a long night for him. So I decided to make polite conversation with him. "Can you spell?" I asked him. He looked very surprised at my question but answered "Yes." so I said, "Good, I need your help." I thought that he seemed to be a kind and gentle young man. Together we managed to write the night report. It was strange because I felt that I was able to trust this man. Eventually the day staff arrived and to my relief I handed over the night report to the Staff Nurse. Then we went off duty and made our way to the dining room for our supper which needless to say I could not eat so I just had a cup of coffee. After Night Sister had left the dining room all the night nurses chatted together and voiced their usual complaints about the work. Then the nurse that I worked with said, "I don't want to work with Nurse Baker any more. It is too hard and there are always too many deaths." So I said, "Thank you, you can take charge tonight." Another nurse said, "Yes, I don't want to work with Nurse Baker either." Then they all laughed. And I realised that they were just teasing. After that we made our way to our rooms to try to sleep, joking as we went along. Once I arrived in my room I was unable to sleep yet again. During night shifts my whole system would be crying out for sleep and then whenever I had the opportunity to sleep then something or someone would prevent it.

I tried to read but I could not concentrate so eventually I got up, dressed and decided to go to visit Mrs. King. I walked to the manse and when Mrs. King saw me she said that I looked worn out. We had a chat, a cup of coffee and something to eat which I enjoyed. I sat in the armchair by the fire and I must have nodded off to sleep. When I woke up it was quite late and nearly tea time. I had a meal with the family and then I made my way back to the hospital, with many gospel tracts that the Kings had given to me which I hoped to give to the patients. When I arrived back in my room I had two letters, one of them was from Ena which was very nice. I found her writing hard to read as she had adult writing, not like my baby writing!

Apparently the Home sister had been to my room and discovered that I was not there so I was in trouble! In those days Night Nurses had to be in bed during the day. If they did go out then they would pretend that they were in bed by putting their pillows under the sheets so if anyone came to look it would appear as though the Nurse was in bed under the bedding. We did not have locks on our bedroom doors. Sister had been into my room and had realised that I was not in bed asleep. On my return Home Sister was waiting for me and gave me a good telling off. But Home Sister was not a problem to me like the Ward Day Sister was, and I would soon have to face her! I tried to put her out of my mind but it was difficult. When I entered the ward with my pockets full of Gospel tracts which Mrs. King had given to me, I was relieved as I realised that Staff Nurse who was in charge and gave us the ward report. The report was getting gloomier by the minute as there were some very ill male patients on the ward. It occurred to me that we would probably not be getting much rest that night. Even before I began my shift, I felt weary. Staff Nurse handed the keys to me and said, "It is all yours, dear and Sister will be on duty in the morning." My heart just dropped.

I enjoyed the practical work on the ward with the patients despite my periodic encounters with the Sister. However, on that particular night I had an upset with one of the patients who was very ill. When Nurse and I entered the ward to start our night routine I gave out some of the tracts to the patients. Some of the men were joking saying about each other, "He is the sinner, Nurse. Not me." So I said, "You are all sinners. Read the tracts and take it seriously." When we approached the ill patient to help to make him feel more comfortable in his bed I began to speak with him about Jesus but this made him angry. I tried to tell him how important it was to turn to Jesus but to my horror he sat up and pointed at me and said, "I do not believe in God!" Just as I started to say that Jesus loved him I realised that he was dead. I burst into tears and the young Policeman came to me and said, "Steady on, Nurse." It turned out that this Policeman worked the same shifts as me and also had the same nights off as me. Our poor suicide patient was still alive, but only just! When we had finished completing the work relating to the death of the patient and the doctor and the Night Sister had left the ward, I was trying hard to keep on top of my work but it seemed to be a losing battle.

When nurse arrived back on the ward after her dinner break I went for my break which was toad-in-the-hole and looked awful so I just had coffee. Then I made my way back to the ward and laid out the deceased. It was very cold on the ward and I still felt upset over this patient. When Nurse and I had finished we sat on the ward with our cloaks on and a cup of coffee and we shivered! I shivered even more when Night Sister appeared! We were stiff with cold and we didn't remove our cloaks quick enough. Night Sister glared at us and told us off. Then she did her usual round of the ward doing her best to wake up the patients with her torch. When Sister left the ward it was almost our tea time but a few patients wanted a cup of tea after Sister had woken them up. I used to find it quite amazing that the Sister would wake up the patients during their sleep!

I took tea and sandwiches to the Policeman because I felt sorry for him having to sit all those hours until the patient died. When I checked the patient I knew that it wouldn't be long before he died. The Policeman smiled at me and I thought it was because he appreciated my cups of tea. Then he said to me, 'Do you need help with the report?' and I said, 'Oh yes, please'. I thought to myself, 'Oh no, I haven't even started the dreaded report, and it looks as though I will have to write the two deaths into the report too.' The other Nurse went to prepare for the morning work and I went into the office and tried to put it all down on paper.

As I was praying to the Lord for help the Policeman entered the office to tell me that the patient had died so I it was my responsibility to ring the Doctor on call to certify the deceased. Then Nurse and I laid him out and I felt sorry for him because all of his treatment had failed. Nurse took him off to the mortuary and then at last, the Policeman and I wrote the reports. I dreaded the morning coming because I would have to face the Day Ward Sister. Eventually we finished our ward routine and I went to the sluice to test the urines for diabetes. As I was clearing up the Policeman came and stood by the door and said to me, 'Nurse, because the patient has died I will not be here tonight. How will you manage with spelling?' So I answered, 'The Lord Jesus will meet my need'. I never saw the Policeman again after that.

Then I tried to make myself look presentable but as I looked in the mirror I could see that my hair was everywhere and looked a mess. I did my best but that too seemed like a losing battle.

As I came back onto the ward I noticed the day staff had entered the office and that also meant the dreaded Day Sister would be in there. As I walked down the ward I felt dilapidated and I could not have felt any worse if I was going to my execution! When I entered the office I could see Sister looking sternly at my night report. The day staff were standing with their hands behind their backs in front of the desk and looking no better than the night before. They had probably been out half the night! As I read my report Sister found fault with everything I had written and I could feel my face going red with embarrassment. Sister did not appear to be pleased with me. At last we arrived in the dining room for our supper but yet again I could not eat it as I still felt upset about the patient who had died during the night, who would not accept Jesus and I felt he had suddenly died on me.

It was not all doom and gloom on the ward as sometimes it was fun with the patients who liked to tease us. Some used to say, 'You are lovely and sweet!' and ask 'Have you got a boyfriend?' So I would answer, 'No' and then they would say, 'Why not, you have a good figure? Do you go dancing?' In those days I was very small and I had a very small waist and I always had remarks made to me about my waist. While the night staff were trying to get something to eat Night Sister breezed into the dining room. Her first words were, 'Nurse Baker, you are to go on day duty at 1:00pm on to the women's medical ward'. I could hardly believe what I had heard. Oh, the joy of it! I was all smiles until I saw Sister glaring at me. Also I had to change my room again. I was not able to sleep during the morning and I went back on duty at 1:00pm. After I reported to Sister I got on with the ward routine. The only trouble was that on the women's ward there was a lot of magic going on and that meant horoscopes and clairvoyants. At that time I did not recognise the danger of the occult. However, I got on well with the patients but because I generally had such a lack of sleep and I did not have much physical stamina I felt exhausted by the time I would go off duty at 8:00pm when I would go straight to bed until the morning. It felt so nice to be off night duty. Sometimes we would quickly look at some magazines but we would have to watch out for Ward Sister because if she caught us then we would have been in trouble.

One evening when I was off duty one of the other nurses who was also off duty asked me to go to the pictures with her but I did not want to go as I had a splitting headache. Eventually I was persuaded to go but it was a noisy, musical film which did not improve my headache. A few nights later I went to a dance with the same nurse and we became friends. Out came the old green dance dress and off we went but when we arrived at the dance hall I found that I was not able to relax so I sat down at a table with a drink of gin and orange and started to muse whilst my friend was on the dance floor. After a while I was feeling as though I wanted to go to bed but a young man came to me and asked me if I wanted to dance with him. I said, 'No, I cannot dance, do not ask me.' But he did not take 'no' for an answer and he dragged me on to the dance floor. While we were dancing I thought that he was holding me too tight which made me feel nervous. I recalled my Mother saying to me, "If anything goes wrong your father will break every bone in your body!" After we had returned to sit down at our table with more drinks I started to relax, the young man told me that I looked like a doll and then called me a kitten. Later that night the other Nurse and I arrived back at the hospital.

We were back on duty the next morning but I felt terrible. The changes in my routine had not been good for me and after coming off night duty on to day duty I was once again plagued with nightmares. One day, during coffee break, one of the Nurses came to me and asked me to go with her to a house meeting. She told me that it was run by one of the Sisters, who was a German lady. I felt a bit sceptical about that but the nurse was very persistent so I gave in and went along with her. I felt a bit apprehensive going to a Sister's home but, when we arrived, Sister made us very welcome. It was a Bible study and prayer meeting and I relaxed and started to enjoy the evening. Alas, this Sister made very good coffee! I have never tasted such good coffee since! I thought it was a change from dance halls so I continued to go to the home meeting for the rest of my time at Croydon. Back on the ward I continued to give out gospel tracts to the patients. The ward routine was hard and very tiring. I either had a headache or my legs ached and I tried to keep out of the Sister's way all the time. We had the uninspiring task of scrubbing mackintoshes and bedpans and sputum mugs; if Sister was not satisfied you had to start all over again. By the time I was off duty I was exhausted.

One day I was on duty and Sister called me in to the office and said, 'It has come to my attention that you are trying to force your religion on to the patients. I don't think it is your place to take your religion to the patients', so I tried to apologise. I found it hard as I thought I was doing it for the Lord Jesus. When I saw Mrs King I told her about Sister and her answer was, 'You will have to pray for the Lord's guidance'. So I did but I had a lot to learn in my Christian life.

During one of my weekends off I decided to go to visit Miss Ena Campbell. When I arrived at her home we had a meal. Ena asked me how I was getting on so I told her about my recent visits to the pictures and also to the dance. Ena was a bit shocked and said, "Louie, I want to read 2 Corinthians chapter 6 verse 17 to you about separation from the things of the world. When you visit the pictures it is like you are giving away your money to the devil." I told her about the home meeting with the German Sister and Ena was pleased about that. Ena also said that if I had any difficulty with reading or spelling then I would probably have difficulty with money. I agreed with her about that point and so Ena helped me to work out what I should give to give to the Lord. As I left Ena's house I decided that I was going to leave Croydon and go to work in North London. A few weeks later I got a Nurse's job in Wood Green Hospital, North London. When I gave in my notice in to Matron she told me that I was due for two week's holiday before I start my new job in North London. So I travelled up to my home in Prestatyn, North Wales, and during the train journey I knew that I would miss my friends in Croydon.

It was not easy being at home in Prestatyn because my Mother continued to remind me that I should not be a Nurse and, as usual, told me that my sister would be a Matron by now. Also I had to be careful when my Mother came back home after she had been for an evening out because I had to sleep with her and had to put up with her mentally and physically abusing me. I also had to beware of my Father who could not tolerate me in his sight. I had to be quick to avoid him and not to provoke him, so I did my best to keep out of his way. However, being at home was not all gloomy as I did visit my relatives and my Grandma who was always pleased to see me. In the second week of my holiday I started to feel restless and I wanted to go back to nursing.

After a sad parting from Grandma I set out for London. During my journey to London had I started to feel very apprehensive wondering what was in store for my life but I need not have worried as I arrived safely at Wood Green Hospital, North London to my new post as an assistant State Enrolled Nurse. The Matron was a very pleasant lady. When the Home Sister showed me to my room it seemed very small. Sister informed that I was to be working on the women's gynaecology ward. When Sister left I started to unpack and then I went into the dining room for my tea. It felt strange being with Nurses that I did not know and I missed my old friends at Croydon Hospital.

When I arrived back at my room I was feeling a bit depressed and I could hear the other girls coming off their day duty as they were banging doors and shouting at one another. I tried to focus on reading but I was not able to concentrate. I began to dread the morning coming. I tried to pray but to no avail. Eventually I was woken up by a loud bang on my door by the 7:00 a.m. Nurse and for a brief moment I could not remember where I was until it dawned on me that I was at Wood Green. It was with a heavy heart that I got up out of my bed, washed and dressed and put my new uniform on.

As I walked along the corridor there were a few other Nurses who were on their way to the dining rooms so I followed them. Unfortunately I did not feel able to eat or drink anything. The Night Sister entered the dining room and announced that the new Nurse should report for duty in the women's gynaecology ward. I walked to the ward, entered the office and listened to the night report from the Night Nurse and then duties of the ward routine were allocated to the team of Nurses.

I very quickly got into the ward routine but I noticed that there was no sign of the Ward Sister. Then I started work in the side rooms. In one side room there was a male patient dying of cancer. While another Nurse and I attended to him I asked him, "Do you know the Lord Jesus?" He looked surprised and the other Nurse stared very hard at me. The patient did not answer me so I decided to keep silent until a more opportune time. While I was in the kitchen after the patients had their dinner I heard two Nurses talking in the corridor saying, 'She is religious' and I realised that they were talking about me. I tried to take no notice of them but when I went for my coffee break no-one spoke to me.

During the evening when I was off duty I began to feel very lonely. I was missing my old friends at Croydon Hospital and I wondered if I had done the right thing by leaving there. I did not feel accepted by the staff at my new hospital. I did not know it then, but the Lord was going to turn the tables.

In due time, and on one of my days off I contacted Ena, who I felt was my only friend at that time. We met in London and had a meal at her home. I did not tell Ena that I was feeling very unhappy. I returned to the hospital and I went into the dining room for my supper, which as usual tasted awful. No-one spoke to me so I just had a cup of coffee and then went to my room. I felt very sorry for myself.

The next morning, when I arrived on duty I met the Ward Sister who was sitting at her desk in the office. I and the rest of the day staff stood very politely in front of the desk to hear the night report. I remember briefly feeling sorry for the Night Nurse, but I need not have done as she was full of confidence. I began to struggle and I often felt in despair and near to tears. My confidence went right down during this time although when I worked with the patients I would feel lifted up in my spirit. I really liked to working with the patients and worked for their benefit.

Another occasion came for me to work with the very poorly male patient in the side ward. As Nurse and I were attending to him I began to tell him once again about Jesus. As I was telling him that the only way was Jesus and of how Jesus loved people the Nurse with whom I was working seemed to be amused by something. I had not heard the door of the ward open and suddenly I realised that the very large, tall and stern Ward Sister was standing by the side of the bed glaring at me. Sister was furious with me and told me to go to her office where she gave me a good telling off.

I returned to my other duties on the ward and the Nurse that I was working with told me that Sister did not like religious Nurses. She also informed me that the male patient was her brother! I had thought that it was strange having a single male patient on a female ward! I responded to the Nurse by saying that I was not religious but I was a Christian and that I felt it was my duty to tell the patients about Jesus. Then the Nurse warned me that I would be in a lot of trouble if I was not careful in what I was saying about religion.

Of course I took no notice of the Nurses' warnings. I did not realise it then but there was a lot that I needed to learn. I was just a 'young' Christian and I just passionately wanted the patients to know about Jesus.

Before too long I realised that the patients on that ward liked me a lot. As I got to know them I started to enjoy going on duty but I had to beware of Sister. The single male patient was very near to death so I decided that I would try to speak to him again about Jesus. I knew that I would have to be very tactful in the way that I approached him. I asked the Lord to open the way for me to speak with him and the opportunity came soon. Sister was having a day off so, whilst I was doing the ward routine during the morning, I managed to speak to patient about his need for Jesus. He did respond slightly and he gave me a smile. That was the last time I saw him. I had a day and a half off from the ward and he apparently died during the night. I returned for duty after my time off and I heard the news that he had died. I was at breakfast and it made me feel very melancholy. I had not found a church that I could attend and I had not found a friend for myself. It was a difficult and lonely time for me. During my next day off, I just wandered aimlessly around London.

On my return to duty the following day, whilst listening to the night report, the Night Nurse reported that two new patients were going to theatre during the day. The Nurse in Charge told me to get the patients ready for theatre. I entered the ward and all of the patients were pleased to see me. I was not sure why as I felt that I was a right misery. I arrived at one of the patient's bedside with my equipment to prepare them for theatre when I noticed there was a Bible on one of the patient's lockers. I picked up the Bible and asked her, "Are you a Christian?" She was smiling as she answered "Yes, I am!" As I was preparing her for theatre we chatted and she asked me how long had I been a Christian. My answer was, "Not long." Then she asked me which church I went to and I told her that I hadn't been to any church since I left Croydon. Then she asked me if I had any Christian friends in the hospital but I told her that I did not have any and that she was the first Christian that I had met in the hospital. At that moment I started to feel very sorry for myself.

After I had given her the pre-med I told her that I would pray for her. Then I left her until the theatre trolley arrived. I had to accompany her to the theatre and I held her hand while the Anaesthetist gave her the anaesthetic. Her name was Joan and she did not seem to be nervous at all. Not all of the patients were nervous; very few people were a nervous wreck like me. I felt quite elevated when I left the theatre but I soon came back down to earth when I arrived back on the ward and found Sister waiting for me to tell me off over a trolley that I had not been cleared away properly. I tried to explain that the reason that I had not cleared it away was because I had not had enough time to do so but it was not possible to argue with Sister! After clearing it up I went to prepare the next patient for theatre. I had to accompany her to theatre as well and I also prayed for her and held her hand. I also got a telling-off from the Anaesthetist! I think he was in a bad mood because he was looking very crossly at me as he said "Nurse, will you stand up! What do you think you are doing, lying and leaning all over the patient?" I just mumbled an apology and left the theatre but I knew that the patients appreciated me because they told me that they thought I was a little angel. Mind you, they did not know what I was really like!

Eventually Joan was discharged and invited me to her home. When I had a day off I went to see her. I also went to the Women's Meeting in the afternoon where I enjoyed the fellowship. One afternoon a lady came to me and asked me to give my testimony. My answer was that I did not know what I should say. The lady replied, "Just say how you came to the Lord!" So I did but I did not say that I was still attached to the occult. I am sure that that was the cause of my downfall because I failed to recognise the dangers of the occult. That church was a Brethren Gospel Hall and I did not hear anyone speak about the occult. One day when I was at Joan's home she told me about her friends who were Raymond and Phyllis Medlock who also attended the Brethren Church. When I met them in their home they appeared to be very friendly people. They also held social events at their home but I found great difficulty in socialising especially if I did not know the people but the Medlocks made me feel at home with them. At last, things in my life were getting brighter! At work I had a friend who was a theatre Nurse and whose name was Joan. We got along well and we had some fun off duty. Joan thought I had an inferiority complex. I was not sure what that meant but I did not like the sound of it.

One morning at breakfast the Night Sister told me that I was on the Women's surgical ward. I felt partly pleased but another part of me felt nervous. I made my way to the ward, in fear and trembling and, as I entered the office I wondered what the Ward Sister would be like. To my surprise, the Sister smiled at me as I listened to the night report. The night staff looked dreadful and I thought that it must be a busy ward. Sister gave each one of us our instructions. My work was to do the bed baths and to help with the dressings. As I started my new routine my nerves receded as I enjoyed the work.

I soon settled in my new ward and I was getting on well with the patients and staff but a big issue arose for me. The nursing staff were not allowed to tell the patients that they had cancer. During my time as a Nurse cancer was like a death sentence. I had witnessed a lot of suffering due to open cancer. The understanding of cancer or of suitable treatments such as chemotherapy was very limited. A lot of patients never thought to ask about it and many of them assumed that they had an ulcer.

After having a day off I returned to find that a new patient had been admitted onto the ward with breast cancer. I started my ward routine, which usually consisted of dealing with beds and bed baths. When Nurse and I came to attend this patient I noticed that she was a middle aged, attractive lady who appeared to be very intelligent. We had a chat with her and settled her down and as I turned to go to the next patient she took hold of my hand and asked me if she had got cancer. For a moment I just did not know what to say but then I answered, "You will have to discuss your illness with Sister." The patient said that Sister would not tell her so I said, "Then talk to the doctor." The patient replied, "He won't tell me either." I just said "Sorry." And then I moved on to the next patient. But that was not the end of it as this patient was so persistent. I found it very difficult to answer her questions as I knew that she was very ill and would soon die from secondary cancer. I told her that I would pray for her. She explained that she was worried about her ten year old daughter so I told her about Jesus and told her that the Lord would look after her daughter after she died. Then I realised what I had said. The patient took hold of my hand and said, "Don't worry." She smiled at me. When I went off duty I felt exhausted and I also felt a bit worried. I made my way to the dining room for my supper which looked disgusting. My friend Jean had told me off for not eating so I tried to eat some pudding.

Afterwards we went to our rooms and had a cup of coffee and a chat. Then I had a bath and went to bed whilst dreading the next morning. During the night I was woken up by the Night Nurse who worked on the same ward as me. She was shining a torch in my face. "Nurse Baker, you are wanted on the ward!" I asked her "What for? It is only 3:00am!" She explained that "The patient who is dying is asking for you and Night Sister has sent me to fetch you." I was only half awake and I felt terrible as I got dressed and made my way to the ward. The Nurse in charge told me which patient was asking for me but I already knew which patient it was.

As I made my way to her bed I was praying and as I went inside the screens I saw a pallid, ghastly look on her face and I knew that she was near death. I held her hand and prayed for her. In a very weak voice she asked me "Will the Lord look after my daughter?" I said, "Yes, but you must accept Jesus as your Saviour and say sorry." She nodded and then she died. I went and told the Nurse and then I went back to bed. I have never forgotten that patient and sometimes I wonder about her daughter.

I told Jean about what happened during the night but there was no sympathy from Jean She said, "You get too involved with the patients. You must harden yourself." During my day off I went with Joan to the Gospel Hall and I told her what had happened and also told her what Jean had said. Joan said, "It is your duty to witness for the Lord and you did it well." I was attending the Gospel Hall Church and I was very happy in the church. I was invited to the homes of

Joan and John who seemed to be very popular in the church and also to the home of Phyllis and Raymond Medlock. Christmas came and all of the Nurses had to give towards the Ward Sister's Christmas gift. It was usually the ward Staff Nurse's job to get the Sister's gift. All of the Nurses had to help to decorate the ward and prepare presents for the patients. I was quite excited because I had realised what the real meaning of Christmas was. The Nurses on the ward bought one gift which was put into a big box or a tub and on Christmas day we gathered round and put our hands into the tub and pulled out a little present. Sometimes I did not like what I received so I kept it towards the gifts to wrap for the following year. Also the Nurses held a carol service when they would visit all of the wards carol singing.

When it was my day off Joan and John took me to Raymond and Phyllis Medlock's home. They had a Christmas party which I enjoyed until we played one game which was a writing game. When I was given a pen and paper I started to panic inside. Fortunately for me, people were getting hungry and they wanted to eat so that game came to an abrupt end.

After Christmas in the hospital I was put to work in the theatre and at first I felt very nervous although the theatre Sister was quite human but firm with nurses. As I became interested in my work my nerves subsided. My friend, Jean, was also working in theatre and we had a good time with the porters as we used to tease each other and we all got on very well. One of the things that would upset me was when the children came to the theatre for their operations. I was appalled by the way one of the Anaesthetists gave children the anaesthetic with a mask which usually greatly upset them. When the child was on the theatre trolley that particular Anaesthetist would put the mask straight on to the child's face and then the child would struggle and then, of course, the Nurse would have to hold the child down, which was hard work for the Nurse on duty. By the time the child was under the anaesthetic I would feel exhausted and very upset from the ordeal especially as I remembered having the mask put onto me when I was a young child.

One morning a young 12 year old boy came in for a tonsillectomy. He was a big, strong boy and we had to hold him down. The Anaesthetist was annoyed with us because we were not doing a very good job of holding the boy down. I was kicked in the stomach. When I went for my coffee break after the boy was under the anaesthetic I was not feeling very happy about all the palaver in the theatre. As I was sitting at the table with my coffee a Nurse came to join me and brought her cup of coffee with her. She asked "Nurse Baker, you don't look very happy, what's up?" I told her about the awful time we had in the theatre holding children down while they were having their anaesthetic. The Nurse replied, "I should not worry about that because children are very resilient and will forget all about it when they recover from the anaesthetic." I was not so sure because I was 24 years old but I still remembered the horror of it all. A week later and I was put back on night duty my heart just dropped at the thought of being back on night shifts. I was put onto the men's medical ward and once again I began to enjoy the work.

One night when I reported for duty in the day Sister's office to hear the day report, Sister reported about two new patients, one of whom was a heart case. When Nurse and I started our ward routine, to my amazement, one of the new patients was one of the leading brothers in the church where I attended. Fortunately he did not recognise me and I decided not to make myself known to him. However this became a bit awkward when I had to assist him with going to the toilet he said to me "Your face is familiar!" I did not make myself known because I did not want to cause him any embarrassment. On the ward there was a Nursing Auxiliary who was a lovely lady and I got on very well with her. Then one afternoon when I arrived on duty, after reporting to the Ward Sister I went into the kitchen to start preparing the patients' meals. The Auxiliary Nurse was standing by the sink and, without thinking; I went up to her and put my arms around her. I was surprised at her reaction because she said, "Nurse Baker, I am not your mother!"

I answered, "Oh no, I did not mean to upset you." She replied, "You have not upset me but I wonder what your relationship is like with your mother because every time you see me you put your arms around me!" I did not know what she meant so I just laughed and turned away.

The patient who was a leading brother in the church was eventually discharged but the trouble was that when I was in the Sunday morning meeting at Church, I saw him so I tried to hide in the back of the church but he had already seen me and at the end of the meeting he came straight down the aisle. As he approached me I felt very nervous. He asked me "Nurse Baker, are you going back to hospital?" I answered him "Yes." We had a brief conversation then he called his wife over to him. She was a very nice lady and they asked me to their home to have dinner with them which was very enjoyable. I felt that I didn't want to go back to my dreary room in the Nurses' home but eventually I had to go back to the hospital.

The next day I was put on the women's medical ward. I was quite happy about that and also the Ward Sister was quite pleasant. Sometimes on that ward I would be working with a Nurse who I got on very well with. She was merry and full of fun and always cheered me up when we were on the ward. She was a plump girl with thick black hair, full of curls. Then, one morning, the Sister allocated the ward routine between the four Nurses and the Staff Nurse. She put one of the Nurses with me who was full of mischief. For example, her mother had cooked some very hot curry pies.

While we were having our coffee break the mischievous Nurse gave me one of her pies and told me to eat it quickly which I did as I had not realised what the pies were like. It felt like the whole of my mouth was on fire! I went straight to the cold water tap but Helen tried to stop me from drinking cold water and kept saying that I would make it worse. I was more worried about the graft at the top of my mouth as I wasn't supposed to eat or drink anything hot. Eventually my mouth went back to normal. One day, when we were working together attending a patient, Nurse Helen was attending to the patient's pressure areas when she suddenly squirted methylated spirits all over me. While I was trying to dry myself off Helen went to get more bed sheets I thought that I would get my own back on her so I waited behind the curtains that were around the patient's bed. I listened until I heard the doors swing open on to the ward. Unfortunately for me, I did not see who was coming through the doors. It was not Helen but it was the Ward Sister and the Heart Specialist. I squirted Methylated spirits all over the Heart Specialist who just laughed but the Sister looked furious. The Specialist said, 'It's alright, Sister, it's only a bit of fun', but Sister did not see it that way. When she discovered who the culprit was, she was even more furious and said to me, "Into my office!" Sister vented her wrath onto me. I tried to apologise but Sister would have none of it and told us that she was going to separate us so that we were not working together due to our frivolous behaviour! I noticed that Helen did not take it seriously but I did not want to get on the wrong side of Sister. After that episode I felt that Sister was watching me like a hawk.

North London General Hospital, Acton

When I went back to church I became friends with a young girl who was also a friend of Phyllis Medlock. Her name was Dorothy and she was going to train for nursing to the hospital. Dorothy wanted me to join her in training to become a State Registered nurse. The only problem was that I did not feel very happy with the idea of more training. I still had difficulty with writing and spelling.

One afternoon when I was off duty I went out with Dorothy for a walk and she approached me once again about training for SRN. I told her that I did not feel that I could cope with any more training but Dorothy was not accepting any of my excuses and persuaded me to think again. I was amazed at her persistence! In the end I gave in and applied to the Acton North London Hospital as Dorothy had been accepted there for her training. After a few weeks I received a letter and some forms from the Matron.

A friend helped me fill in the forms but I left out the question about school education as I was afraid it did not look very promising. I did not feel encouraged by my completed application form and I did not think that the Matron would accept me. But, to my surprise, I received a letter from the Matron for an interview.

The day arrived for me to meet the Matron in her office and I felt very nervous, as the Matron looked strict and she did not smile. She was looking through my forms and, of course, Matron asked me about my education and wanted to know why I had left it out of the form. Then Matron asked me which school I went to so I told her. Then I had a shock as Matron said, "I will get in touch with your former Headmaster." It was at that point when I decided to tell her that I had missed a lot of school although I did not tell her why. The thought of Matron getting in touch with Mr. Owen filled me with horror and also made me feel hatred towards the school. Then Matron said, "I am sorry, Miss Baker, you have to have a high standard of education. I cannot accept you for training." Then Matron left her desk and proceeded to open the door and say, "Good afternoon, Miss Baker." I did not move. Something within me rose up. I said "Matron, I am not leaving until you accept me.2 The Matron tried to be firm with me and she said "No, I am sorry I cannot accept you until I have heard from the Headmaster of your school."

I could not believe what Matron was saying so I said, "Matron, a good Nurse doesn't have to be all brains!" Then I thought I saw very faint amusement on her face. She returned to her desk and then she said to me, "You appear to be very determined to be accepted by me so I have decided to put you on a month's trial and see how you get on. I will get in touch with you. Good afternoon!" As I left the office I felt very shaky after my performance with the Matron. I made my way to a café and ordered a cup of coffee. Whilst I sat at the table drinking my coffee I started to think about what the Matron had told me. Matron had received excellent references from previous

Matrons of the hospitals where I had worked so I prayed that she would not get in touch with my school headmaster in Rhyl, North Wales. As I made my way back to the hospital where I worked I made the decision that if Matron did accept me for SRN training I would fight to complete the training. I did not tell anyone at my hospital but just got on with my work on the ward.

After a few days I received a letter from the Matron of the North London Hospital accepting me on her staff as a probationer and soon after receiving the letter I went to see the Matron of my hospital to inform her of my intention to leave and to give one months' notice. Then I told the Ward Sister who seemed to be very surprised and sorry that I was leaving the hospital. But Sister did smile at me and say, "I'm sure, Nurse Baker that you will get through the training."

When I told my friends of my decision to leave they seemed to be surprised about my news. When I told my friends at church they seemed to be pleased for me and also prayed for me. I felt that the Lord was with me. Then I had to tell my friend Ena Campbell about my news so on my next visit to her I told her about my decision. Ena didn't seem very enthusiastic about my plans for more training as she thought it would be difficult for me. After a bit of an argument Ena wished me well. In those days I was very strong willed and I had a lot to learn. Eventually my months' notice came to an end and on my last day on the ward Sister called me into her office and the other Nurses and Sister said that I would be missed although they believed that I would get through my next training if I worked well. Then Sister gave me a hard-backed book called, 'Born Free' by Joy Adamson. It was about a lioness of two worlds called Elsa. The staff knew that I loved lions and animals and I was very pleased with the book. At last I left the hospital and went back to Prestatyn for a short time and back to my Mother who kept telling me that I was making a big mistake. I took no notice but when I went to visit my Grandma I felt disappointed because Grandma told me that I should listen to my Mother. I was glad when the day came for me to leave home and make my way to the North London Hospital.

I travelled by train to London Euston station. I was feeling very apprehensive when the train arrived in London and I made my way to the underground station. On my arrival at the hospital I reported to the Home Sister's office and the Sister took me to my new room in the Nurses' home. The décor of my room was very simple and consisted of a wardrobe, one chair and a dressing table. When I had unpacked my case and put my things away and a few things on the table and the sink I sat down on my chair and I started to have qualms about my new situation. Then I started to read my Bible.

I read Joshua chapter 1, verse 3: 'Every place that the sole of your foot shall tread upon I have given unto you'. After reading that I prayed and I felt more encouraged to go into my unknown future. Then I heard a lot of noise in the corridor caused by the Nurses who were going off duty. I decided to venture out into the corridor and find the dining room so that I could have my supper which was not very appetizing. To my surprise my friend Dorothy entered the dining room with her friend. After supper I went with Dorothy and her friend to our rooms for a cup of coffee. However I had a problem as Dorothy's friend did not appear to like me.

'Two is company but three is a crowd!' I decided to leave them and I went to find a phone box to let my Mother know that I had arrived at my new hospital and then I retired to bed. I found it difficult to sleep in a strange bed and I dreaded the morning but eventually sleep came. And then I was awoken at 6:30am by a Nurse banging loudly on my door. I arose quickly although I was not feeling very good. I washed and dressed in my new uniform which was the usual white dress, starched cap, flat, lace-up shoes and black stockings. When I went for breakfast the Night Sister appeared in the dining room and instructed me "Nurse Baker, report to the Men's surgical ward." My heart dropped because I would have preferred to go on the women's ward. Not only that, it was also my birthday, 1st April 1961 and I was 25 years old. Fortunately for me, no one knew it was my birthday so I thought I would make my way to my new ward. I reported to the ward Sister's office where the Sister smiled at me, which was an encouragement as much of my confidence had gone. After listening to the night report Sister told me to work with my friend, Dorothy. I will never forget that morning! When we started to make the beds we came to a patient who I felt was laughing at me and I soon discovered why he was amused when I started to bed-bath him. When Dorothy turned him towards her I could clearly see that he had opened his bowels. As I started to wash him he started to laugh and also Dorothy was doubled up laughing and all the male patients who could walk came inside the curtained area for a moment to see what was going on. I felt a bit alarmed until they all said 'April fool!' which made me laugh too. The patients had put artificial faeces inside the sheets of the patients that we were attending. Sister told Dorothy and me to go for our coffee break. Dorothy told me that she had a present for me. It was a picture with a Bible text on it,

> "Believe in the Lord Jesus,
>
> and you will be saved - you and your household."
>
> Acts chapter 16 verse 31.

What a pleasant surprise! It was the only present I received on that birthday and I did not receive any cards either. As I became interested in the hard work on that busy ward my nerves began to subside. It was not possible to have a conversation with the patients because the Ward Sister would watch us all the time and then she would give you more work to do.

The Sister would also ask us why we had not finished the work that she had already allocated to us. It seemed as though we could not win and we certainly did not argue with a ward Sister!

After a month's trial the Matron asked to interview me so I changed my uniform and made by way to Matron's office feeling very nervous indeed. I entered Matron's office in fear and trembling, with my heart beating like a race horse. I stood in front of Matron's desk with my hands behind my back. I was surprised when Matron told me that she had accepted me for the three year state registered nurse training. I signed a form and left her office feeling a bit more secure in myself as I returned to the ward. However, I did not realise what I had let myself in for as there would be a lot of exams and lectures.

I did realise that it would be a very difficult process for me as I would have to cope with the theory side of the training and all of the writing. I thought that I would probably cope very well with the practical side of the training although I still felt like a nervous wreck about it. Even so, I was determined to fight to complete the training and I thought "What is the point of giving in to difficulties?" I felt that I had to fight while there was a will and a hope in me. I also loved the hospital and I could not imagine myself anywhere else but in a hospital. In addition to all of this I was very stubborn. What is more I knew that I had the power of the Lord Jesus with me. In many circumstances I had recognised that the Lord Jesus was with me and that he had sent his angels to me during so many of the difficult times in my life.

One day, a Nurse invited me to the Nurses' Christian Fellowship which was held in the Nurses' sitting room. I enjoyed the Nurses' Fellowship and it was a good opportunity for me to get to know the other Nurses. About this time, a new nurse came into my life. Her name was Maureen and I got on well with her. She used to take me to her home where her parents always made me feel very welcome. The only trouble was that her brother wanted to go out with me. I refused to go out with him because I was so involved with my work in the hospital. Because of this I felt that I had to stop going to Maureen's home. I settled well into my work on the ward and I enjoyed the work immensely. A lot of the male patients were friendly towards the Nurses and they were always telling me what a lovely figure I had. In those days I was very small and my waist measured only 18 inches. Patients told me that I had an hour-glass figure and I felt uncomfortable having to hear so many remarks about my figure. In those days some patients were in hospital a long time and so they wanted to know all about the nurses. But there wasn't much time for gossiping because we would have ward Sister on to us.

The ward work was hard! The practical work was not new to me due to my training at Bristol and my experience but to some probationers it was new. The routine was so rigid and the ward work had to proceed along with everything else. The lockers had to be scoured and clean beds had to be made. The corners of the counterpanes had to be geometrical and also the wheels at the end of the beds had to be straight and facing each other. When I went off duty my body used to feel that it was in a state of chaos and fatigue and all I wanted to do was to go to bed. However, I continued to go to church at the Gospel Hall and I continued to visit Miss Ena Campbell. If I went with her to the evening meeting at church on a Sunday I would usually find it very beneficial.

The problem I had then was that worry would gnaw at my mind about the theory side of the training. I couldn't ask for prayer because I did not want to let anyone know the situation that I was in. I said my own prayers and the first chapter of the book of Joshua helped me.

At last the dreaded day arrived when I and my first year set had to face the classroom and the Sister Tutor. The night before I found it difficult to sleep but when I did eventually drift off into some kind of sleep it certainly wasn't refreshing! At 6:30am there was a loud bang on my door and I stumbled out of bed feeling awful. When I looked in the mirror to do my hair I did not recognise myself! Eventually I was ready to go to the dining room for breakfast where I tried to eat some corn flakes but failed. Night Sister entered the dining room and I could not concentrate on what she was saying because I was nervous in a bad way. I watched Sister leave the dining room and a young Nurse jumped up to open the door for her. The etiquette was still very strict and you had to stand aside for a senior staff member.

I entered the classroom as a first year student Nurse. I had not realised the immensity of the training! Sister Tutor appeared pleasant but I do not think that I looked intelligent! I had not much confidence and I felt awful. Sister did try to put us at ease and told us that we would be working towards the prelim exam which Nurses would take after a year's training.

I do not think that Sister was very impressed with me. For a start, when she asked a question I gave her the wrong answer! I thought that I had made a very bad start on my first morning. We were to be in that class for the next six weeks and were studied anatomy and physiology. I found it very hard, especially trying to keep up with Sister's dictation notes, which were far too fast for me to keep up with so I just scribbled page after page. I could not remember how to spell words about anatomy and I found it very difficult as I watched Sister pointing with one of her canes. My mind started to wander as I tried to write about the skeleton which was hanging in front of our desks. My mind went back to the warehouse in Bodfor Street, Rhyl where I worked for Clarke & Sons and I remembered I had bought a small book about the skeleton. When I showed my workmates my book they had just laughed at me and had said, 'You will never get to be a Nurse', but I was determined to learn the names of all the bones in the body. Then I suddenly came back to earth as Sister was looking at me as she asked, 'Nurse, are you paying attention?' I just replied, 'Yes, Sister', but I quietly thought to myself, 'The battle had begun to finish what I had started training for!' During the afternoon Sister demonstrated the practical side of our training. I did not have a problem with that side of nursing. Sister gave us lectures on the usual practicalities of bandaging each other and making beds using a dummy figure. We also had lectures about hygiene which I did not like very much. All of this information was essential to become a good Nurse although I could not always make the right connections between the information and the practice. I noticed how fast the other students were taking notes. Relying on my memory was not a good idea either as it was not always very reliable which I found difficult. When we went for our coffee break I got to know the other girls but I used to feel awkward particularly as I was older in age than the others. Some of them were only 18 years old and I was 26 years old. However, I got along well with the Nurses in my group and they said that I did not look my age. They thought that I looked about eighteen or twenty years old.

At last the day came which I had been dreading as we had a test paper and also a practical test which I passed. As for the written paper, it was a nightmare! I did know the answers but I did not answer them correctly on the paper. The next day I was in for a big shock. Sister Tutor handed out our papers and when I looked at mine it was awful. I saw a lot of red ink all over my blue ink! I just stared at my paper in dismay.

Sister discharged us to go for our dinner break but just as I was leaving the classroom Sister said, 'Nurse Baker, I want to speak to you about your test paper', and my heart just skipped a beat. I gave her my paper and Sister said, 'Nurse, you really must try harder than this. I couldn't make out what you had written and you have made so many mistakes. You must concentrate more or you will fail'. I tried to make an apology to Sister but I do not think she was in the mood to accept my apology. I felt upset and I could not eat any dinner so I just had a cup of coffee. I had a new friend, a girl who was in my group who was training for her SRN. She was very pretty and attractive and she was also a Christian. We got on well together and it was not long before we went into town and for walks together. We also joined the Christian fellowship. Around that time I was still being plagued with nightmares although I was still attending church

I did not ask for prayer because I did not want to tell anyone about my problems.

My younger sister Jo was very clever and went to the Grammar school before joining the RAF. Once, while on leave she came down from our home in Prestatyn to stay with a friend in London. One evening she came to visit me in the hospital and she looked very smart in her uniform. Whilst in training we were supposed to spend our evenings studying but, because my sister had arrived I did not do any study. After our conversation about our parents I decided to take her to the dining room for our supper. On this night it was our favourite meal of pork chops. All the Nurses were coming into the dining room for their supper and were wolfing down their meal along with thick white bread. My sister was amazed at the spectacle and said that the meal was disgusting. After leaving the dining room we went to my new friend Pam's room for coffee. Then my sister went back to her friend's flat leaving me feeling very low.

The following day it was back to the classroom. I did my best to work very hard and study and try to remember but I still could not keep up with Sister's dictation as it was very difficult. Sister was pleased with my practical work though. The usual procedure then was that no-one spoke to Sister unless you were spoken to first.

One day Sister gave us a lecture on how to give injections intramuscular. She demonstrated with an orange and I found it very interesting as it was all very familiar to me. Sister also demonstrated to us how to pass a gastric tube through the nose into the stomach so that analysis could be carried out as an aid to diagnosis.

I always enjoyed the practical side of training and I found it all fascinating. Eventually the six weeks came to an end and we had to take our test paper and practical test. I came top of the practical test which I thought was due to Nurse McNamara who had trained me so well in Bristol Hospital. I'm afraid I was bottom in the written paper and Sister Tutor was not very pleased and told me that I had to make more of an effort with my written work. When Sister handed me my paper as usual it was covered in red ink where she had marked all of the errors. I felt as if I was hanging on by the skin of my teeth. I went to my room feeling very low and by now I was realising that I had some serious problems even though I was convinced that the Lord was with me. My friend came into my room and tried to get me out of my low mood by trying to make me laugh which worked eventually. After this I decided to visit my friend Joan from the church. I had not told anyone at the church about my problems, my family or my mouth.

Eventually I was working back on the men's surgical ward which I was quite pleased about which did not last long as when I arrived on duty I discovered that a different Ward Sister was in charge and she was very hard to please. It seemed as though I could not do anything right for doing wrong! The days were long as I was on duty from 8:00am to 8:30pm but we got three hours off during the day, either morning, afternoon or evening. I found the morning off duty was the hardest. I left the ward at the 10:00am coffee break and tried to do some studying and then I went for lunch and then reported back for duty at 1:00pm which was a long shift. My legs ached continually. Then I would go off duty at 8:30pm and go for my supper. But I was so tired that I could not eat anything and I would go to my room and just collapse on my bed until someone made coffee.

One morning, while on duty Sister was furious with me because I threw a patient's toes away! I didn't realise that the pieces of wood in his bed were his toes. Also the Surgeon was on his way to examine the patient. I tried to apologise but Sister did not accept my apology and told me to go and find the toes, which I did but they were not recognisable as toes. When the Surgeon came onto the ward and examined the poor patient he just nodded at Sister and then left the ward. As for me, I was still trying to cool down my blushing face.

One morning when Matron was doing her ward round accompanied by Ward Sister, I was just walking down the ward after scouring the sluice. Matron beckoned me to her so I went and stood respectfully before her. She said, 'Nurse, your hair is on your collar; either get it cut or tie your hair back'. So I said, 'Yes, Matron', and Sister just stared at me. So when I was off duty I tried to tie my hair back after deciding that I did not want to have it cut. The trouble was that I had baby-fine hair which did its own thing. In the end I succeeded in arranging some kind of roll behind my head. Then one lunch time when I entered the dining room for my dinner some of the Senior

Nurses said, 'Here comes Jane Eyre'. I just laughed and said, 'Oh, dear, I can't win'. That was the hair style for the remainder of my time in hospitals.

Then one morning, while on duty I answered the telephone. The call was for a Doctor who was doing a ward round with Sister. Without realising it I did the wrong thing. I walked up to the Doctor with my hands behind my back and said, 'Excuse me' and then I delivered the message. Sister gave me a terrible look and the Doctor just nodded. I felt stupid because the hospital etiquette was strict and so I hid away in the sluice. Eventually when the Doctor left the ward Sister came into the sluice and started to tell me off about addressing a member of the medical staff directly. You were supposed to go through the medium of someone more senior to yourself. Then Sister made a sudden move towards me and I quickly raised my arm across my face to protect myself. Sister exclaimed "Good heavens, girl, I am not going to hit you!", and she left the sluice. However, I never made that mistake again.

One morning when I was on duty I was told by Sister that I was to help the Senior Nurse with the dressings which I found very interesting. Medical treatment was very different in my time and wounds were always well covered. The Nurse told me about the patient's wounds but I already knew although I chose not to say anything. After the Nurse finished with the dressing I was given the task of clearing the trolley with Savlon disinfectant.

One evening when I was off duty a Nurse asked me to go to a dance with her. I did not want to go as I was so tired after coming off duty but I was soon persuaded. So off we went to the dance hall. I was wearing my old green dance dress. I thought my friend wanted a boyfriend and she soon got a nice young man. I just sat by a table feeling like death and all I could think about was my bed because I felt so tired. As I was waiting for my friend to call it a night (no chance there!) my mind started to wander back to Stoke Mandeville Hospital. Then a young man came towards me and took my arm and almost dragged me on to the dance floor. He soon realised that I wasn't very co-operative and when the dance finished he asked me if I would like a drink, to which I replied, 'Oh, yes please'. My head felt terrible so I went outside thinking that I was going to collapse any minute. The young man brought the drinks out and we sat on the seat and just talked. After some conversation he asked me to go out with him but my answer to him was, 'No!' because I wanted to put Nursing first. Then at last my friend came to me and said, 'We have a lift back to the hospital'. When we arrived back in the grounds we found an open window and kept a watch out for night duty Sister. My friend appeared to be happy and told me that she had a date with the young man with whom she had been dancing. Well, that didn't surprise me by the way they were all over each other at the dance! But I was not feeling happy, I was feeling annoyed because by that time I had started to feel wide awake. So we had a cup of cocoa. Then I tried to sleep for the rest of the night. When morning arrived at 6:00am it was far too early. I felt dreadful and when I looked in the mirror I looked absolutely ghastly. When I entered the dining room and sat down with my tea and cornflakes, I noticed a Staff Nurse enter the dining room who I thought seemed lovely so I asked the Nurse who was sitting next to me, 'Who is that Staff Nurse, isn't she lovely?' The Nurse answered and said to me "You will not think she is so lovely when you work under her!"

When I reported for duty Sister divided the ward work. After we heard the night report from the Senior Night Nurse (who looked dreadful) we started our work. After bed making my next job was to scour the bed pans and everything else in the sluice. The ward Sister would always inspect our work and if she wasn't satisfied you had to do it all over again until she was satisfied. It was unbelievable, the number of times I saw my face in a shiny bed pan!

On that particular day Sister was behind me all the time and my arms ached with scrubbing the sluice and the bathroom. I thought no germ or dirt would stand a chance on that ward. After I had finished the cleaning, Sister gave me another job to do and my heart failed because I knew that I would not be able to do what Sister was telling me to, so I prayed.

Afterwards, when I arrived back on duty after my dinner, which I couldn't eat, a Nurse who was sitting next to me remarked, "If you don't eat you will disappear down a drainpipe!" I had remembered my own medical test as the Doctor had not seemed to be very impressed with me and told me that I was far too thin. I was only 6st in weight but, fortunately for me, he passed me. He said that the next time he saw me he would expect me to have put weight on. So I had decided to eat Mars bars!

When I went into Sister's office, Sister was not very pleased with me and said, "Nurse, I am going for my lunch. When I come back I expect you to have done the charts and forms which I have told you to do." This made me feel anxious as the other Nurses were busy in the ward. Also, I knew that the Ward Sister could report a Nurse to Matron if any of the nursing staff disobeyed her on the ward.

I looked at the papers and put my hands on my face and prayed. When I opened my eyes there was a Nurse by my side and I knew that she was not one of the ward staff. I noticed that her face was very pleasant. She did not speak, but just pulled the papers towards her and did the job which I supposed to have done and then she left. I was puzzled! I left the papers on Sister's desk and went into the ward and asked the other Nurses if they had seen a Nurse with me in the office, but they all told me "No!" I did look everywhere in the hospital but I never saw her again. I now believe that the Lord sent an angel to help me because I was desperate and the Lord heard my prayer.

One morning, while I was making the beds with a Nurse I accidently caught one of the patient's drainage tubes and pulled it out. I tried to put it back in but it didn't work. It was too painful for him so I went and told Sister what I had done. Sister was not pleased with me and asked "Oh, Nurse, why are you so careless?" and came to examine the poor patient who was not a bit upset! But Sister started telling me off and asked "Oh dear, whatever will the Surgeon say?" However, when the Surgeon did his ward round with another Sister and a Doctor I started to feel nervous. I knew Sister would tell him who it was that had been so careless. It turned out that the Surgeon decided to leave it out!

Christmas was coming soon so I tried my best to keep out of Sister's way which was never an easy thing to do.

When Sister was off duty the Staff Nurse was in charge. I always looked forward to Christmas in hospitals as it was the usual routine which Sister organised. The Nurses would decorate the ward and arrange the presents for the patients. The Nurses would put money together towards the Sister's present and they also bought a present to put into the tub. The patients seemed to be in a good mood and some of them would like to tease us which we did not mind. Sometimes we would make them apple-pie beds and then they would chase us and one patient even put his feet through his sheet! Of course, all of this fun was had while Sister was off duty. Sometimes, when I got the opportunity, I would tell the patients to the Lord Jesus. I also became aware that some patients were very nervous about going to theatre and sometimes a patient would ask me to pray for them. Only the patients who were full of confidence thought that they did not need praying for.

When Christmas day arrived Sister was in a good mood and we had a good time as long as the ward work was done we could go to visit the other wards. Nurses did not usually have any off duty on Christmas day but we would enjoy ourselves. Also, the Surgeon would always come on the ward to carve the turkey and we would wait with trays while Sister served out the vegetables. Then we would carry the trays to the beds. The patients were allowed to drink what they wanted, even the ones that were on special diets. They also had Christmas pudding although some regretted having it the next day! By the time I went off duty I felt very tired and when I had my day off I went to visit my friends from the church and had my Christmas dinner with them. The Christmas dinner for the Nurses was quite good that year and for once and I managed to eat that too!

One morning soon after, as I entered the dining room I saw the Staff Nurse who I was in awe of. I watched her as I ate my cornflakes and wished that I could be like her. I did not notice the night Sister enter but suddenly I heard Sister's voice penetrating into my ears, "Nurse Baker is to start night duty at 8:00pm and come off day duty at 1:00pm!" What a fright I had! I knew night duty was coming but had I hoped it would be not quite so soon. I came off duty at 1:00pm and went to the dining room for my dinner which I could not eat so I just had some pudding and coffee and then went back to my room to pack my belongings and move to the night nurses' quarters.

After unpacking, I eventually got into bed but, most annoyingly, I was wide awake and I could hear noise all around the corridors, which was a nuisance. I felt depressed and I tried to read but I could not concentrate. I tried to study but that was even worse. I pulled the covers over my head and started to think about the Bible. I sat up and read the 'Daily Bread' reading notes and started to pray but it was only 'skin praying' – just thinking about oneself. I must have dozed off because I was aroused by a bang on my door at 7:30pm. I dragged my body out of bed feeling awful. I got washed and dressed and tried to do something with my hair, which was always a headache. I made my way to the dining room and tried to eat cornflakes and a cup of coffee. The Senior Night Sister entered the dining room and we all stood up. Then Sister nodded and we all sat down. Sister was tall and had a mass of dark hair and looked very strict. To say that I felt nervous was an understatement - I was terrified of her! I never saw her smile and she spoke very sharply, "Nurse Baker, report to the men's surgical ward!" I was relieved as I knew the patients on that ward. As Sister left we stood up and made our way to our wards to face the long night. As I entered the office Staff Nurse was finishing the day report which seemed to me to be endless. The ward appeared to be very busy and the day Nurses had not finished their work. At last the day staff went off duty, and they looked more dead than alive, then my Senior Nurse and I started the ward work. The patients who had had their operations during that day had drips attached to them and two patients were dying. Also that day there were two motor bike accidents (In those days motorcyclists did not wear helmets). The patients who knew me seemed pleased to see me. When I went around with the night drinks I got mixed up with the Gastrics. My Senior Nurse was not too pleased and said that I must concentrate on what I was doing but the patient did not mind having the wrong drink as he was all smiles. My Senior Nurse went off for her break, leaving me in charge of the ward, I checked the dying patient and checked the patients on drips and everything appeared to be well and they all seemed to be asleep. But not for long! I decided to do some clearing up in the kitchen. Then I heard a sharp voice asking "Nurse, why are you not in the ward?" It was the 'terror by night Sister.' I just stammered my reply to her "I am sorry, Sister" but she was having none of my apology. Her answer was, "Nurse, you must remain in the ward at all times. While you were in the kitchen something serious could have happened!"

By the time Sister had been round the patients shining her torch into their faces half the patients were awake and wanting cups of tea. So when Nurse arrived back on the ward after her break she was surprised to see so much activity. Then I had to explain why and she just raised her eyes in annoyance and sent me off for my break, which was our dinner time. It was usually stew or some kind of salad. I could not eat the meals as they tasted awful so I just had coffee and some pudding, if it was nice which wasn't very often.

I made my way back to the ward feeling dreadful and reported to my Senior Nurse who gave me some jobs to do. I tried to finish my work in the kitchen but not for long because we had another motor bike accident admitted. He was a very nervous young man who kept asking me if he was going to die. So I said, "Not if I can help it!" Then he laughed and we tried to make him comfortable. After the Doctor had left I prayed for him just as Night Sister approached down the ward determined to find me more work to do. I was trying to get through my work but as usual half the patients were awake and wanting cups of tea, due to Night Sister. The night staff always had their tea on the ward whenever they had the chance. By the time we had our tea I felt on the point of collapsing. During the early hours of the morning my body would go into its lowest ebb. We had just finished our tea and Marmite sandwich when Night Sister entered the ward. I tried to stand up but I felt numb with cold. Sister shone her torch into my face. Fortunately I heard a patient call out at that moment "Nurse!" so I staggered down the ward to the patient. When I saw Night Sister leaving the ward I went to prepare the morning cup of tea and washes, while Senior Nurse wrote her night report. Eventually the day staff arrived and I was relieved to see the Staff Nurse in charge, not the Ward Sister. I wearily took myself to the dining room for my so-called supper which was awful. The food on night duty was atrocious so I decided that I would go into London. When I was getting ready and changing into 'mufti' one of the night duty Nurses came into my room and asked why I wasn't going to bed so I told her that I was going into London as I no longer felt tired. The Nurse asked "Can I come with you?" so I replied "'Yes." and we went to Oxford Street and afterwards went to Lyons Corner House coffee bar. While we were eating our meal a man remarked to us "You girls are eating as if you haven't eaten for a month!" which made us both laugh and replied to him "We haven't!" Afterwards we went back to the hospital by Underground. I knew later that I would regret going out to London.

I went to bed but sleep was impossible. Then I must have dozed off as I awoke to the sound of a bang on my door by the 7:30pm nurse. Once again I dragged myself out of bed and got ready for duty. When I arrived on the ward which again looked very busy the patient who was dying the night before was still there, dying. Nurse and I stood either side of Sister with our hands behind our backs while Sister went through the day report. It seemed to be endless. Just before Sister went off duty she told me off for using too much tea during the night (there were no tea bags in those days!)

On my nights off I usually went into London just to wander around the shops and visit Ena and my friends from the church who were kind enough to put up with me. One night they told me how tired I looked. After having an evening meal, I would go back to the hospital feeling very tired and I would have a night drink, which was usually cocoa or coffee.

Some days my sister would come to visit me and my friend, Pam, and we would go out together. My Sister had a friend in the RAF with her who was called Colette who was in the RAF. When I arrived back on night duty I was on duty with another Senior Nurse who looked rather strict and I felt a bit apprehensive. Also the ward looked like a mad house as there had been a lot of operations and new admissions during the day and I realised that the night was going to be busy! After the day report which seemed to be longer than ever I went into the ward to relieve the Day Nurses who looked half dead with tiredness and they looked glad to see me. Then the Senior Nurse gave out the night drugs and I started to prepare the evening drinks. When I went round the patients giving out their night drinks one patient kept telling me how much he loved me. Of course, I did not take any notice of him and told him "I know what you are after!" The patient in the next bed asked "What is he after, Nurse?" So I said, "A cup of tea during the night!" and he laughed.

I had brought two surgical books with me hoping to do some studying but there was no chance. We were too busy with a patient who had collapsed. The Doctor came to revive him but failed to do so and we had a death on our hands. The Senior Nurse went for her break and left me in charge. The ward seemed very eerie at night. I was glad when the Nurse arrived back on the ward and I could go for my dinner break. I could not eat my dinner and also there was rice pudding which I had never liked.

I remember my father shutting me in a bedroom until the next day because I would not eat rice pudding, so I just had coffee and some bread which was stale. I leant my head on the table feeling as though I was going to die at any moment. Then the Nurse told me how awful I looked and told me to get some Yeast Vite tablets. Eventually when I was off duty I did buy some Yeast Vite from the Chemists. I think they did help me generally as I gradually had more energy in my body. When I arrived back from my dinner break Nurse and I had to lay out the deceased. When we had finished I had to go with the porter to the mortuary which was not very pleasant during the night! When I arrived back on the ward I thought that I had turned grey. I went to the kitchen to prepare the morning teas and also our 4:00am tea which we had on the ward. Just as I was recovering from my visit to the mortuary, which was very eerie, I heard a sharp voice saying, "Nurse, come into the ward!" It was night Sister, (the terror by night!) I followed her into the ward. Senior Nurse stood up to do the ward round while I stood with my arms behind my back feeling very cold and wondering how many patients would wake up! Eventually we managed to have our tea and I felt stiff with cold. At last we started the ward work and the Senior Nurse wrote the ward report while I started the ward routine. Before long the day staff arrived but before I could go off duty I had to make sure that the kitchen and sluice were clean and tidy. Eventually I wearily reported off duty and went to the dining room with the other Night Nurses hoping that there would be something to eat but I must have been fooling myself! I just had some pudding and coffee. After some conversation with my colleagues I made my way to my room and to my annoyance I started to feel awake so I decided to go out and visit my friend from church. After a meal I fell asleep in an armchair and when I arrived back at the Nurses' home I tried to sleep for another few hours. Then I reported on duty and I did not feel too bad after taking two Yeast Vite tablets. We listened to the night report, which wasn't very encouraging as Sister told us that that one of the patients, who was an elderly man called George, was discovered smoking in his room and the cigarettes were taken away from him. Sister told us to watch him closely, (as though we did not have enough work to do on the ward!). On that night, the ward routine was finished and all the patients were settled down and I had attended to George who was already asleep; Senior Nurse gave out the drugs whilst I did some jobs in the kitchen and Night Sister came to check the dangerous drugs.

Everything was peaceful when Night Sister left the ward. Then the Nurse went for her dinner break and I was just enjoying a few minutes peace when a patient who was coming back from the toilet said, "Nurse, I can smell smoke coming from a room in the corridor!" My feeling of peace just evaporated. George was smoking a cigarette which he had taken from us and he was on fire! His clothes and bed linen were burning and I felt panic inside me but I managed to put out the flames and get George out of his room but I could not cope with the bed mattress. Then I remembered the patient who kept telling me that he loved me, so I went to him and asked him, "Do you still love me?" And his answer was, "Yes, Nurse!" He was going to regret that because I told him that I needed him in one of the side rooms. He looked a bit startled and asked "What for?" I whispered loudly to him "I cannot tell you here!" I was concerned in case another patient heard and I started to pull him out of bed as he asked "Whatever will my wife say, I am a happily married man?" I told him "You must not tell your wife or anyone!"

He was a young man who had an appendectomy and had recovered well and he was due to be discharged. When we got into George's room the patient asked me "Oh dear, whatever has happened here?" Then I told him why I wanted him to help me with the bed mattress. I was going to put it in the corridor but when we turned the mattress, it was not too badly damaged so I cleaned the room up and put clean bed sheets on the bed and settled George down for the rest of the night. I thanked the patient for helping me and he said, "I would like to have a talk with you in the morning."

I knew that I should have reported the fire but I was so fearful of Night Sister. After opening the windows wide the smell of the smoke had evaporated. When Nurse came back from her break she asked "Is there something burning?" I replied "No, Nurse!" but I could feel my face going red. Fortunately the lights were very dim so she didn't notice. I was really glad to go for my break then.

In the morning after we had done the ward routine I went to thank the patient who had helped me in the side ward during the night. He was all smiles and got hold of my hand and said, "It was a pleasure, Nurse." I asked him what he wanted to talk to me about but he just said that it was not important and started stroking my face. Eventually I went to the dining room for my supper which looked disgusting. As I sat down I noticed a Staff Nurse who I admired. I wished she was my friend. Then I thought, 'No chance, forget it!"

Just as I was day dreaming Night Sister appeared and her sharp voice penetrated into my mind, "Nurse Baker, you are to come off night duty and start day duty on the women's surgical ward at 1:00pm." I felt very happy about that until I discovered that I had to go back to the classroom on Monday morning. On the Sunday I went to church and then I spent the rest of the day with my friend. I was dreading going back to the classroom as I had forgotten that Sister wanted us to write case notes about a patient. Of course, I had done the practical work so I wrote just one page on what I could remember. When we arrived back in the classroom Sister was not impressed with my one page of written work. The other Nurses had done a lot more written work. When we were going for our dinner break Sister called me back and said, "Nurse Baker, you really must put more effort into your written work!" Sister handed me my paper back which had more red ink on it than blue! Then Sister said, "What you write is correct but you put it in a nutshell. You must spread it out more." As I made my way to the dining room I prayed that Sister would not report me to Matron. During the afternoon we did practical work which I was good at. Once a week we had a Doctor who gave us a lecture on diseases. I had to keep a lot in my head because I was too slow writing it down on paper but I did find the lectures very interesting. We were studying towards the prelim exam which consisted of Part 1 written paper and Part 2 practical. We had the weekends off during times in class so I attended church on Sunday mornings and evenings. One day, while I was out with my friend we came across another Gospel Hall. I became interested and decided to attend the hall on the following Sunday. I arrived there on my own only to discover that it was 'Closed Brethren', but I didn't mind. When I entered the hall I just wearily sat down and enjoyed the peace and quietness after the turmoil of the hospital. At the end of the meeting a lady came to me and wanted to know who I was and where I came from so I told her that I was from the hospital (no pens and cards in those days!). Her name was Mrs Bick and she invited me to their home in Hounslow. Her husband was a kind man and I was allowed to go to their home anytime I wanted. In the meantime my friends from the 'Open Brethren' were a bit surprised that I had gone to the 'Closed Brethren' hall but in those days I did what I wanted to do although I had a lot to learn. During that time I was still plagued with nightmares. I also dreaded going into the classroom and having to face Sister Tutor and I felt a nervous wreck.

Then, one day, Sister Tutor called me aside and told me that I must work a lot harder with the theory and, as Sister was telling me all about my mistakes on my test papers, I felt as though at any moment I was going to collapse, although I did not. Then the dreaded day came when we had to take the part 1 written paper prelim exam. I found that the questions were not easy to answer especially as I had to write about tracing waste from the lavatory pan to the main sewer and all of the other hygiene matters. Although I found it difficult, I answered what I could remember but I did not feel happy as I left the exam room. After a week it was the practical exam and, of course, I felt I could do that with my eyes shut. I found it easy to lay up trolleys and answer questions on General Nursing. One examiner looked very strict and I did not feel very confident with her. After this was the awful wait for the results.

In the meantime I was back on the men's surgical ward which pleased me because I was interested in surgery and to my surprise the Staff Nurse that I liked was working on the same ward. That meant that I worked very hard to please her and she was pleased with my work, unlike the Ward Sister who never seemed to be satisfied with anything I did.

Then, one afternoon, I was in the linen room as Sister had told me to tidy it up. I was busy putting linen on the correct shelves because Sister got annoyed if the shelves were untidy. The Staff Nurse came to me and asked me to do a job and I informed her "I have already done it, Staff." She smiled and gave me a kiss on the side of my face and said, "You are a sweet girl" and then she sent me on my tea break. Staff was working a month's notice as she was going to do Midwifery. I felt a bit sad as I knew I wouldn't see her again. However, I had a lot more to be concerned about! The dreaded results had come out and I had failed Part 1. I was really surprised and I dreaded seeing Sister Tutor which would be very soon!

I went to see the Sister in the classroom. I felt very apprehensive but Sister was quite nice and told me that I could have another chance. She also said that I must concentrate more and I must put more effort into the theory.

I went to my room feeling very upset. My friend came into my room and I told her that I was going to give in my notice. Her answer to me was, "You are not giving up!" and she started to tickle me.

After my friend had left my room after trying to cheer me up (which had not worked), I sat on my bed with my hands over my face praying, "Oh Lord, please help me." I usually had my quiet time with the Lord first thing in the early morning before I went on duty but in between I was 'skin praying.'

I turned my radio on and to my amazement a song was playing and the lyrics were, "Pick yourself up, dust yourself down, and start all over again. Nothing is impossible! Start all over again! Remember the famous men who had failed and had to start all over again! So, "Pick yourself up, dust yourself down and start all over again!" After hearing that song I felt encouraged. The next night Sister told me that I was to come off day duty to start night duty. That night I didn't feel very happy about the thought of going back on the dreaded nights especially when I found out who my Senior Nurse was. She was a third year student who appeared to be very strict.

We were working on the children's ward and after hearing the day report Nurse went with the day Sister to check on the ill children while I went to the fridge to get a bottle of baby's milk to feed a baby suffering from the disease of Spinal Bifida. When I took the baby out of his cot I noticed that he didn't react to me. As I sat him on my knee to feed him, he died. He just felt like a rag doll. Sister came over to me and said, "It's alright, Nurse, we expected it" As we put him back in his cot I felt upset. After that it was the usual procedure of Doctor, parents and mortuary. In those days children did not have their parents with them in hospital.

When Nurse and I finished our main work, whilst having a cup of tea and toast and as I was relaxing, Nurse said to me "Tonight bring your notes so that I can go over them with you if we have the time."

I nearly choked over my tea! I silently thought, "Help, Lord, I haven't got any notes!" Before I came back on duty to face another question I prayed that the night would be busy, and so it was! We were rushed off our feet. The Lord heard my prayer! My Senior Nurse was a clever person, not like me. My confidence was low and I always felt useless compared to everybody else.

When we wearily went off duty the Night Nurse reminded me about bringing my notes (which I didn't have!) and said to me, "I shall expect you to bring your notes tonight so I can help with some studying."

When I got back to my room I sat on my bed with my hands over my face and asked in prayer "O Lord, what am I going to do?" Just as I was going back on duty there was a knock at my bedroom door and when I opened it I was shocked to see Staff Nurse standing there. For a moment I wondered what I had done wrong but she smiled at me and came into my room carrying a pile of folders. She sat down beside me and said, "I am giving you my notes because I don't need them anymore, and I feel that you should have them." I was very pleased and told her how much I appreciated her. Also I couldn't stop praising the Lord because her notes were so easy to read and her diagrams were so neat. I started to study immediately and I felt so happy. I also started to study with another Nurse for part 1 of the prelim exam.

My sister had come to live in London with her friend, Jim. Collette was in the RAF and they lived in Kilburn, London.

At last my Sister Tutor was slightly more pleased with my written test paper but there was still a lot of red ink on it and Sister told me that I must put more effort into study and improve my spelling. This was two weeks before the prelim exam. So when I took the prelim exam I did my best work and after a few weeks I heard that I had passed Part 1. What a relief! My friends were very pleased and so was Sister Tutor. I don't know what I would have done if I had failed because the hospital was my life, having spent almost all my life in hospital. But I also knew deep down that it was all due to the Lord Jesus, O I praise His name! I was now going into my second year of training and I realised that the theory was going to be a lot harder for me.

One evening while resting on my bed a Nurse who was also off duty came into my room and asked me to go with her to gate crash a Doctor's party. I did not feel very happy about that but in the end she persuaded me so I dragged out my old green dress and at 9pm off we went to the Doctor's party uninvited. I felt very uncomfortable and also a Doctor recognised me and asked me if I had been invited. I went brilliant red and the Doctor just laughed. After a few drinks I started to relax but I was very relieved to return to my own bedroom.

I received the good news that I had passed the prelim and because I had a Staff Nurse's notes I was feeling more confident in myself. But my feelings of happiness were short lived due to having to work in the theatre. O, how I missed the men's ward! I was in my second year's training.

One afternoon the second year students had to have a lecture from the Head Theatre Sister. We all gathered around Sister because she was going to demonstrate about the theatre instruments. Sister expected us to remember what she had told us. The other Nurses did remember but, as usual, I was slow to remember the names of the general set. Then Sister asked "Who is Nurse Morgan?" When Pam told her who she was Sister was pleased. Pam was my friend and also a very bright, attractive girl. We went out together and we liked shopping and going for walks. Then Sister said, "Who is Nurse Baker?" I put my arm up and then Sister said, "Well, Nurse Baker, I shall expect you to know what I have told you on Monday morning!" I felt her wrath had come down on me.

Over the weekend I stayed with my friend from the church. After spending all Sunday at the church I arrived back at the hospital dreading the next morning. To say that I was nervous was an understatement, I was petrified! I could not sleep but eventually I heard a loud knock on my door by the 7:00am nurse. I dragged my body out of bed. I got washed and dressed and when I looked in the mirror I did not just feel like I had died but I also looked like I had! After trying to do my hair neat and tidy, which as usual was a losing battle, I made my way to the dining room for my breakfast which I could not eat. I met with my friend Pam as we made our way to the theatre. I felt very pessimistic as we entered the theatre to report to the 'terror of the theatre', Head Sister. I felt as though I was about to collapse at any moment. Sister sent us off to get changed into our theatre gowns and boots which, as usual, were too big for me. I knew that the two theatre porters were laughing at me, so I said, "Oh you're only jealous because I am only 5ft tall and 6½ stone in weight and you both look like giants!" They just laughed. Then Sister gave me the dispensary to write out the order for the different disinfectants. The only problem was I made a mistake and Sister gave me a good telling off.

The next day one of the theatre porters seemed to take a liking to me, I could not think why but he came to my rescue every morning.

I was not very popular with the Anaesthetist due to the fact that when patients came into the anaesthetic room for their operation I would pray for them.

One morning, while a patient was receiving their anaesthetic, I suddenly felt very tired and when the Anaesthetist asked the patient to count to five and did they feel sleepy I said, "Yes, I feel very sleepy." Then the Anaesthetist was annoyed with me and retorted "Nurse, will you please stand up! What do you think you are doing, leaning all over the patient?" One morning a patient was in the anaesthetic room with a Nurse from the ward when the Porter called me over and we were looking through the window at the anaesthetic room. I asked the Porter what he wanted and he said, "Now look at the Ward Nurse. She isn't leaning all over the patient. She is standing by the side of the trolley with her arms behind her back. Not like you leaning all over the patient!" I knew he was laughing at me but I did not mind because the Porters helped me not to be harassed by the Theatre Sister.

I was interested in the operations whenever I could escape from the work in the sluice. One morning Sister told me I was to assist the Surgeon who was doing tonsillectomies. I felt very apprehensive but he was quite kind to me. Some Surgeons there were bad tempered and sometimes threw their instruments across the floor in temper. I found it very irksome as it was usually me who had to sterilise the instruments all over again. When working in theatre we had to take a turn at being on call during the night which I dreaded.

One weekend I was on call on the Sunday. I spent all day with my friend in church and at her home so when I arrived back at the hospital I prayed that I would not be called to the theatre. The Lord Jesus did not answer that prayer as I got into my bed feeling dead tired and the next thing I heard a loud knock on my bedroom door and a voice saying, "You are to go to theatre, Nurse!" I dragged myself out of bed and got washed and dressed. When I arrived in the theatre, to my horror, the Head Sister was also on call. She told me what jobs to do so I got on with my work thinking that I was going to collapse any minute. Eventually the patient arrived in theatre. He was a male and was wheeled straight into the operating room still awake. The Anaesthetist was at the head of the patient because the patient was unable to take the anaesthetic.

So Sister informed me that I had to talk to the patient during the operation. I was aghast because I was not very good at conversation. I stood by the Anaesthetist who looked how I felt, more dead than alive. He did not appear to be in a good mood due to being dragged out of bed at 2:00 am. On the arrival of the Surgeon Sister told me to start talking to the patient just as the Surgeon was making an incision in the patient's abdomen. As for me, I hadn't a clue what I was going to talk about so I decided to tell him about what I knew about Jesus. After I had said, "Are you prepared to meet the Lord your God?" The atmosphere in the room changed dramatically. I thought the Sister was going to explode and she said, "Go to my office, Nurse!" But the Surgeon said, "Oh no, Sister, let's hear what Nurse has to say." So I carried on trying to point out the gospel of the Bible. I never saw that patient again after the operation was over.

I was in the sluice clearing up when the Surgeon was standing in the doorway and asked me which church I went to. I told him the Brethren. When I eventually got off duty I was walking down the corridor to my bedroom when the Night Sister was walking towards me and told me off for looking untidy and told me to change my apron. I had to go back on duty at 1:00pm. When I looked in the mirror I looked like a ghost, and I looked haggard so I decided to have a hot bath. When I arrived back at the theatre I was on duty with the second Theatre Sister who was a lot easier going and was quite pleasant.

During this time I still attended the Nurses' Christian fellowship. This Sister was also a Christian. One day when in conversation Sister said to me "I have decided to tell a Nurse to give her testimony in a meeting." So I asked "Who is that, Sister?" Her answer was "You, Nurse Baker!" So I said "Oh no, Sister, I can't!" Sister said, "Oh yes, you can and you will be alright." Sister gave me a week to prepare what I was going to say. I felt terrible as I had never spoken to an audience in my life. Well, when the evening arrived I had not prepared anything. I could feel my heart going like a race horse and I kept asking "Oh God, help me." I do not remember what I said but it wasn't a long talk and Sister appeared to be pleased with whatever I had said. When I visited Ena and told her about how nervous I had felt Ena told me that I would get used to it.

One morning, while in theatre I caused a commotion during the operations. Some swabs were missing and the problem was that I was responsible for counting the swabs and I could not account for them. Sister was furious with me although it was obvious that I was praying. Then I said a stupid statement. I suggested that the Surgeon might have stitched the swabs inside the wound. I cannot describe the atmosphere that morning! Everybody was cross, except the patient who was still unconscious on the operating table. In the end the swabs were found behind a radiator. I cannot even imagine how unpopular I must have been on that morning!

I found the most annoying thing was that Sister would snap a demand for something from behind her mask and if we did not understand her hissing way of speaking we were in terrible trouble. Sometimes I would misunderstand her or I might make a mistake. If sister did not tell me off immediately and on the spot verbally her wrath would come later after the end of the operation.

One very busy day, during surgery operations, I knew Sister was in a bad temper and everyone else appeared to be nervous or irritable, including myself. Sister was assisting a Surgeon when she suddenly shouted an order at me. I just did not understand what she was saying and I was too nervous to ask her to repeat what she had told me to do so I thought I would guess what she wanted. But, of course, it wasn't what she had asked for! She had wanted a jug of hot water and so Sister was furious with me. Most of the time the

Theatre Porter helped me and I knew that the Lord Jesus was with me.

One morning during the operations I was overcome by nausea and dizziness. I think it was due to the heat and also the fumes of the ether. Fortunately I was near the end of my shift and I managed to drag myself to the sluice room and push my head under the cold water. I put on a dry gown and I survived. I always had a bath when I came off duty as other Nurses had mentioned that people stank of ether whenever they came off duty.

One day while I was off duty I decided to go into London shopping, although I did not have any money, but it was a nice way to get away from the hospital. While I was waiting for the underground train I felt that the passengers were looking at me and one old lady asked me if I worked in a hospital theatre because I smelt of ether. I was a bit amazed because I couldn't smell any ether on my body. I had most probably got used to it.

I was having my breakfast one morning when Night Sister announced, "Nurse Baker, you are to start duty on casualty!" I felt a bit alarmed because I was thinking "What if I kill someone accidentally?" I was just getting used to working in the theatre, and keeping apart from the Head Sister. I had tried hard to keep out of her way although I often failed. Sisters never seemed to expect us to have some initiative of our own. They always seemed to me to be dissatisfied with me and the other nurses.

During this time my Mother's Step-Father died. He lived in America with his second wife and he was very rich. He left my mother £1000 which was a lot of money in 1963. My father had always wanted a Public House and eventually they moved to the Park Place in Ruthin, North Wales.

Louie's father, Philip Baker Park Place Hotel Ruthin

Oh dear, what a mistake it was for them to leave Prestatyn but, of course, my father thought he was in heaven due to all the alcohol around him! Eventually he drank all the profits. My mother was suffering from Arthritis and she was in a lot of pain.

At this time my sister, who was working in London and living with her friends Jim and Collette with who she had been in the RAF, decided to come home to Ruthin to help my mother and father in the pub. Then she met her husband, Peter Jones, who was a plumber. They had a band that played music in the pub.

One morning while I was on duty Sister came to me and said, "Nurse Baker, Matron wants to see you." I nearly collapsed with fright. I was desperately trying to think about what I might have done. My main concern was Sister Tutor and I wondered if she had complained to Matron about me. So I decided to go for my coffee break which I could not even drink as I was anxious, and then I went to my room hoping that I would have a clean apron to put on.

I went to Matron's office feeling that I might die at any moment. Outside Matron's office there were two more Nurses waiting to see Matron and they looked how I felt! All sorts of thoughts were going through my mind and one of these questions was "Had the

Anaesthetist complained about me leaning and praying over the patients"?

When it was my turn to face Matron I tried to stand politely with my arms behind my back. Matron was writing, as usual. She looked up at me and said, "Nurse Baker, you are due for two weeks holiday." At that new, my heart sank because that meant I would have to go to Ruthin in North Wales. As I left Matron's office I was not feeling very happy. I did not want to go to Ruthin because I thought I would not be able to see my Grandma as she lived in Prestatyn. While I was packing my case ready to catch the Holyhead train from Euston Station I decided to go to Rhyl to visit my Aunty who worked in a furniture shop in Queen Street, Rhyl. When I arrived my Aunty appeared pleased to see me but she told me that I looked ill. When my Uncle came to take Aunty home after work he also gave me a lift so that meant that I could see Grandma who looked quite well. The next day my Uncle took me in his car to the Park Place pub in Ruthin. When I arrived at what had become 'home' my Father was standing behind the bar of the pub and did not seem to be pleased to see me. My sister showed me to the bedroom which I had to share with her. The rooms in the Park Place Pub were quite big and there was also a large sitting room upstairs. My youngest brother was still at school and another sister was at work.

Living in a pub seemed strange to me. In the evening there was a band playing until 11:00pm. There was one young man called Gordon in the band who was tall with fair, curly hair. I think he took a liking to me. He was always asking me to go out with him but, of course, I always said "No." Then one night my sister and her boyfriend and Gordon and I went out just for a drive in the car. I was in the back seat with Gordon and he was trying to kiss me and I was feeling fed up with him and I said, "Gordon, you will feel sorry in the morning. It is only the drink talking and you will regret this in the morning." He took no notice of what I said and so I told him that I would never marry as I wanted to be a Nurse and live in a hospital for the rest of my life. Gordon just laughed.

I also remember an old lady who always sat in the bar by the fire and always wore a shabby fur coat down to her feet and who always drank a bottle of gin. My parents and everyone else just ignored her until, one day, she was sitting by the fire, which was an open coal fire, and her fur coat caught fire. She was in flames and my father had to put out the flames.

One Sunday when I was at home in the pub my mother had put a notice board outside advertising, 'Hot lunch served daily'. My Mother had cooked a beef dinner for the five of us family members, but, just as my Mother and Sister put our dinners on the table in front of us we heard the doorbell ring. My Mother went to answer the door and came running back to us. Just as we were about to start eating Mother shouted, "Stephanie, quickly pick up your dinners and take them to the five people in the dining room before they get cold!" One lady in the group remarked, "I have never been served so quickly in all my life!" and they seemed pleased with my Mother.

Business men would often travel through Ruthin and they would stay for the night in the Park Place Pub. One night my Mother mistakenly locked one poor business man in the outside toilets which were like a blockade of toilets in the back yard. My Father, who heard the sounds of banging and said to my Mother, "If that is Charles, I will kill him for coming in so late!" however, when my Father went to investigate he found the poor man locked in the toilet! The business man forgave my mother, eventually!

Very soon after that my holiday came to an end. When I arrived back at the hospital I was put in the Casualty department which I was apprehensive about as I did not know who the Sister would be but I reported for duty although it was in 'fear and trembling.' The first patient that I saw was a heart attack but I comforted him by telling him that he would not die and after that I prayed for him. Fortunately, he recovered! Later on when my nerves eventually settled down, I became quite interested in Casualty work.

One morning while I was on duty one of the Doctors on duty asked me if I would like to learn how to stitch a wound. I felt really excited at the idea of stitching a wound. I soon learned how to stitch and the Doctor said that I was very good and that I would make a good dressmaker! I remember a boy of about 12 years old who had a wound on his leg. I actually thought quietly to myself that he was a big baby and I warned him that if he did not stop crying I would go to his school and tell his classmates what a big baby he was. He soon stopped crying!

Another day one patient was very depressed and crying so I told her to cry and bang the wall which she did and then Sister came and asked what all the noise was about. The patient said to Sister, 'That little Nurse told me to shout and cry'. Sister was not very pleased with me but the patient told her husband that I was an angel!

Then one morning the Night Sister came breezing into the dining room during our breakfast and announced, "Nurse Baker, you are to start duty in Casualty." This news frightened me. When I arrived on duty it was quite busy and I found that I was working with a Staff Nurse who I did not like because I thought she was a bit strange, although as time went on we got on well. I think I was the only Nurse in the country who prayed for drunks to come into Casualty because I believed the Lord would help those drunks and then they would help me with my spelling!

One night two drunks came into Casualty swaggering so I went to them with my pen and pad and asked them how to spell certain words. One of the men asked "Didn't you ever go to school?" and my answer was, "Not if I could help it!" I think some drunks thought that I was putting them through some kind of a test.

Eventually I finished in Casualty and went back to the dreaded classroom having to face Sister Tutor in fear and trepidation. One good thing was that after working in the theatre I became very interested in surgery and as I was in the third year of my training we had doctors giving us lectures. The only problem was that every time a doctor asked me a question my brain automatically went on strike and I was dumb with agony. One morning when the doctor was giving a lecture on tapeworms I liked the word TAENIA SARINATA so when the doctor asked us the name of the beef worm I remembered it. No one else could remember it and he looked at me and said, 'Nurse, your lips are moving. Answer the question'. After thinking I was going to collapse at any moment I gave him the right answer. After our time in the classroom we had a test paper on surgery and I came second in the group. Sister Tutor was pleased with me. My paper did not have any red ink on it and she had even written 'excellent' on it. I could hardly believe it and it was at this moment that I decided that I would fight for the rest of my training.

I had been transferred to Central Middlesex Hospital and was on the Gynaecology ward. I remember one patient who had a total hysterectomy. She nearly died because she lost so much blood but I told her that she would not die because I was praying for her. The lady did not die. I enjoyed the work very much and got along well with the patients and staff, apart from the ward Sister who filled me with fear and trepidation. Then, to my horror I was put on night duty.

I made a new friend who lived in the Nurses' home in the room next to me. I felt very happy but, as usual, my happiness was short lived as Night Sister one morning announced that Nurse Baker was to go on night duty on the Women's Medical ward. I had to work until 1:00pm and then try to sleep until 7:30pm, which was almost impossible with the noise around the corridors. I tried to read and study but it was useless and I would just doze off. One evening I was woken by a loud knocking on my bedroom door. I dragged myself out of bed feeling ghastly and then reported for duty. My Senior Night Nurse was a nice girl and we got along well together but I was still in trepidation of the Night Sister. The hospital food was different from the other hospitals, slightly nicer but it was still atrocious!

The ward was quite busy with a number of ill patients and when the Senior Nurse went off for her meal break I was left in charge. The ward was also subjected to strange, eerie noises, especially in the sluice. When I was working at night the most annoying thing was that Night Sister would come creeping into the ward with her torch determined to wake up as many patients as she could which meant I would then have to make lots of cups of tea and then give out bedpans - the usual round of hard work! One night I reported on duty with my Senior Night Nurse and, after hearing the day report, which seemed to go on forever, I decided to tell the patients who were dying about Jesus. I remember one patient on the ward who I got on with very well. She was a Christian. She was suffering from cardiac failure and always called me 'angel'. We became friends and she invited me to visit her at home when she was discharged but it wasn't meant to be. One night I was on duty and I had given out the bedpans we were talking about names. Her name was

Louise and my name was Louie. Then when I went to collect her bedpan she was dead. She had had a heart attack. It was a terrible shock and I was upset. I became even more upset after I had to lay her out and go to the mortuary. I felt thoroughly depressed. I did know that Nurses should not become attached to patients but it did happen sometimes. Louise's daughter gave me her cameo brooch.

I would always try to be as friendly with all of the patients as possible and make them cups of tea. Then one day Sister asked me what I had been doing with all the tea. Whenever I was on duty too much tea was being given out. In those days there was only loose tea leaves available to make a cup of tea, there weren't any tea bags then.

Soon afterwards I went back on day duty on the Women's Medical Ward. When I told my friend which ward I was going on she said

"Bad luck, Old Thing, you will be with Sister Barford and you will need your wits about you!" My friend never said a truer word than that! Sister Barford was a nightmare and I could not seem to do anything right!

I was still attending the Nurses' Fellowship and I thoroughly enjoyed the meetings. I was also still attending the Brethren Church and I would visit my friends frequently during my time off work and I was also in touch with my friend Miss Campbell.

I was looking forward to Christmas once again as I always enjoyed Christmas in hospital as it was not the usual routine. We would help to decorate the ward and put up the Christmas tree and prepare small presents for the patients. We would also have a collection towards the Ward Sister's present and buy presents for the Nurses on the ward which we would put into a tub or box and then each one of us would have a turn at picking one out. The presents were only cheap items and I usually threw mine away.

I am sorry to say that our Ward Sister was not in a good mood for Christmas. She usually found fault with everything we did. All Nurses on all of the wards had to be on duty on Christmas day. I did not mind though as I enjoyed it so much. On Christmas Eve all the off duty Nurses had to go carol singing and one particular Christmas

Eve I was off duty. In the daytime I was working with a Nurse who was a friend and we used to often play tricks on each other. This Nurse told me that she would get her own back on me which she did on that particular Christmas Eve! When we assembled together with the Sister who was in charge of the carol singing, her first announcement was that the Nurse who was going to sing a solo was off sick. I was not taking much notice of what was being said until Sister asked if any of us would sing a carol. For a minute no-one answered. Then, to my horror, the Nurse who I had played a trick on said, "O, Sister, Nurse Baker has a lovely voice." Sister then announced "You, Nurse Baker, you will sing a carol!" I had such a shock! I remembered that when I used to work at Clarks in Rhyl and I would sing during my work Mr Clark would say, "I think the cat has got his tail caught in the door!" I knew that he was laughing at my singing. I told Sister that I could not sing but Sister appeared to be frustrated and told me to sing and stop thinking about myself. She told me to get on with what she had told me to sing so I had no choice but to sing. Fortunately for me it was an easy carol. I sent an SOS prayer to the Lord! After I had finished singing, I could hear some of the patients saying, "How sweet." The patients always appreciated the Nurses singing carols.

After Christmas I returned back to class with Sister Tutor who appeared pleased with me. I knew that the Lord was with me.

After studying in class, I was on the Men's Surgical Ward and I was very happy there and I was getting on well.

Then one day I got into trouble with the Ward Sister about giving injections although it was a job that I never used to mind doing because I would be gentle and never hurt the patient due to my own experience. I recalled inwardly how as a patient in Chepstow under a Plastic Surgeon named Mr. Emlyn Lewis, he would always prescribe penicillin injections after my operations and they were quite painful. One evening I remember that I was dreading the Nurse coming round with the penicillin injections. That particular evening it was a German Nurse. I had climbed out of bed to watch her giving a girl an injection. What I saw horrified me and so I quietly got back into bed feeling very nervous but, to my surprise, when it came to my turn I had not felt a thing. The Nurse would always throw the needle, attached to the syringe, into our buttocks just like throwing a dart. Things were different during my training and we were taught the correct way of giving injections by Sister Tutor.

As I worked on the ward, it soon became apparent that the patients who had been prescribed injections only ever wanted me to bet eh one to give them their injections.

One day a young man was admitted to the ward who had been prescribed a lot of injections and he was also in a lot of pain. The Ward Sister gave me the job of giving injections and when I went with my receiver to the young man he didn't look very pleased to see what was coming. After I had given him the injection he turned round towards me and asked "What have you done with my injection?" I replied that "I gave it to you here into your buttock." Then he said "I will only have you to give me my injections." This patient would then inform any new patient that was admitted to the ward to only accept injections from Nurse Baker. Then one day a new patient arrived and the Ward Sister told one of the Nurses to give him his pre-med but as the Nurse approached him he asked her, "What is your name?" When she told him her name the patient said, "I want Louise to give me the injection" and he kept refusing the treatment from the Nurse. The Ward Sister noticed an argument between the Nurse and the patient and asked, "Is there a problem, Nurse?" The Nurse answered, "He keeps refusing his pre-med and wants Louise to give him the injection." So Sister asked "Who is Louise?" and then she found out it that he meant me. She was furious and she called all the Nurses to the patient's bedside and said, "Nurse Baker, please demonstrate how you give injections."

I sent an SOS prayer up to the Lord and fortunately I gave the injection the way I was taught in class. One of the Nurses was smiling at me because of the way that I gave an injection.

I was then very near to my final exams. During this time in the Sixties a Typhoid Fever broke out in part of the country so as I was near my finals I decided to study about Typhoid Fever. I was right and we did have a question on Typhoid fever.

During this time I was still babysitting for my sister's friends Jim and Collette who were in the RAF with my sister and who were all living in London. Poor Jim had to drive me back to the hospital next morning even though he was suffering from a hangover.

I found the Ward Sister very irksome because she did not appear to like visitors and also she had to have the ward to her satisfaction which meant that the wheels at the end of every bed had to be aligned and also the Ward Sister would only allow the patients to have water on the top of their lockers.

During the summer my friend Dorothy and I had some holiday due and Dorothy invited me to go to Switzerland as it made a change from going home. I decided to go with her and I enjoyed the holiday a lot. We stayed with some friends of Dorothy. I felt excited because it was the first time I had travelled by plane and I enjoyed the journey.

When we arrived back in the hospital I was in the class room and I found the theory difficult. The day arrived when we took our final practical exam. I decided to go to a hairdresser in Chiswick, London but I didn't give myself enough time as the hairdresser was a young man in training and he was very slow setting my hair. He wanted to set my hair in a cottage loaf style but I began to panic because my exam was scheduled for 2:00pm and it was then 1:30pm. At last the lady in charge came to help him. I arrived at the exam room just in time and everybody admired my new hair style. One of the examiners looked very strict but I didn't feel nervous and when the exam results came out I came top with very high marks. However going into the classroom to get the theory was different. I was nervous but I knew that the Lord was with me, and the reading for that morning also confirmed that. On the morning that I was taking my final exam 4th June 1964, I was feeling very apprehensive.

I had been nervous throughout the previous night but I reminded myself that the Lord drove the sea back (Exodus 14:21) and I knew that the Church was praying for me. The Nurse sitting at the side of me in the exam had written two pages at the same point in time I had not even started! I muddled through the Anatomy and Physiology which I always found difficult, especially when I was trying to draw diagrams. I just prayed that the examiner would be able to recognise my diagram. I was fortunate with the rest of the questions and somehow I managed to answer them. Of course, we all thought we had failed! It was an anxious six weeks as we waited for the results and our anxiety was increased by the fact that there was a postal strike. Eventually we received our exam results and I had passed as a State Registered Nurse! I could hardly believe that I had passed especially as two of the Nurses had failed. Sister Tutor was very pleased that I had passed and so were my friends. When I went to visit my friends from the church they said, "This is the Lord and it is marvellous in His sight."

After hearing this good news the Ward Sister told me that Matron wanted to see me. After having a quick cup of coffee and changing my apron I made my way to Matron's office feeling very apprehensive. However, Matron appeared to be in a good mood and told me that she had received excellent ward reports from the Ward Sisters about me and informed me that I was due for two weeks holiday. So I went to Germany with a friend called Pat. We went by plane but I did not enjoy the holiday and I wanted to go back to London. We were staying in a hostel and we were sleeping on bunk beds which I thought were awful. My friend was enjoying it and told me that I was far too fussy. There was a young girl called Esther and we became friends but I was very annoyed because there was a young man on this holiday who took an interest in me and he told Esther that he wanted to go out with me. Of course I said "No!" as I did not want to get involved with any male! One day whilst going out to the shops I saw an ornament which I liked in a shop window. The only trouble was that the man who was serving did not speak any English and I did not speak German. Then the young man, who spoke fluent German, bought the ornament for me and he still wanted me to go out with him! I was not interested and I told him that I was going to be a Nurse for the rest of my life and that I would never get married. I never saw him again.

When I arrived back at the hospital I was a Staff Nurse on the Men's Surgical Ward and I enjoyed it very much. After a few weeks I was moved to the Women's Surgical Ward. One afternoon when I was in Sister's office trying to work something out two young Nurses came into the office with a big bunch of flowers and a box of chocolates. I said, "Which patient are those for?" The nurses said, "These are not for a patient, they are for you because you found it hard and you did so well." I was quite amazed at that but also very pleased.

I was still having difficulty with spelling words and I remember that one night while in charge of a ward I had written in my night report about the ill patients and put at the end of the report, "Remaining patients no change." but I had actually written, "Remaining patients no chance." Apparently the Ward Sister had laughed about it with Matron. However, Matron did not laugh about it with me because I got a good telling-off! Apart from these problems I enjoyed my work on the ward.

I was still plagued with terrible nightmares and it was not until many years afterwards that I was eventually delivered from the nightmares. It happened when the Lord Jesus brought me back to North Wales and eventually through the ministry of a lady called Mrs. Jean Boswell who was speaking at a meeting in the Rhyl Baptist Church. Since then, I have been free from nightmares. Praise the Lord!

While I was still on the Women's Surgical Ward in the hospital in London a patient had come into the ward for her operation of a radical mastectomy for breast cancer. I was prepared to get her ready for theatre and I decided to pray for her. After praying I told her that the Lord Jesus would help her and she recovered well. Two days after her operation she invited me to her home. After her discharge from hospital Matron wanted to see me. Of course, as I made my way to Matron's office I was expecting the worst along with some other nervous looking Nurses. When it was my turn I knocked on her office door and a voice said, "Come in." I entered her room and stood in front of her desk with my hands behind my back and my heart going like a racehorse [only faster!]. To my surprise Matron smiled at me and said, "The patient who had the radical mastectomy for cancer is a friend of mine and wants to thank you for praying for her and for your kindness towards her."

Matron also told me that she was pleased with my reports from Ward Sister and said that I was a good Nurse. After my time with Matron I went back to the ward. I did not find being in charge on the ward easy and there was always one thing or another that I found difficult. Then one day a Nurse took advantage of me. I discovered her lying in the patient's bath reading a newspaper! I told her that if she wasn't on the ward in two minutes I would report her to Matron. I found out later on that she had been having bad ward reports from

Ward Sisters. The other Nurses got on well with her, but there is always one bad apple. Matron gave her the sack.

I remember one patient who liked me called Celia. She was a Brethren Christian and after her discharge from hospital invited me to her home where she took me after we had met in town. I met her Mother and Sister who had a lot of friends who were always at their home. One evening they were watching Coronation Street and we all had an argument as I said that Christians should not watch soaps. We still remained friends and if I was off duty on a Sunday then I would go to church with her and stay at her home. One Sunday, I had been working in the morning, but I was off duty during the afternoon. I was resting on my bed feeling very tired when my door opened and Celia's friend Shirley stood by my bed saying "Come on get up!" Celia has asked me to fetch you for tea and church. I made excuses, saying that I felt so tired and my hair was very untidy, Shirley was not accepting any of my excuses and so I reluctantly got up and got ready to go out. During tea time one of Celia's friends said to me "You look a bit too delicate to be a Nurse." I replied "I manage." After tea we all went to the Brethren church.

During this time I was feeling that I needed a change and considered Midwifery. I applied to a London hospital and received a letter from the Matron inviting me for an interview. I prayed that the Matron would not mention my education and fortunately she didn't. After answering the questions that Matron put to me, she told me she had received very good references from the Matron at my hospital. So the Lord Jesus opened the door as I received a letter from Matron accepting me for Midwifery with a start date. Initially I felt excited after giving my months' notice to Matron but my life came crashing down soon afterwards. I had a week's holiday due, so I decided to go to Ruthin for a week. As usual my Mother told me I looked terrible. I tried to keep out of my parent's way and I felt sorry that I had not gone to Prestatyn instead to see my Grandma.

A New Hospital

My next move was to arrive at my new hospital. This was a new experience and it seemed strange to me. When we arrived in the classroom we were taken to the Labour Ward by Sister Tutor to watch the delivery of a baby, I thought that birth was the most wonderful thing. I recalled my time at St. Asaph hospital how I was naive in those days but there would be no more mixing babies up! Back in the classroom I found it difficult to study the theory but in I got on very well with the practical. I felt the Lord was with me during my first delivery (it was a girl). Towards the end of part one I had delivered 28 babies. I got on well with the staff and the patients.

The Head Sister was to be feared as she gave the Nurses a terrible time. During one delivery Sister came rushing in, stopped and said, "Oh how peaceful!" I even did an episiotomy, which was done when it was too difficult for the baby's head to come through the second stage of labour. However, I was more interested in the condition of a new born baby's mouth than what the sex of the child was!

One morning when I got out of bed feeling awful, I found it difficult to get washed and dressed. I made my way to the dining room for breakfast but I could not eat anything. I arrived on duty on the Labour Ward and I measured and recorded all of the women's blood pressures without any problems. After that I went to help with a delivery and then I took all of the sheets into the sluice. Then I just started to cry and I could not stop. One of the Nurses and the Ward Sister came into the sluice to see what was wrong with me as they were not able to get any sense out of me. A Nurse took me to the Nurses' home and the Sister sent for a Doctor who was also unable to get any sense out of me. After a week in bed and with no improvement in my condition I was admitted to Rothay Park in Horsham, West Sussex.

I settled down quite well and soon began treatment which started with an interview with the Psychiatrist. After a conversation, which was mainly about my life, he prescribed Largactil which did not suit me. It made me feel like a zombie and a bit out of my environment. During my stay in Rothay Park I started to take an interest in mental illness, I also became friends with another patient whose name was June who turned out to be good friend. She lived in Kent.

During this time my parents had left Ruthin where they had run the pub for three years and they moved to a little village called Henllan near Denbigh. Back in Rothay Park I was getting healthier. I remember one patient who would not stop washing her hands and always left the tap running, so I would always turn the tap off after her, and she always said "Thank you." Eventually I was discharged from Rothay Park and given two weeks sick leave from work by the doctor. My new friend June did not want me to go home, but I did not have any choice. I went to visit my Grandma in Prestatyn where I met my Uncle who took me to Henllan in his car to stay with my parents. What a terrible mistake! I was still mentally vulnerable and I did not manage to get through the two weeks. My Father was very unwelcoming towards me and he made it obvious that he did not want me to stay with them at home in Henllan. It was not easy with my Mother either. The effect on me was disastrous and due to my mental state I collapsed. My Mother was so worried about me that she went to see the minister at Henllan church who came to visit me at home, and after seeing the awful state that I was in, he sent for a Doctor.

When the Doctor arrived he carried out an examination and came to the conclusion that I was to be sectioned under the Mental Health Act. I was then admitted to Gwynfryn Mental Hospital in Denbigh. I was examined by a doctor who then prescribed me anti–depressants drugs and I had ECT (Electro Convulsive Therapy]). At that time I refused to have the treatment unless I had my Bible with me. I held the Bible on my chest before receiving the anaesthetic treatment. When I regained consciousness my memory was temporally affected but it usually returned after two days. The treatment worked for a few days but my depression returned, only this time it was much more severe. During my time in Gwynfryn I became very interested in the other patient's illnesses, I kept asking them questions about their mental illness, and I also made many friends there. As our illnesses improved we were allowed to go into Denbigh where we would go shopping and visit a coffee bar. On one occasion I met my Mother there and I told her about a patient whom I had met and we had become good friends. This friend had told me that her Mother had only to get into bed and she became pregnant! My Mother slapped me across my face with full force and I felt my head reeling. I felt glad to get back to the hospital!

Eventually I had an interview with the Psychiatric Doctor who told me that I was well enough to be discharged. He also told me that I would not be able to go back into Nursing. I was so shocked by what he was saying to me, I told him that Nursing was my life and that I could not imagine doing anything else. I also told him that I wanted to do Psychiatric Nursing. His answer was "You can't because you will be in and out of hospital all your life." My answer to that was "No, we will see about that." The doctor was taken aback by my answer. The next day my Mother came to see me and told me that she had seen the Doctor who had informed her that I would not be able to go back to nursing. I felt very upset at this, and I told my Mother that I was going to do psychiatric nursing. I cannot write what my Mother's reaction was to my news! When I next saw the Doctor he suggested that I should go into private nursing, so in my mind I decided to apply for private nursing.

When I was discharged from Gwynfryn Hospital in Denbigh I felt that I did not want to go home, so I decided to go to London and stay with my sister's friends, Jim and Collette. I turned up uninvited on their door step with my suitcase and lots of drugs and a small amount of money. They were very surprised to see me but they accepted me into their home. I became useful to them as a babysitter. They had a lot of friends who were in the RAF and one Sunday afternoon a family came to visit them with two little boys. After we all had a meal I was sitting in the armchair. One of the little boys was staring at me. I thought "Why doesn't his mother tell him it was rude to stare at people?" After a while he came over to me and said, "Please can I sit on your knee?" So I said "Yes!" and then, to my amazement, he told me that he loved me and he put his arms around me. Of course I was not used to all this loving attention! When it was time for him to go home he started to cry and told his mother that he did not want to go home and that he wanted to stay with me (Louie). I took him to their car and whilst we waited for his

Father he began to scream. As I bent down to comfort him, he kissed me and caught hold of me. He was telling me how much he loved me. I tried to tell him that he would soon forget me. When his father tried to get him into the car he was screaming and kicking but eventually they managed to get him in the car and drive away. When I went back into the house Jim and Collette were teasing me about it. I have never forgotten that little boy. I expect he is grown up and married now.

I had now started private nursing in London. The only trouble was that I found it boring just being with one patient in their home. Then one day I received a phone call from head office saying that they wanted to see me. When I arrived at the London office the lady who was head of the agency asked me would I go and nurse in Harley Street Clinic. She told me that I would get lots of tips because the patients were film stars. I replied that I could not bear the thought of it. I was suddenly very conscious of my lips but lady accepted my answer.

I kept in touch with my friend June who I had met at Rothy Park, Horsham, West Sussex and June invited me to her home in Orpington, Kent. I got on very well with her family. The agency sent me to a private house to nurse an elderly lady. The trouble was that her daughter liked women but when one of the Nurses told me about her, my answer was, "I don't think she will bother about me!" When I arrived at the house I found that it was very old and creepy with old fashioned furniture. I was also living in the house, which did not help my nightmares! After a time I started to feel bored and restless so when I had finished my nursing duties I would clean the house to pass the time away. The daughter told me that she was very pleased with me and also asked me how I had such a tiny waist.

After a few weeks the agency sent me to a nursing home in Tunbridge Wells. I also lived in this home. It was quite a good home but I was still plagued with terrible nightmares which always left me thoroughly depressed. After another few weeks I went to another home where the Matron was very strict. I made friends with another Nurse who liked to go out dancing and drinking. One evening I was off duty and having a peaceful time in my room when my friend appeared and asked me to go to the dance with her but I declined because I felt very tired. My friend persuaded me as she said that I looked depressed so I gave in and found my old green dance dress and we made our way to the dance hall. My friend was soon on the dance floor with a young man. As for me, I dreaded going to the bar for a drink and all I could think about was going back to sleep in my bed! Then I spotted a big bowl of punch so I had several glasses of the punch. Then a young man came over to me and said "Be careful, that punch is very strong. Can I have a dance with you?"

As I made my way to the dance floor I felt light headed. Then suddenly the young man got hold of me and lifted me up. I felt as though I was touching the ceiling. Then the next thing I knew I was on the railway platform and it was 4am in the morning. Then a man appeared from nowhere and asked me if he could help me so I said that I had to be on duty at 7:00am at the nursing home. Whoever this kind man was he took me outside the station and he rang for a taxi. When I arrived on duty I felt dreadful and the Nurse who I went to the dance with wanted to know what had happened to me. My answer to her was, "I do not want to talk about it!"

Another episode was when I went to London to see a film which did not finish until 11:00pm. The trouble was that the buses stopped running by that time and there were no trains so I decided to walk. As I continued I found myself out in the countryside where there were no lights and it was very dark. Then I heard the sound of a car approaching. The car stopped, the driver wound the window down and he shouted to me, "What are you doing standing in a field?" I told him that I was lost so he told me to get into his car and he would give me a lift. I arrived back at the home at 3:00am.

The agency sent me to another nursing home. This was a very big place and the Matron was a really nice lady. I was put on night duty. The home was a very eerie place and the staff told me that it was haunted. There was one resident who had an Ouija board and I had watched it being used. Many years later I was going to regret that.

During the time I was doing private nursing I did not go to church and I had no desire to go. When I went to visit my friends in London I got the feeling that they did not understand why and that they also thought that I did not trust the Lord. I was still reading the Bible but I had no real relationship with the Lord Jesus. I still had a strong interest in Psychiatry but I had no interest in Midwifery at that time.

I was dependent on anti-depressive drugs and my favourite was Librium but I also liked Valium, Stelazine and anything else I could get the Doctor to prescribe for me.

One evening while I was on duty in the nursing home another Nurse was in the office. We recognised each other as she had trained with me in London. She had failed her final exams although she was clever. She was pleased to see me and we worked well together. The only problem was the creepiness of the home and the feeling that it was haunted. I think that one gets what one believes! The resident who had the Ouija board sent shivers down my spine as she also wore a mask. I didn't know until one evening when I was on duty I heard a strange sound on the second floor and when I went to investigate and as I got to the bottom of the stairs I saw a figure standing at the top wearing a mask. It reminded me of the awful facial injuries and disfigurement of the World War Two pilots who I had seen in Gloucester Hospital when I was a young child and also again when I was in Chepstow as a girl. However, I did not feel frightened but I was annoyed and I said to her "Please go back to bed and take that silly mask off." She was a very dominating figure! I did talk to her about the Lord Jesus but she did not want to know! I gave her my daily reading book called "Streams in the desert."

During this time I was still very interested in Psychiatric Nursing so I applied to the mental hospitals which were in London, Birmingham and Colchester. One of my friends helped me to fill in the application forms which I received from these three hospitals. I decided that I wanted to go to London or Birmingham and decided not to apply to Colchester so I threw those forms into the waste paper basket. During the night I felt a strong desire to retrieve the Colchester forms from the bin and the next day a friend helped me to fill them in. After a few days I received a letter from the Matron asking me to go for interview. During the journey to Colchester I prayed that the Matron would not ask me about my education as I did not have any! By this time 'A' levels had been introduced and hospitals expected a Nurse to have 'A' levels. Fortunately for me the Matron at Colchester, who was a very nice lady, did not mention the fact that I had not filled in the section about education but she did say that she had received very good references from my previous Matrons and accepted me. I was given a date to start on the training programme for Psychiatric Nursing.

I gave my notice in to the private agency and, as I had another week off, I decided to stay with my friend June in Kent. She was very pleased with my good news and we got along well together.

One day June asked me to pass something to her out of a drawer. When I opened the drawer I noticed my name on the top of a magazine, which was a humanist paper.

June had written about my testimony and we discussed this.

I explained that I had evidence in my life that the Lord Jesus was real and that he was alive to help people in their lives because Jesus was raised from the dead and Christians love Jesus because he loved them first. When we said our 'Goodbyes' I did not realise that would be the last time that I would see June alive. I set off for Colchester and whilst I was travelling from London on the train I decided that I was going to have a good time and was going to the social club! I had come to enjoy a drink of alcohol. I was serving two masters at that time in my life! Fortunately for me, God had mercy on me!

Louie Brighton SRN at Colchester Hospital

Severalls Hospital Colchester

When I arrived at the hospital I made my way to the office in the Nurses' Home expecting to see a Home Sister but I was met by a lady in a different uniform. This lady was the warden of the Nurses' Home and she was a very pleasant person. After a short conversation the warden said to me, "I feel that I should put you in the room next to Nurse M." I did not take much notice then but while unpacking my case there was a knock on my bedroom door. When I opened the door it was the Nurse from next door. I knew straight away that she was a Christian. She was tall with dark hair and she was all smiles. She introduced herself but my response to her was quite rude. I asked her where the social club was as I needed a drink. After this I felt very uneasy in myself so then I went for my tea and rang my mother to tell her that I was in Colchester.

The next day I was back in the dreaded classroom but this time it wasn't a strict Sister Tutor who would make me feel that I had no confidence. I never had any confidence in myself. The students were allowed to wear mufti [plain clothes] and, to my surprise, the Tutors were male. Our Tutor was a very nice man but I still had the usual problem of getting the information down on paper while the other students wrote very fast.

Even though I had a problem with writing I was determined to get through the course as I was very interested in Psychiatry.

One night I had a terrible nightmare. I was dreaming and when I awoke I saw something black at the side of my bed and it went behind my bed so I jumped out of bed and ran into the next room. My friend said, "O Louie, not again!" so I told her about my dream.

During the daytime I was normal but during the night times I would feel wretched because of all that was going on. However, I got on very well with the staff and I also enjoyed the lectures.

At the end of the period in class we had a test. I was top in the practical but I only just passed the theory. When we were on the wards in our Nurses' uniforms I loved the work. One day my friend said to me, "Louie, I think you are ill." I had not told anyone that I had a mental breakdown but my friend said to me, "You do not eat much and you are losing weight and you don't sleep. I want you to see a Mr. G. W. North in Liverpool who has a gift of healing from the Lord." So, I agreed and set off for Liverpool by then my friend was already in Liverpool. I travelled by bus and my destination was 16 Devonshire Road which was a big house where the church meetings were held that were run by Mr. G. W. North and Mr. Norman Meeten. The church was called 'Fellowship'. As I entered the meeting I was amazed at what I saw and heard. The entire congregation were shouting "Hallelujah!" and "Praise the Lord!"

I thought that I had entered a mad house! When I sat down someone spoke in 'tongues' a language that I did not understand and then I started to feel a bit scared. At the end of the meeting I was taken to see Mr. North in his office and little did I realise that I was in for a shock. He appeared to be a nice man and when I sat down he started to talk to me but before I could reply, to my amazement, he said to me, "You have been involved in clairvoyance and drugs and drink." I started to feel uncomfortable but I answered "Yes." Then he also said that I had been involved with some spiritualists and I thought of my Mother and my Aunts on my Mother's side and I said, "Yes." Then Mr. North said "I am going to pray now. I am not shouting at you, only what is inside of you."

He was ruthless. Then I felt something come out of my mouth and from between my legs. He asked me if I had seen a dark figure during the night that disappeared behind my bed and I said "Yes."

I also told Mr. North about the awful nightmares that I was plagued with and the strong attraction to horoscopes. After all the praying from Mr. North I felt a bit exhausted but apart from that I enjoyed my week with the girls in their flat. I also felt more peaceful in my mind.

When I arrived back in Colchester I was on the ward giving out the drugs to the patients when I realised that I had not taken any drugs myself for a week. When I told my friend this she appeared to be very pleased at the news. Then I decided that I must throw away all my drugs which I did. I have never taken anti depressive drugs since. The Lord had healed me through Mr. North.

There was a very pretty Nurse working on the same as me. One day as I entered the ward and made my way to the office I heard the patients saying as we passed through the ward "Oh isn't she pretty." As I passed through the ward they said "Oh she is plain." I did not know then that the Lord Jesus was going to turn the tables for me. The pretty girl I was working with did not seem to have much patience towards the patients. Then the next thing that I heard was how much the patients liked me.

One day when I was on duty during the evening a young girl who had learning difficulties came to me in the office and asked me if she could have her boyfriend in. Without thinking I said "Yes." I am afraid in those days I was very naïve about physical relationships. Anyway I made Sheila very happy but the ward Sister was not too pleased when she discovered that I had allowed patients to have their boyfriends in their rooms.

One evening while I was in charge and I was struggling to write the ward report one of the patients came into the office to tell me how much she liked me as a person and said that she was sorry that she did not like me when I first came on the ward. During my time at that hospital I did not have any qualms. I took to Psychiatry like a duck to water. I loved the work and enjoyed the practical side of it and I got on very well on the wards and I got along well with the patients. Usually when I went off duty the ward was very peaceful. The theory side was a bit difficult at times. One afternoon I was trying to do some studying and there was a knock on my door. It was a Nurse from the ward who said "You are wanted on the ward. One of the patients has gone berserk."

When I arrived on the ward it was chaos. The Nurses who were on duty were trying to hold a girl down whilst Sister tried to administer the Paraldehyde drug by injection. The Sister said to me "Nurse Baker, you have got lovely shaped legs." My reply was "Sister, this is hardly the time to admire my legs!"

This remark brought back to my mind an incident from my terrible school days. I recalled that one morning I had been in a Maths lesson and the teacher had called me out to the front of the class to do a sum on the board. I knew that I would not be able to do the sum as my mind had gone blank. My friend Shirley had tried to help me by holding up the correct number of fingers but it was useless. Instead, I had decided to get undressed. By this time the boys were going berserk, banging on the desks and shouting. When I was just about to pull my knickers down the teacher, who was furious, got hold of his cane, (in those days teachers were allowed to use a cane). He brought the cane down on me with such force and shouted at me to get out of his class and go to Miss Lewis the Headmistress. I hated her so I didn't go but went to the toilets instead and lit up a cigarette. On the way home from school one of the boys from my class had said to me "I noticed this morning what a good pair of legs you have!"

Back in the hospital I had far more to concern me than legs! Although I was very interested in Psychiatric studies I would usually have a quiet time spent in prayer with the Lord Jesus before going to face the day. On this particular day I was on my way to the dreaded classroom. When the Tutor started the lecture I noticed that the other Nurses were writing their notes down very fast. As usual I could not keep up with them and I put my head in my hands and prayed "Oh, God, please help me." Then I suddenly realised that I would have to use my memory. Since working on the wards I started to realise that some of the Psychiatric illnesses were demonic and I would write this as my answer on a test paper. The Tutor was not very impressed with my answer and, one day, while in class the Tutor came to me and said "Nurse Baker, if you write about the devil or demons in your exam papers you will fail." So I had to be careful with what I wrote on my test paper. Apart from that I did well. Fortunately for me, I just passed the theory, which was amazing because not only did I have to learn about all of the mental illnesses but I had to remember the spelling which I found difficult. We also had lectures from the Psychiatrists which I found very interesting, especially about Schizophrenia. I had learnt about the three types and received good marks for that on my test paper. The Tutor was quite satisfied but not entirely because he told me that I had to expand my answers a lot more when writing my test papers.

Eventually I finished in class and went back to work on the wards. I enjoyed the work and the discipline. The etiquette was also easier because we were encouraged to speak to the patients as long as the ward work was done. I was relieved to be back on the ward. The ward was a mixture of chronic mental illnesses and one patient became a serious threat to me. This patient was a psychopath and was mentally deranged. At first this patient appeared very friendly towards me. I did not know which was worse, Ethel being friendly or disliking me! Heaven help any Nurse that she took a dislike to. I was soon to find out what it was like to feel her wrath!

One morning while making a bed with another Nurse, Ethel came up to me and told me to do a job for a patient which I knew I could not do without the ward Sister's permission. Ethel was livid with me and said to me "You have scars on your face. By the time I have finished with you, you won't be recognised." The Nurse I was with said "You should be frightened. Are you?" My answer was "No, I am not frightened of Ethel." Mind you, I should have been nervous because I had heard that she attacked Nurses. After that episode her attitude towards me was very threatening.

Apart from Ethel I got on well with the other patients and staff. I also had a new friend, who was a lovely Christian girl from London who took me to her home for the night when I was off duty. We went to the Nurses' Christian Fellowship which was run by a Sister from another hospital. I was in a happy state of mind until one day. It was my day off and I heard from a nurse that Ethel had gone berserk and was taken to the locked ward where very disturbed patients were admitted. Little did I know what I was being protected from and also of the power of God who protected me from danger.

One morning while eating my cornflakes Night Sister appeared and announced "Nurse Baker, report for day duty on 'A' ward" which was the Female Locked Ward. I felt slightly apprehensive after hearing about Nurses being attacked and ending up in hospital. I arrived on duty deciding to trust in Jesus.

I'd had a quiet time with the Lord before going on duty. When I arrived on the ward, after the Night Nurse had unlocked the door so that I could enter to the Sister's office, we listened to the night report which was quite alarming and appeared to be going on forever. At last the night report ended and then Sister turned to me and said, "Nurse Baker, go and get Molly up." I felt very afraid as I had heard how dangerous and disturbed this patient was towards the staff. Without warning she would punch the nursing staff in their faces so I was a bit concerned about the bone grafts in my nose. As I entered her room I was wondering what the best way to approach her might be. I thought that if I said "Good morning." She might say "What the hell's good about it?" So I decided to open her wardrobe and say, "You have very pretty dresses, Molly."

I noticed that Molly was staring at me but I did not trust her so I was praying silently.

When I bent down to help Molly with her shoes she suddenly caught hold of my face in her hands and said "You're new, I haven't seen you before. You are tiny and you have a poor mouth. If anyone threatens you or attacks you come and tell me and I will tear them apart." I said "Thank you, Molly."

One morning a Nurse and I were bathing a very disturbed patient. This patient was always locked in her room because she could be very violent. It was quite a struggle to get this patient into the bath. While I was trying to wash her and getting soaking wet the Nurse who was helping me started to tell me that she loved me and made a sudden move towards me. My answer to her was "Don't be so silly, we have work to do." Then one morning the Nurses were due to be changed to different wards. My friend and I went to have a look at the notice board and to my horror I was due to start night duty on the same ward that I had already been working on.

I was just about to go to my room when I saw a group of patients coming towards me saying "I can't wait for her to come on night duty and she will not leave the ward conscious!" The strange thing was that I did not feel fearful by her aggressive attitude towards me. When I entered the ward after ringing the bell the Nurse came and unlocked the door to let me in. I prayed quietly "Please, Lord, my feet are in the water. Please part the waves." I was going to know the power of God in my life that night! As I entered the office the Ward Sister looked very agitated. I thought the day report was never ending and then, to my amazement, Ethel was standing in the office and said, "Sister, I don't need any sleeping tablets as I feel so tired."

Ethel was on very strong medication – 200mg of Sodium Amytal. As she went staggering off to her room Sister said "I don't trust her."

and, without thinking, I said "Tonight, Sister, they will be like lambs." Sister's answered "Well Nurse, I hope for your sake they will be!"

When the day staff went off duty I locked the door leading out. As I walked past the side rooms I looked in Ethel's room and to my amazement she was flat out over her bed. I did not dare wake her up when I went round with the night drugs. Some of the patients were asleep and the ward seemed very quiet and peaceful. Of course, I was praising the Lord Jesus. During the night I read the previous night reports which were disturbing. Then I heard someone unlocking the main door to the ward. It was Night Sister who was very agitated and asked me "Nurse, you haven't rung. Why?" So I said "Sister, I did not need to ring you. They are all asleep."

I do not think that Sister could believe what I was telling her!

After Sister had left the ward I went into the kitchen to prepare the morning cups of tea for the patients who were still asleep. Fortunately for me the ward was still very silent so I went into the office to write the night report.

When I sat down I put my head in my hands and thanked the Lord for hearing my prayer. Then it occurred to me that I would have nothing to report so I just wrote that all patients slept well. When I had made the teas and was opening the hatch leading to the ward two young girls came up to me with some of the other patients and asked "Who are you?" So I replied, "Nurse Baker, the Night Nurse." But they would not accept my answer. Then, while giving out the teas, again the patients asked me "Who are you?" So again my answer was the same. So then the patients told me it was the first night's sleep that they had for three weeks. Then I said that I was pleased that they had slept well. Their reply was "You are not a Nurse, you are an angel!" So I was called an angel for a long time. I also knew in my heart there was an angel and it was the Lord's protection for me.

When the day staff arrived on duty and came into the office they asked what had happened during the night. My answer was "Nothing! All the patients slept well and that is what I have written in the night report." The day staff could not believe what I had written. When I left the ward Ethel was still asleep on her bed and I thanked the Lord Jesus for His protection over me during the night.

I went to the dining room and afterwards I made my way to my room with the thought of trying to get some sleep.

After a hot bath I settled down and was just dozing off when, to my horror, I heard heavy footsteps coming up the stairs. Then my bedroom door was flung open and, to my horror, Ethel entered my room and stood by my bed. I felt frozen with fear and I thought I would be badly hurt but to my astonishment Ethel stood over me and said "You were praying for me during the night." So I said "Yes, I was." I was wondering how she had got out of a locked ward and then she left, leaving me feeling a bit shocked.

After that night I acquired the name of 'Angel' and it certainly protected me from attacks from patients. One night while giving out the sleeping drugs I went to enter a side room but I heard a male voice shouting "Don't come in" so I left them. Eventually the man came out of the side room as I was unlocking the main door. He said to me "You are very kind." When I went to see the female patient she was looking very happy and she put her arm around me. At that time I did not realise what they had done as I was extremely naïve about physical relationships!

My next ward was an open ward and I enjoyed the work. One morning while on duty a Staff Nurse asked me "Who did the operations on your mouth?" I told her it was Mr. Emlyn Lewis. She told me that Mr. Lewis had died through liver disease (cirrhosis) and I felt very sad to hear that news. He had been a very clever Plastic Surgeon. He operated on the British and American fighter pilots. He trained under Sir Harold Gillies who was a top Plastic Surgeon in Harley Street, London.

To my surprise I received a letter from Westminster Hospital in London asking me to go for a check-up by a plastic surgeon called Mr. J. P. Reidy. As usual I took the letter to Matron who was a very nice lady and appeared very understanding. At this time I had a very prominent scar on my lower lip. I arrived at the hospital clinic and was waiting to see the Surgeon and some people asked me why I had the scar on my lower lip. The reason was that it was where my top lip had come from. I sat in front of Mr. Reidy while he examined my mouth and then he asked me had I any problems so I replied "Yes, I am not very happy about the scar on my lower lip." Mr. Reidy said "I will admit you to Stoke Mandeville Hospital." I felt really pleased about going back to hospital and on my way back to Colchester I felt so excited!

Then one day, while off duty I received a phone call which gave me a terrible shock. It was the husband of my friend June from Kent and he rang to tell me that June had committed suicide. I felt very upset as June was a very good friend. A few days before I heard this sad news I received a letter from June. I thought at the time that what she had written in the letter seemed strange because she kept telling me that I would do well. I wasn't so sure about that but I found it hard that I would never see her again.

During this time I was on duty on the Locked Female Ward but I did not mind as I knew the patients. One day when I had unlocked the main door to the ward and I was walking to the staff office I noticed a patient swinging the very long window pole and she was just about to smash the windows in the ward which were really high up. Then two of the other patients caught hold of her and I heard them say "Behave yourself, the Angel is on duty!" After that episode there was peace until I went off duty.

After a few weeks I received a letter from Stoke Mandeville Hospital saying that I was to be admitted to ward six. Oh, the excitement!

As usual I took the letter to Matron who was very nice and told me that I was due for my holidays. So I decided to take the remaining time after my discharge from hospital.

Back on evening duty in the Locked Female Ward a young girl was admitted on to the ward and was diagnosed suffering from schizophrenia. She was very agitated when the doctor arrived. He prescribed Paraldehyde. I knew this patient and she also started to beg me not to give her Paraldehyde so I decided that I would pray for her. When she started to calm down I told the Doctor that she had become quiet. After getting her into bed I went into the office and the Doctor was sitting at the desk writing notes. Then he said to me "What is the answer?" So I said to him "The answer is the Lord Jesus Christ." The Doctor just put his head in his hands and just looked at me. Then he left the ward.

All the Nurses were due for a move to different wards and I was moved to a female open ward which made me very happy. I was also overly in awe of the Ward Sister and one of the Nurses said to the Sister "Nurse Baker loves you, Sister." So the Sister said to me, "That is very nice of you, Nurse Baker" I felt embarrassed.

When I next went to church I asked the leading brother to pray for me and I told him about loving the Ward Sister. He asked me what the relationship was with my Mother so I told him. His answer was, "You are looking for a Mother figure" That was the end of that!

One morning when we were on duty, while we were having our morning coffee Sister received a phone call from the Sister who was on the Locked Female Ward wanting help from some of the Nurses because one of the patients had gone berserk and was threatening with a carving knife in the kitchen. So two of us made our way to the locked ward. As we arrived two Nurses and a Sister were standing outside the kitchen door looking very anxious. I decided that I would enter the kitchen because Sister was in charge and the other Nurse had a young family. The other Nurse was very attractive and, as for me, I would be seeing the Plastic Surgeon very soon anyway, so I went into the kitchen. The patient looked at me and remarked "The Angel!" and immediately dropped the knife. I asked her "Are you making a sandwich? I will make a cup of tea." My Mother taught me how to make a nice cup of tea. While the patient and I were making tea and sandwiches the staff standing outside the kitchen door, were getting worried because it was so quiet in the kitchen. Eventually when we came out of the kitchen I noticed that the patient looked very angrily at Sister so I calmed the patient down and got her into her room with the tea and sandwiches. The Sister thanked me and then I went back to my own ward.

The day came for me to go into hospital. I felt very excited as I made my way along the corridor to ward 6. I went into the ward office and the Nurse in charge admitted me onto the ward and took me to my bed. After unpacking my case it was tea time. When I sat at the table I noticed two patients with facial disfigurements and one poor girl had no nose. Even at my age it was still a slight shock but I soon got used to it.

After tea I decided that I wanted to go for a walk about so I asked the girl in the next bed to me if she would like to go for a walk. She appeared to be a bit hesitant but gave in and we went off without permission. I decided to visit the Men's Ward to find out if any fighter pilots were on the ward. My new friend did not seem very happy about going into the Men's Ward but I encouraged her to come with me. As we entered the ward we were confronted by the ward Sister who asked us "Can I help you, girls?"

I asked her if there were any fighter pilots among the patients on that ward. She looked surprised and instructed us "Go back to your ward, girls." But we did not go back to our ward as we decided to go to the canteen instead.

Next morning we were all sat by our beds waiting for Mr. Reidy, the Plastic Surgeon, to do his ward round. He arrived with his entourage and when he came to me he examined my mouth and told me what he was going to do. I also had to go to the dental department and the Speech Therapist. She was a very nice lady, not like the Speech Therapist who attended to me at Chepstow hospital. After two days I was on the list for my operation and I began to feel nervous. When the day arrived I got myself ready and the Nurses pulled my bed to the front of the ward. While I was waiting for the Nurse to give me an injection of Omnopon and Scopolamine I wondered if I had done the right thing. Of course, it was too late then so I prayed and then the theatre trolley arrived and I was off to face the Anaesthetist.

The next thing I remembered was being back in the ward feeling very thirsty. A Nurse was by my bed and refused to give me a drink because I was feeling very sick.

My lips felt very swollen, especially the lower lip. I could not drink out of a cup and I also found it too difficult to eat. I did not leave the ward until my stitches were removed by a Staff Nurse. I remember the Staff Nurse having a long talk with me and telling me that I had to accept that they would not be able to do any more for my mouth and lips. I did accept what the Staff Nurse was telling me but I felt very sad because it would mean that I would not be going to Stoke Mandeville Hospital any more. My lower lip was still swollen and also my lips would not grip the cup when I tried to drink. I had to make sure that I had a lot of tissues on me, even today, after all the years, I still have to concentrate when I drink out of a cup.

The day arrived when I was discharged from Stoke Mandeville hospital but I felt very sad because no one will ever know what the hospital meant to me. I did not have any money and the hospital in Colchester sent me a closed cheque. That meant that I had to go into Aylesbury. When I was in the bank the man behind the counter refused to accept the closed cheque because I did not have a bank account. Oh dear, I was in trouble because I did not have any money. I said to the young man behind the counter "I am not going until you accept my cheque." He asked me if I was a patient at Stoke Mandeville Hospital. So I told him that I was and it was quite obvious anyway because my lower lip was so swollen. In the end, after I had prayed very hard, he decided to ring the hospital in Colchester. I do not know what was said but the young man accepted my cheque and gave me the cash. I was so pleased!

When I was going back to the hospital on the bus a little boy asked his Mother "What is wrong with that girl's lips?" I heard his Mother say "Be quiet!" the little boy just stared at me all the way until I got off the bus. When I arrived at the hospital I was just in time for tea and while eating a jam sandwich I looked at the other patients who were sitting at the table with me. One girl had no nose and another had a disfigured face and I wondered what the little boy on the bus might say if he came on the ward.

The next morning I felt sad when I said "Goodbye" to the patients and Nurses. As I walked down the long corridor with my case I turned to look at all the Nissen huts for the last time. I travelled on the bus to Aylesbury railway station to catch the Euston train and from there I caught the Holyhead train to take me to Chester.

When I arrived at Chester station someone was supposed to meet me but no one came so I waited and waited. After some time I went to the phone and rang my Mother who said that my Father was on his way to Chester. Eventually he arrived outside the station to meet me. He was not in a good mood and he did not speak to me at all. At that time my parents lived in Henllan which was a small village near Denbigh. The doctor had given me two weeks sick notice so I was at home and at times it was difficult.

One day I went to Chester on the bus with my Mother who said, "Your lips are a mess, I think you should take that dressing off."

My lips were full of scabs.

At last the two weeks came to an end and I made my way back to Colchester feeling quite happy for a change. When I arrived back in the Nurses' home I reported to the Warden who told me that I was still in the same room. It seemed strange to be back! I was assigned to the Men's Ward.

When I went on the ward I saw some patients lying on the corridor floor. The Nurse who was with me told me to just step over them. A lot of the men patients were epileptic and some of the patients had very strange behaviour. Anyway I soon got used to it.

During my time in that hospital I attended a Nurses' Christian Fellowship and they held meetings in the Nurses' sitting room. They were run by a Sister from another hospital.

One evening I made my way to the top sitting room and I could hear someone playing the piano. When I entered the room I saw that it was a male Nurse who was playing. When he saw me he came over and caught hold of my hand and kissed my hand. I thought it was funny and it made me laugh. The next day was my day off so I decided to do some long overdue study in the morning and to go out in the afternoon. I got my notes out to start studying but, to my horror, I could not make out what I had tried to write out in the classroom so instead I turned to my Psychiatric books. Then just as I had settled down to study there was a knock at my bedroom door and when I opened the door there was the man who was at the Nurses' Fellowship the night before. His name was George and he asked me to go out for a walk with him and have coffee. I declined.

I explained to him that I was trying to study but he took no notice and said "I will make a cup of coffee and come back to your room." In those days male Nurses were not allowed in the female Nurses' bedrooms. When I tried to tell him about the rules he took no notice. He was a tall man with black hair and brown eyes and I heard from the other Nurses that he was in a university and from an upper class family. Soon we went for a meal and a coffee and soon I found it to be a bit of a nuisance because I was trying to study for an exam.

Eventually I fell in love with him and he kept telling me how much he loved me. I was always a bit confused about the issue of love and there was no intimate relationship with each other. We only kissed and that was when my lips were not hurting! The result of all this was that we started to argue.

One day I received a letter from a very nice lady who led a Bible study for teenagers. She wrote that she had heard about me and asked me if I would get in touch with her and she explained the reason she was asking me. In her Bible class there was a young girl who was born with a cleft lip and was unhappy about it.

The lady's name was Joyce and she invited me to her home for tea and in the evening turned up for their Bible class. I just sat and listened and I noticed the young girl that Joyce had mentioned. I thought that she was a pretty girl with long fair hair and blue eyes. I also knew that she had a single cleft lip and also a very long flat nose. Joyce introduced me to the girls after the meeting. I went to speak to the girl and told her to ask her Mother to take her to the Doctors so that she could get in touch with a Plastic Surgeon. I had a long conversation with her and she was surprised to hear how many operations I'd had.

Back at the hospital I was put on night duty on an Open Men's Ward and I quite enjoyed the work. When I arrived in the ward office to hear the day's report a tall male night nurse entered the office and he clicked his heels together and asked who the Night Nurse was. I told him that I was to which he replied "Nurse Baker, the Bible basher." I ignored that remark. While I was giving out the night medication he came to me and put his hands around my waist and remarked that he thought I was very tiny. My answer to his remark was "Please don't underestimate me. I am quite capable." We worked well together.

One morning he was missing so when he came back to the ward I asked him where he had been. His answer was "I have been to tell the other staff how good you are to work with." But I was in for a terrible shock! After a few weeks of work together one morning, when I was having my nights off, I was lying in bed thinking what I would do on my night off. I thought of studying but I didn't feel like it. I was just about to get out of bed when there was a knock on my bedroom door. It was my friend who came to tell me that the male nurse with whom I had been working on night duty had committed suicide. I could not believe it because he was always cheerful. I remembered one night when we were working together we spoke about religion. He also invited me to his home for tea and to meet his wife who was a Staff Nurse. She was a very attractive girl and they also had a little daughter.

After that I was working with another male Nurse who was tall and quite big. He came into the office, looked at me and said "Nurse Baker, supernatural" to which I replied "Oh, no, just a Nurse." He was a catholic and he was very easy to work with.

He wanted me to go out with him and, of course, I kept saying "No!"

One lunch time, as I entered the dining room he was behind me. He picked me up and ran all round the dining room. I said "Please put me down!" Then the next time I saw him he was on the same train as me when I was going to London. We had some conversation and then he told me that Geoff was not suitable for me. My answer was "I will be the judge of that." By that time I thought I was in love with Geoff although we had started to argue because I was not very good at kissing and also my lips were very tender. The result of that was an argument but he still came to see me and we still went out together and also went to church together.

Then the time came for another period in the classroom where we received lectures from the Psychiatrist. I found the lectures interesting. Then one day I was in trouble for writing what I thought about mental illness as it did not go down very well with the Tutor although I was top of my practical exams and the other Nurses wanted me to help them with the practical work. Next I was on the E.C.T. unit which I enjoyed. E.C.T. is an abbreviation for Electro Convulsive Therapy which was used for patients who suffered from clinical depression and I found it very interesting because I had received the same treatment myself.

There was a problem though because I was working with a male student Nurse who also wanted to go out with me. One day while I was on duty I was singing a hymn which was called, "When heaven came down and glory filled my soul." The male Nurse picked me up and sat me on the sterilizer and he threatened to put me in the sterilizer if I did not stop singing. Then he said that Geoff was not suitable for me. I did not feel very happy about him telling me who was suitable for me and I'm afraid that he became very annoying to me. When I was helping the other Nurses with their practical work he would always watch us through the window. He was a married man with a pretty wife and they had a little boy.

One day when I was on duty and the patients had received their E.C.T. treatment, Sister sent me to check outside in the corridor to make sure that there were no more patients. I checked the list and I thought we had finished but when I went into the corridor there was a smartly dressed lady. I thought she was a patient. I encouraged the lady to come with me into the treatment room. Eventually, I persuaded her into the treatment room only to hear the very amused Doctor say "Nurse, this lady is my mother!" I felt a bit silly.

I enjoyed the work on the E.C.T. unit. One morning when I was going for my coffee break I went back to my room to change my apron and found that I had received a letter from the Westminster Hospital in London. It was an appointment to see Mr. Reidy, the Plastic Surgeon from Stoke Mandeville hospital for a check-up after my last operation. I took the letter to Matron to get permission for a day off for my appointment. I had never been to Westminster so it was a bit strange after Stoke Mandeville Hospital. Mr. Reidy seemed very pleased with his work and asked me if I had any problems. I told him that I had some difficulty drinking out of cups. His answer was "You will have difficulty for a time."

After my interview with Mr. Reidy I decided to go to the restaurant for a cup of coffee. When I sat down at the table with my coffee a young man came to the table and asked if he could join me. I replied "Yes." He was smartly dressed in a black suit and carried a brief case. He asked me if I had been to see Mr. Reidy. Again I answered "Yes." and then, just as I was about to put my coffee cup to my lips my lower lip did not grip the rim of the cup and the result was that the coffee went everywhere except in my mouth.

Then the young man said "Oh dear, your lovely dress." He went to get some cloths from the restaurant kitchen to wipe my dress, which was a very nice new woollen one. I felt embarrassed but he was very kind.

When I got back to the hospital I was put on duty on the Geriatric Unit on the Women's Ward. I shall never forget one patient there who suffered from Alzheimer's disease. The sad thing was that this lady had been a missionary in India and had worked with Amy Carmichael of Dohnavur. The patient was quite attractive and she was tall. She had been a school teacher in Dohnavur but when I met her on the ward she was very confused and kept thinking that she was still in India. She kept saying to me, "My dear, you are very pale I think you should see Amma", who was Amy Carmichael. Whenever I could I would read to her from the Bible. I am sorry to say that I did not get on very well with the Ward Sister who told me to keep my religion off her ward.

Then, one weekend, when Sister was off duty I thought it would be a good idea to tidy her untidy office. I thought that she would be pleased but I am sorry to say that she went mad when she came back on duty and told me to put things back the way I had found them. Also one of the patients was having difficulty with her walking but when I discussed the patient with Sister during the ward report she was convinced that the problem was all in the patient's mind but I was not so sure about that.

One morning while I was on duty the patient was lying on the floor. Sister shouted at her to get up. I could see the patient was having difficulty in standing so one day while I was in charge of the ward I decided that when the Doctor came to do the ward round I would ask him to examine the patient. He did an examination and the blood tests showed that the patient was suffering from bone cancer. Sister was livid with me because she thought that I had gone over her head. I started to think that I would have a bad ward report from her. Then one evening while on duty Sister decided to tell me that she thought I was a good Nurse, and, because I knew that already, I said "Yes, Sister, I know." Sister responded by saying "Do not over estimate yourself, Nurse Baker."

My close friend in the hospital who knew all about me suggested that I should go and see Matron to tell her about my past but I did not take to this idea. This friend was the only Nurse who knew all about me and I knew that she would not gossip about me because she was a lovely Christian girl. I decided to visit Matron during coffee break so I put on a clean apron and made my way to

Matron's office in fear and trembling. I knocked at the door and I heard her say "Come in!" I entered and stood in front of Matron's desk with my arms behind my back. My heart was going so fast like a race horse. Matron smiled at me and said "Yes, Nurse." Then I started to tell Matron about my nervous breakdown and lack of education. I noticed Matron's eyes going wide and looking very surprised. Then Matron said "Nurse Baker, I accepted you on your previous references from other Matrons, which were excellent. Please go back on duty." Oh, I felt so relieved because I loved the work so much.

On my next Open Ward I got on with the staff and the ward Sister and in that hospital the etiquette was not so strict.

One morning when I was on duty the Ward Sister asked me to do a job which I was against because I did not agree with it so I said "Yes, Sister, but I won't like it." Sister replied "Do as you are told and get on with it." My answer was "Oh, I suppose I will have to." Then Sister said to the other two Nurses "Get hold of her and put her on the bed." So I said "Oh, please don't hurt me, I am only little!" Sister said "Rubbish, on the bed!" Then Sister lifted my dress up and sprayed me with fresh air spray. I said "Oh, Sister, you've wet all my pants!" Sister just laughed and said "Tough!" That was a bit of fun at my refusing to obey Sister!

One day a new Staff Nurse came to work on our ward. While the patients had gone to their different departments, (Physiotherapy, Occupational Therapy) I was putting the clean laundry away in the airing cupboard and the Staff Nurse came to me and asked me who did the repair to my mouth. When I told her it was Mr Emlyn Lewis at Gloucester and Chepstow, and we discussed the sad news of Mr. Lewis who had died.

During that time I was still going out with Geoff although I was not sure about my feelings for him and I did not want close contact with him. One evening while we were in the upstairs sitting room he tried to kiss me but my lower lip was still tender. I could see that he was annoyed and then he walked away from me. I thought then that the relationship was finished as he did not come near me.

Then one day I was in my room trying to study, but it was a losing battle because I was tired and finding it too difficult to concentrate. There was a knock on my door and it was Geoff who asked me to go for a coffee with him. So we went into town to a café and had tea and cakes. On our way back to the hospital I needed to go to the toilet. Geoff complained that I was worse than the patients but we found the toilets. Geoff waited outside for me. As I went into the toilet I could hear singing and shouting in the next toilet. I realised who was making the noise and my first thought was, how on earth did that patient get out of a Locked Ward? I went out to Geoff and we had to ring the hospital to tell them that a patient from the Locked Ward was in the toilets. (We had no mobile phones in those days) We had to wait until transport came because she would not leave the toilet.

Geoff asked me to go to a dance with him but I said "No, I haven't danced for years." He came up to my room in the Nurses' home to tell me that the dance was only in the dining room. At that time I was trying to study and I was trying to improve my spelling, which I found very hard although I had no problem remembering the names of the illnesses or diseases. I decided that I would go to the dance with Geoff. I found my old green dance dress, ironed it and off we went to the dining room which looked quite different for that occasion. A Nurse told me that I looked very pretty and that my dress was lovely. After dancing with Geoff and treading all over his feet he left me in disgust. I did not think that it was my fault as I had told him that I had not danced for a long time. Then suddenly everybody stopped dancing and in the centre of the dance floor there was a couple who were doing a strange kind of dance. I recognised the male as he was one of the Doctors and I also knew the Nurse who was dancing with him.

She was crawling up his legs and then would fall wriggling at his feet then the Doctor would dance all around her. To me it looked weird. When the dance was over Geoff came to the Nurses' home with me and at the main door he did a low bow, took my hand and kissed me.

When I arrived in my room my two friends came to me and told me that they had been praying for me. During that time I was still attending the Brethren Church But in my mind I thought that I loved Geoff. Sometimes Geoff would come with me to the church.

One day I was working with a Nurse with whom I got on very well. She was married and she asked me to go out with her and her husband one evening. So I went with them to a pub but I did not drink any alcohol. During the evening my friend started to tell me that in her opinion Geoff was not suitable for me, her reasons being that he was too big for me and that he would kill me because I was so small. I felt a bit upset. I did not realise it then but in just one year's time I would be married; but not to Geoff!

One day, while reading the Nurses' notice board, I discovered that I was due for a week's holiday so after seeing the Matron, I set out for Chester. My father met me outside Chester station. He was in a very bad mood and when we got in the car he said to me "Don't speak!" so I didn't speak a word but he did not take me straight home. Instead we went to a pub and my Mother was there in the pub so I just sat and waited quietly until they decided to go home.

A middle aged man who I knew was sitting by me and he started to talk to me and asked me to go out with him. I said to him "No, you are married and have six children!" At last my parents wanted to go home. We got into my Father's car and drove off but my Father was driving very fast and we did not have seat belts on in those days. Suddenly my mother shouted "Philip, slow down, there is a police car coming behind us!" Eventually we arrived home safely. As I got out of the car I said a prayer "Thank you, God, for a safe journey." My Mother grabbed me, slammed me against the car and hit and punched me with her fist. I was concerned about my nose and lips, and then I heard my Father shouting in a very stern voice "Phyllis, what do you think you are doing?" Then my mother stopped hitting me but I knew that it was because of the drink and also because of what was inside her due to her involvement with clairvoyance and spiritualism that was causing her to behave like that. However the week was not all gloom as I had opportunities to visit my friends and relatives.

At last it was time to go back to Colchester. I arrived back at the hospital feeling quite happy until I discovered that I was back in the dreaded classroom and the Tutor wasn't pleased with me. We had to write an essay about a patient on the ward. The patient that I chose was a music Teacher who was suffering from depression. This patient was a Christian and a very nice lady but she had not been able to get a job because she told them about her illness so I told her not to fill in that section of her application form and also not to tell lies on the form. She was very surprised when I told her about her about my previous illness. I did not usually speak about my illness to anyone so I knew that I was 'putting my head on the block' as mental illness carried a terrible stigma at that time. I also believed what the Bible said about mental illness and, of course, I wrote about that in my essay which did not go down very well with my Tutor!

One morning the Tutor called me as we were leaving the classroom. He told me again "Nurse Baker, if you write about the devil in your exam paper like you have done here in this paper then you will fail!" Then he handed me back my paper which seemed to have more red ink on it than my handwritten blue ink. While we were waiting to take our final practical exam; I was feeling a bit nervous the Tutor came over to me again and reminded me to keep the devil out of my answers. The problem was that when the examiner started to ask me some questions he asked me what I would do if I was faced with a patient who was threatening me with a knife. My answer was that I would pray and then I saw his eyes narrow and he said "Nurse, while you are praying the patient could kill you." Then he dismissed me.

I was never very good at answering questions in the classroom and when we had lectures from Doctors and Psychiatrists my brain seemed to go on strike! I did not have much confidence in myself apart from when I worked on the wards. Anyway I took the final exams and I passed. After a few weeks I received my Nursing badge and certificate to say that I was a qualified Mental Nurse.

Back on duty I was on the Locked Ward and the patients remembered me. One day one of the patients fell and hurt her arm and had to go to the Fracture Clinic. I was the only Nurse that she would allow to go with her.

It was a nerve racking experience because she was violent. I managed to keep her calm by telling her that the Doctor was our friend. When we got in to see the Doctor he asked her if her arm was hurting. Then she shouted at him "Of course it bloody hurts, why you think I am here?" Her shouting made me jump and the Doctor didn't look too happy either! After examining her arm and having an x-ray he referred her to an Osteopath. I was more than glad to arrive back at the hospital as I felt mentally drained.

One morning we heard that Lord Snowdon was visiting the hospital. I did not take too much notice but then Sister asked me to take two of the patients for a walk. One was Molly who was very unpredictable in her behaviour. As we started to walk in the grounds I noticed a group of men. I did not take too much notice of them and we carried on walking. Then Molly said very suspiciously "Who are those men?" As usual I said "They are our friends, Molly."

One of the men was the Lord Mayor and then I realised that one of the other men was actually Lord Snowdon. As he approached us he said very politely "Good morning, Nurse." and smiled at us. I responded by saying "Good morning." The Head Nursing Officer was also with them and he looked very pleased. I was relieved to get back on the ward. I did not tell any of the staff on the ward otherwise they would have asked too many questions.

One evening when I attended the Nurses' Fellowship which was held in the Nurses' sitting room one of the Nurses who worked in another hospital asked me if I would go on holiday with her to Scotland. She was going to stay in a castle called Kilravock Castle in Croy, Inverness. I said that I would go and so we arranged to have our holidays together.

I began to feel very excited about the trip to Scotland. We had booked two weeks holiday but my friend's Father died just before we were due to go away. She suggested that I went for the first week on my own. I did not have much money so on my way to buy my train ticket I prayed that the fare would not be any more than £11 or £12. The Lord answered my prayer and so I was able to set off on my way to Scotland, but I got on the wrong train and got off at the wrong station. The station porter told me that I was seventy miles out of my way and told me to go to Glasgow and then I would have to travel over night to Inverness. It was 5pm so after an hour's wait I eventually got the right train and I was on my way to Glasgow.

When I had settled into my seat a group of young sailors came into the carriage. They were very noisy and were drinking alcohol so I decided to go into another carriage but in there was a young couple who were all over each other. They were kissing and caressing each other so I prayed to the Lord to stop them going any further. I thought that they were going to eat each other! Then suddenly the girl sat up and looked at me and said "Have you eaten any food? Would you like a sandwich?" So I replied "Yes please" as I had not had any food since 6am that morning and it was then 12 o'clock, Midnight. Eventually we arrived in Glasgow and then I had to find the train for Inverness. While I was standing on the platform I noticed a large written text on the wall opposite saying "Fear not for I am with you. I will hold your right hand." I recognised this as the words of the Lord from a verse in the book of Isaiah in the Bible.

After a long journey I reached Inverness. It was 5am, very cold and raining hard. I sat on a seat in the station and wondered what to do at that moment a porter appeared and asked me if he could help me. I showed him the address of the castle and then he told me that it was a long way and there would not be any buses or trains going that way. Then I think he felt sorry for me because he said that he would ring his friend and ask him to give me a lift. By that time I was feeling a bit tired and hungry as I had not had much food.

After a while a young man arrived and I got in his car and told him about my long journey. The drive seemed to take ages and I didn't realise how far the castle was from the station. At last we entered the grounds of the castle and the driver refused to accept any money from me. He suggested that we should wait a while because it was only 7am. Then a door opened and a tall man with grey hair came out in his dressing gown. He came to the car and asked "Are you Louie Baker?" When I told him that I was he asked "Where have you been? We have been to meet three trains from London and your friend rang up and was really worried about you!" So I told him about my journey. Of course, that opened the door for a lot of teasing! Every time I went in the dining room he would tell all the other guests about my journey. Either he or his wife would bring my breakfast to my room every morning. One day I went into the kitchen to get some cornflakes but the staff told me that Mr. Duncan did not allow guests in the kitchen at which point he came into the kitchen and said "Louie can go where she wants." I just sat at the table and ate my cornflakes.

One evening I went to my room accompanied by two young ladies who were also guests in the castle. When we entered the room Mr. Duncan was in there and he started to make excuses as to why he was there. When he left the girls told me to lock my door. One night I forgot and I was just lying in bed reading the biography of Florence Nightingale, which I enjoyed, when the door opened and in came Mr. Duncan. He sat down by my bed on a chair and asked me if I had got a boyfriend. I told him that I had, meaning Geoff. I was not afraid of him because I was so naive and I trusted him as Mr. and Mrs. Duncan had been missionaries. Mrs. Duncan was a very nice lady and Mr. Duncan's brother, George was a gospel singer.

One day, Mr. Duncan decided to take me on a tour round the castle which was interesting because it was a lovely building. Back in my bedroom I tried to fix the lock on my bedroom door because it did not work properly but I was unable to do this. I climbed into bed and tried to sleep when once again Mr. Duncan came into my room and sat on my bed and told me that he was going to pray for me. Then he held my hand and started to pray.

One morning while we were having breakfast one of the guests stood up and announced that he was going to organise a walk up a mountain called Ben Nevis. The next morning we were waiting for the guide and the transport to take us to the mountain, the guide looked at me and said "You are not suitably dressed." The other people were wearing suitable clothes but I just wore a straight dress and a pair of court shoes. I told the guide that I would be alright and took my jacket and joined them in the transport bus.

When we arrived at the mountain we all got out of the bus and then I noticed that everyone was wearing boots. I walked at the back of the party but as the path got steeper and steeper the guide was really worried but I was determined to go on. As we ascended higher up towards the top of the mountain some people in the group turned back because they said that they had had enough of climbing mountains.

Eventually they all went back to the transport except me. I wanted to carry on up but then it started to pour with rain and then the guide looked at me and said that we were going to go back down because I only had court shoes on. As we were descending I started to slip so the guide held my arm until we reached our transport. I expect he was glad to see the back of me! When I arrived back at the castle I was soaking wet so I went for a hot bath and then I went into the dining room for my evening meal. Mr. Duncan was in the dining room and started to tease me about going up the mountain. The castle belonged to a Miss Margaret Rose who had inherited it. The castle was idyllic and the scenery surrounding it was beautiful. At last my friend arrived from London and said "Louie, what on earth is going on? I've spoken to Mr. Duncan and he told me about your journey and how you almost got lost!" I just replied "Please, don't ask, I just made a mistake!" They just stared at me in disbelief.

At last I could leave the castle with my friend because Mr. Duncan would not allow me to leave the grounds. I only went out once in the first week and that was with a lady called Margaret Rose who took me to Glasgow in her own car.

My friend and I went out on day trips and I enjoyed the second week of our holiday. On our last morning we had to pay for our stay at the castle. When it was my turn I went into Mr. Duncan's office. He smiled at me, but not for long when I told him that I had no money. He took a deep breath and said "Louie, I am not going to charge you anything." I promised that when I had my next wages I would send it to him but he replied "No, Louie." I left his office.

On our last day we were waiting in the entrance hall with our suitcases for Mr. Duncan who was going to give us a lift to the railway station. I got in the back seat and my friend sat in the front and I did not speak during the journey to the station but just stared out of the window. As the train approached the station Mr. Duncan shook hands with my friend and then he pulled me towards him and kissed me full on my lips, which was quite painful. I was glad when we were on the train. My friend was astonished and said "Louie, what was going on?" My answer was "I do not know, don't ask!"

My lips were still smarting. I thought that Mr. Duncan liked me but I did not realise until afterwards that he liked me a little too much!

Eventually we arrived back at the hospital and I was back on duty on the Surgical Ward, which consisted of half women and half men. One day a new patient came in suffering from breast cancer. When I arrived to attend to her needs I noticed a Bible on her locker so, feeling pleased, I said to her "You are a Christian?" Her answer was "Yes and you must also be a Christian?" I replied "Yes I am!" Her name was Ruth, and she was a lovely lady, tall with thick wavy hair.

One day, after her operation I was removing all her stitches when she invited me to her home. Her husband was also very friendly and asked me to their home so one weekend when I was off duty I went to stay with them. I also went to their church which was open Brethren. I soon found out how popular Ruth was in the church because she had so many friends and I enjoyed my stay with them very much. When I was working on the ward I used to give Christian tracts out to the patients.

The male patients would laugh and make fun of me but I didn't take any notice of them. Then, one day, while preparing a male patient ready for the theatre he said to me "Please pray for me. I feel very nervous about going for my operation." So I did pray there and then.

One day when I was off duty Geoff came to see me. He took me to the male Nurses' sitting room and we watched television. It was 1969 and the day that Neil Armstrong took the first steps on the moon. When we went to the dining room for our tea I was sitting with Geoff and two other Nurses at the table started an argument. One of the young women who worked in the dining room had a mental problem and some of the Nurses had said that she was schizophrenic so I said "No, she is a high grade subnormal."

In those days they did not say someone had learning difficulties. One Nurse said that I was right. When I left the dining room and went outside with Geoff he caught hold of my shoulders and started to shake me and said "You always think you are right!" I said "Don't Geoff! I love you!"

One day, on my day off, I went with two Nurses from another hospital to Frinton-on-Sea in Essex. It was a very hot day and I had to be very careful because my skin would get sunburnt very easily. I did not dare take the risk of getting sunburnt because Home Sister always thought it was my fault, so while the girls were sunning themselves on the beach I decided to go into town and try to escape the sun. However it was a losing battle because I had a very short dress on and no stockings. As I was walking along the High Street I came across a Bible shop so I went in and looked at the books. I came across a big book called the 'Biography of James Hudson Taylor' and decided to buy it. While I was paying the lady for the book I asked if I could use the toilet. The lady said that I could and that it was right at the top of the stairs but, of course, I took the wrong turning and I went into a bedroom and, to my amazement, on the bed there was an old man with a very long beard and a mass of grey hair (but more the colour of silver). He was asleep so I quickly left the room and went downstairs again. I told the lady that I had gone into the wrong room and apologised to her and asked who the old man on the bed was. She replied "Oh that man is my Father and I am his daughter Olive." Her father was called Ernest Luff and he had written a book called, 'He dared to believe' which I had a copy of back at the hospital.

Next morning I was in trouble because I could hardly walk because of my sunburn. When the Doctor came to see me with a Sister from sick bay she was furious with me and scolded me "Nurse, don't you ever learn?" I did not answer her but I was in sick bay for two days!

Next I was on the ward where the patients with mental problems were admitted. One day a young girl was admitted who was a heroin addict. She was very agitated when I went to her room to give her a dose of the drug Methadone and I handed her the receiver that held the injection but she said "I am not allowed to inject myself." So I said to her "As you have been injecting yourself for months I am sure that you can manage this injection!" She then asked "Do you trust me?" I answered her "No, I don't trust you, I trust the Lord Jesus." Then, to my amazement she wanted to know more so I told her about Jesus and then astonishingly she said "If Jesus is all you say He is ask Jesus to heal my husband, he is on the Men's' Ward." I told her that I would go and see her husband so in my break I went off to the Men's' Ward.

I had a terrible shock when I got there because the Charge Nurse told me the man was dying and would probably be dead within the hour. I thought to myself "Oh, no, Lord!" I went to see the man behind the curtains and I could see that he was very near to death. I put my hand on his chest and prayed for him and I kept praying while on duty and the Lord answered my prayer because he recovered. The couple had a two year old child who was more like a baby due to the heroin drugs. Eventually, the three of them went home together, Praise the Lord!

One day I had a shock when the Nursing Officer told me to go on night duty on the Surgical Ward and to be in charge. I tried to rest during the day but sleep was impossible. After trying to eat a breakfast at 7:30pm I made my way to the ward. As I entered the ward to my annoyance I saw two Doctors which was a bad sign and the day staff had not finished their work. As I was listening to the day report from the Staff Nurse I started to wonder what was going on as it all seemed surreal. The Nurse who I was working with appeared to be calm and she was very helpful to me as she knew all the patients.

When we had settled the patients down and given out the drugs we had a cup of coffee and I went over the day report. Then the Nurse went off for her dinner break. I was just thinking about writing the night report when I started to hear noises. I checked the patients who were all asleep until the night Sister arrived on the ward with her strong torch.

When the nurse came back from her break I went off for my dinner break but the dinner did not look very appetising. I could not eat dinner at 1:00am so I just had a cup of coffee and a chat with the other Night Nurses who looked awful. There was a particular night duty look about them! When I arrived back there was a Doctor on the ward examining the operation cases.

Apart from that everything was quiet. While Nurse was in the kitchen preparing for the morning teas I started to write the night report. Then I heard footsteps and thought "What is that?" It was night Sister doing her last ward rounds. Night Sisters in my time were very strict and I always felt a bit scared of them as they usually looked for faults in everyone's work. A few weeks later I was due for a week's holiday so I decided that I would like to go to Rome because of what I had read in the Bible in the book of Romans.

When I went to the Travel Agents I did not have enough money for the fare to Rome so I booked to go to Italy to a place I had never heard of! Also I had an insurance policy which was coming to an end. I could not find anyone who would go with me probably because I did not seem to know where I was going. When I told my Mother she said "You cannot go to Italy on your own!" So my Mother came on the holiday with me. We went by ship from Dover. On the ship my Mother made friends with two ladies so I did not see much of her. Most of the time she was propping up the bar with her new friends while I just wandered about the ship thinking about Geoff. By that time I thought that I was in love with him.

One day while I was sitting in a deck chair by the pool I noticed three people talking by the pool. I noticed one of them, a man who had black curly hair that curled around the nape of his neck. He also had dark skin. After a while I went into the dining room for the evening meal. During the evening my mother went to play Bridge or Whist.

When we arrived in the hotel after leaving the ship I woke up one night to discover that my Mother was missing. When I found her she was propping up the bar having had quite a few drinks. I tried to get her away from the bar but she became aggressive so I left her to it. When my Mother eventually came to bed I pretended to be asleep.

The next day we went on a day out to Yugoslavia. It was not very nice! We saw some shops but they were empty and it all looked a bit depressing to us. We also went into some caves. As I was going into one cave the man with the black curly hair was coming out of the cave with two other people. The next morning when I went to get my passport the one under mine belonged to the man with the black wavy hair. It seemed as though I could not get away from this man and all of the coincidences seemed a bit strange. Whilst we were waiting for the coach to take us to board the ferry for our return journey to Dover my Mother seemed a bit put out because a lady told her that she thought that I was very delicate, but my Mother replied "Rubbish, my daughter is not delicate!"

Whilst I was waiting on Euston station for the train to go to Colchester the man came over to me and asked what work I did. I just said "Nursing" and I walked away from him. I was not interested in him because I was too busy thinking about Geoff and wondering what he was up to. I would feel jealous if he went out with someone else.

Back at the hospital I was on the Surgical Ward. I was happy to be there as the ward Sister was nice. The male patients kept putting their hands around my waist. I was only 18 inches around my waist. Also the men asked me if I did dancing because my hips seemed to sway when I walked. One patient picked me up and carried me down the ward. I shouted "Put me down. If Sister or Matron saw me I would be in trouble!" Anyway it was only fun on their side.

One day I saw a tiny kitten in the hospital grounds so I picked it up and took it to my room in the Nurses' home. The only problem was that it was wild. I got some milk for the kitten to drink as I came off duty and as I entered my room the kitten was going berserk. My friend came into my room and when she saw the kitten she said "Are you completely mad? If Home Sister discovers the cat you will be in trouble!" The next day I went on duty after a bad night's sleep.

I had no sleep because the kitten was walking all over me during the night.

When I went back to my room to change my apron the Sister came to my room. She was furious with me because apparently the cleaners had discovered the kitten crying under my bed. While Sister was telling me what she thought of me, which wasn't very encouraging, I could hear a radio playing in someone else's room through the open bedroom doors. The song that I could hear was, "Kiss me, Honey. Honey, kiss me. Thrill me, Honey, thrill me. I don't care if I blow my top, Honey, Honey, don't stop." I could hardly control myself not to laugh! Then Sister left my room and walked briskly down the corridor and I just collapsed on my bed laughing. The next day a notice was put on the Nurses' notice board saying that if any cat was found in a Nurse's bedroom it would mean dismissal.

By this time in my career I had decided that I would like to do a course in Plastic Surgery or Tropical Diseases. However I did not realise how circumstances would shape the course of my life.

One day I received a letter and, to my amazement, it was from the man with the black wavy hair. I thought that he did not know my address or the hospital where I was working. I just ignored it and tore the letter up.

One afternoon when I had time off I was planning to have a nice rest and quiet. There was a knock at my door so that put paid to my rest! I thought it was Geoff wanting to go for a walk. I did not want to go out as I was feeling tired after a busy morning. Also I had made a mistake with two patients having the same name. However, once again the Lord came to my rescue.

I gave in to Geoff and we went for a walk. It turned out to be more like a hike because Geoff was a tall man, about 6ft in height, and as I am only 5ft, I found it hard to keep up with him. As we walked through a muddy field my shoes sank into the mud. Geoff started to complain. He took hold of my arm and said "You are too slow. Try and keep up with me." By that time I felt a bit cross so I said "I am going no further!" To which Geoff replied "Please yourself!" So I left him walking away into the distance. I felt furious with Geoff but when I reached the road I did not know where I was and it had started to rain. I was completely lost and my feet were wet and cold. I stamped down the road thinking to myself "I never want to see you again, Geoff." Then I came across a house and knocked on the door and, to my great surprise, the Ward Sister opened the door. Sister also looked taken aback and said "Nurse Baker!" I said "Sorry, Sister, I am lost." Sister invited me in, made me a cup of tea and gave me a piece of cake. After that Sister's husband gave me a lift to the hospital. Later, when I saw Geoff in the dining room I asked him why he had left me. His answer was that I was too slow and, of course, it was my entire fault.

One morning while I was on duty I went to get some milk out of the fridge. There wasn't any there so I went to the nearest ward, Locked Ward. A Nurse had a key which opened all of the other doors so I was able to unlock the main door leading to the Locked Ward and went in. I noticed that the Nurses were busy so I went to the kitchen. There was a woman standing by the sink and I thought she was the cleaner. I saw a crate of milk by the fridge so I asked the 'cleaner' to tell the Nurses that I had taken two bottles of milk. During the morning a Nurse told me that there was a phone call for me. It was a Nurse from the Locked Ward saying that a patient had told her that I had taken milk from the fridge. I said "No, it was the cleaner." Then the Nurse said "No, Nurse Baker, you saw in the kitchen a very violent patient who had got out of her room. Someone was looking after you!" I know that the Lord was looking after me.

I remember on one ward where I was working there was one of the male patients who was a diabetic and also had a mental problem. He was also very aggressive towards the staff. He was always filling his pockets with sugar, so one day I tried to empty his pockets and suddenly he turned and put his hands around my neck and squeezed my neck very hard and also verbally insulted me. Just as I was thinking that my last hour had come I saw a fist go past my eyes and hit this violent patient. The person who came to my rescue was a male Charge Nurse and he gave the patient such a hiding. I tried to stop him but he said that he would not allow the patient to insult me.

One morning I received a letter from the man with the wavy, curly hair. At last I knew his name! It was David Brighton. His letter suggested that we met in London so, in my mind, I decided to meet him to put a stop to our friendship as I did not want him in my life. I thought that it was Geoff that I wanted.

As I was on my way to London I thought to myself "What am I doing meeting a man I do not even know?" I had the weekend off but I only got a day return ticket. David met me in Euston Station. I felt very nervous but he soon put me at my ease and, after going out for a meal, he told me that he had booked two rooms at a hotel. I did not feel very happy about that and I told him so and I also told him that I had a return ticket back to Colchester. Then he said "Louie, I am not going to hurt you, just try and relax." We settled into the hotel which was very nice and all we did all night was talk. He wanted to know a lot more about me, so I thought "Good, this will put him off me!" I told him all about my lack of education and all my faults and about the scars on my body. Well, it didn't work! He wanted to see me again so I told him about Geoff. He knew that he had a rival. As I was on the train going back to Colchester I thought that I would not hear from David Brighton again.

The next morning I was back on duty and, while making beds with another Nurse who I was friends with, she asked "Well, how did you get on with a strange man in London?" I told her that we had stayed in a hotel and just talked. Also all the male patients wanted to know about him so I just said that we had a nice time going round the London sights. Then my Nurse friend said "You mean to say that you spent a night in a hotel and nothing happened?" To which I replied "Yes!" By this time the male patients were doubled up laughing. Then one patient said "I believe her." By that time my face was going red. I told the patients that I did not believe in having a physical relationship before marriage and that brought on more laughter. Then I told them that Sister had put me down to give the injections. That soon put a stop to them laughing at me. Patients in those days were in hospital a lot longer and liked to have some fun with the Nurses. I thought that if David had done something that I had not approved of then he would not see me again. I also remember my Mother saying to me "If you do anything wrong your Father will break every bone in your body."

One day my friend from another hospital asked me to go horse riding with her so I went. My friend had a horse and I had a pony which I kept falling off! Then, one day, I got it right and I enjoyed my pony. Then, one day, I went riding on my own because my friend could not come with me. The lady in charge came with the pony and she was also holding the reins of a very big horse. The lady then left me while she went away to see someone else. I started to pray because the big horse was a bit awkward. Eventually the lady returned and was surprised to see the horse so calm as the horse usually reared up when it was nervous.

Back at the hospital I received another letter from David Brighton. He always wrote long letters. I went into the dining room for my lunch but I was not very hungry. I saw Geoff and sat by him and then he came back to my room with me but I did not tell him about David. There was another male Nurse who wanted me to go out with him but I refused. It always amazed me because after working with male Nurses they always wanted to go out with me. Before that they wouldn't even speak to me!

One evening while on duty I had a strange incident. A young male patient was admitted suffering from acute appendicitis. I prepared him for theatre and, after his pre-med I went with him to the theatre. We were in the anaesthetic room and the Anaesthetist arrived and asked me to get a drug for him. I did not know what he wanted but I went into the room where the drugs were kept and I was praying hard. To my amazement I saw a Nurse in the drug room. She did not speak at all but she pointed to the drug that the Anaesthetist wanted. I went back to the patient and the drug was administered and then the patient was wheeled into the operating theatre.

I did feel a bit puzzled about the Nurse in the drug room because I had never seen her in the hospital so I asked the porters who worked in the theatre. They said that the only Nurse they saw was me. I said to them "You must have seen the Nurse because she was quite near to you." The porters were adamant that they had not seen another Nurse. I have never forgotten that Nurse as I think that it was an angel sent to help me from the Lord Jesus.

I received a letter from David Brighton telling me that he loved me but I thought "He doesn't know me." Because the patients were always saying that they loved me so it must be that kind of love.

I did not want to get involved with David. One day during tea time in the dining room Geoff and I had an argument over something trivial. I would not give in to him nor would he give in to me. Anyway, he came to my room and sat on my one and only chair as I was reading another letter from David.

One day I was on an Open Ward working with a Chinese male Nurse who was a Communist and I found it difficult to work with him. When I told Geoff he threatened to trash him but I would not let him hurt the Nurse as it would have caused a lot of trouble. Then a couple of days later I had another letter off David wanting me to meet him in London. Then in the dining room I was sitting with two nurses having coffee and Geoff came in and sat by another Nurse which I wasn't pleased about and I told Geoff that he should sit by me. He answered "Don't be so possessive!" I replied by saying "Don't worry; I won't be possessive any more as I have met someone else." To which Geoff replied "Good!"

I wrote a note to David telling him that I would meet him at Euston Station. I met David in London for one day each week on my day off. He took me around the sights and the museums. We also went to the museum for tropical diseases which wasn't very nice, but interesting. I started to notice how kind his personality was and the effect on me was like someone giving me doses of medicine.

One morning, back at the hospital I received a very long letter from David saying that he was serious about me. The problem was that I thought I was still in love with Geoff.

West Bromwich

I had made the decision to leave Colchester and so I applied to a hospital in West Bromwich in the Midlands. I got the job as a Staff Nurse and David was pleased because that was his home town and I would be near to him.

I worked a month's notice in Colchester and then I was on my way to West Bromwich but there was quite a shock in store for me as the Matron at that hospital was very strict. I think she was the last Matron to leave after the changes in the NHS. I was missing my friends and I was also missing Geoff! I could not understand the other staff on the ward because the dialect was so different from the Essex dialect.

The Matron had put me on the Children's Ward and that was a fright because I hadn't nursed children for years, and, on top of everything a young baby collapsed. When the Doctor arrived to examine the baby he wanted to know about things that I just did not know. Then he asked "You must be new here because I haven't seen you before?" I replied "Yes" The Doctor put the baby on a drip and I had to give a Penicillin injection which I felt a bit nervous about as it had been a long time since I had given an injection to a child, let alone a baby! I didn't mind giving injections to adults; in fact it was one of my favourite jobs. The cleaner on that ward was a little woman who was very fat and looked like a barrel on two small legs. But she was very kind and that made a change after some of the cleaners I had met. I remember one cleaner who gave me and the other Nurses a lot of trouble. The Ward Sister was nice but firm with the staff and the Sister expected me to know everything. The only problem was of course that I didn't know everything! After five years of Psychiatric Nursing I felt like a fish out of water.

Two babies were seriously ill in the main ward. I helped two Nurses make the little children's beds. One little girl was dying. One of the Nurses asked me where I came from and I answered "Prestatyn, North Wales." To which one Nurse said "You are never Welsh!" My answer was "No, I am English!" The Ward Sister gave me a list of jobs to do and drugs for the children and I also had to check the ill babies. Sometimes parents would only stay with their children during visiting times.

I went to check on one baby and after I had changed him I held him carefully in my arms but then he died. It was a strange sensation holding a dead baby in my arms. I laid the baby down and went to tell the ward Sister who told me that it was expected and rang the Doctor to come to confirm the death.

It was my duty to lay out the baby. The cleaner came over to me and asked "Can I help you, Staff, as I have had seventeen children?" That sent shivers up my spine! I thought to myself "How on earth could a woman have so many babies?" Because she was being so kind to me I let her help me lay out the little baby.

After this when David came to meet me once I had finished duty, I burst into tears and said that I wanted to go back to Colchester. David's answer was "You will get used to it."

Marriage And Family

David and Louie Brighton and David's friends
who were witnesses at our wedding.

A month later David arranged for our marriage. We got married in 1971 in a Registry Office. I did not like the man who married us as he was very cold and he did not smile at all. We only had three people present and one of those was David's mother. The other two were friends of David's, and one of them used to a girlfriend of his before we got married. A lot of Nurses would show each other their engagement rings but I wanted a watch instead of a ring so that was what I received from David.

On the day that I was getting married the ward Sister asked me to work but I said no because I had an appointment. Sister asked "Can't you cancel it?" But I replied with a firm "No!" Sister asked me why not and so I told her that I was getting married.

Sister looked taken aback at my news and asked me "Does Matron know?" When I told her that Matron did not know Sister said that I had to tell the Matron.

The next morning, in a clean apron, I took myself off to Matron's office and joined two Nurses who were also waiting to see Matron. When my turn came I knocked on the door in trepidation especially because Matron did not look in a good mood. I stood with my arms behind my back waiting for Matron to stop writing and then she asked "Yes, Nurse?" I told her that my Ward Sister had sent me to tell her that I was getting married. Matron looked at me and asked "Married! Who is this man?" So I answered her "The man I am going to marry!" Matron then asked me how long I had known him. I answered her "Three weeks, Matron."

After our wedding David and I went on honeymoon to Italy. We went to Rome one day on a coach trip. I was enjoying the journey but I suddenly thought in my mind that that the coach was going far too fast. We were travelling over the Dolomites and the driver was driving very fast around the bends. Then suddenly the coach crashed into a big maroon German car. The coach skidded to the edge of the cliff. There was a very deep drop in front of us and the front wheels of the coach were hanging over the edge. Usually the drivers had an argument as to whose fault it was but this time the drivers were so amazed at the angle of the coach and why it had not gone right over the edge. Everybody had to leave and we all left the coach very gingerly. Once I was off the coach, I stood still just looking around two ladies came over to me and asked me "Do you believe in God?" My immediate answer was "Yes, I am a Christian!" Then they said "That is why the coach didn't go over the edge!"

I really needed to 'spend a penny' but there weren't any toilets. I started to look for some place to use and when I discovered a wide silver pipe going into the ground. I decided to ask the women if they needed the toilet. They all said yes so I told them about the pipe I had found. Then we all stood around the pipe with our coats and cardigans in front of us and took it in turn to spend a penny.

After four hours of waiting in the hot sun the police arrived on the scene of the accident and were amazed at the way the coach was situated. They interviewed the drivers and then we were allowed to carry on with our journey back to the city of Rome.

We enjoyed the holiday but it was too hot for me! David had very dark skin so he could stand the heat better but I was glad to get back to the Midlands in England and get back to work.

After we were married we lived in David's home until we had a place of our own. Eventually we got a nice flat in Walsall, West Midlands and David taught me how to love, which did not come easily to me at all but David was very patient.

One morning while having my coffee break I was sitting opposite a young Nurse whose name was Rene and in conversation she told me that she was a Christian and attended the Assemblies of God in Walsall. She was expecting a baby and I didn't know it then, but I also was going to have a baby. Also I wasn't going to any church at that time so, in my mind, I decided to go to Rene's church and David came with me. I felt very happy in that church and then, one day, the Pastor of the church asked me if I would give my testimony, which I did. At the end of the service as I made my way to the main door to go home, a young man who was unknown to me came towards me and said, "Your testimony is exceptional. I have recorded it and it will be in the church magazine." I thanked him and continued on my way home.

Soon afterwards I discovered that I was expecting a baby. O the happy days that lay ahead! One morning while I was conducting the ward round with a young Doctor, he looked at me and remarked "You are going to have a baby!" I just laughed and said "Oh no!"

When I first found out that I was pregnant and I phoned my mother to tell her the news her reaction was not pleasant. She said, 'You know you don't like children. You are not capable enough to have children'. When I told David what my mother had said he wasn't pleased and said, 'Take no notice'.

By that time I was settled in that hospital and had adjusted to the Birmingham dialect. I also had my new friend, Rene, whose husband was a school teacher. I started to go off tea and coffee and I felt nauseous in the evening. I decided to visit the Doctor who told me that I was nearly six months pregnant. He referred me to the Gynaecologist because of my history of Poliomyelitis.

He hit me on the head with my case notes and asked me how long I had been married. When I told him he asked "Whatever did you do?" I just stared at him as he said "You are very fertile! You will be here again this time next year." Then he hit me again with my case notes. The Clinic Sister said to me "Take no notice, Mrs Brighton, he's doing a survey about women in their thirties and you came along, only married for a few months!"

One week when I went to the Antenatal Clinic to see the Gynaecologist there were two young Nurses training to do Midwifery there. He asked the Nurses if I was carrying a foetus or a tumour. I interrupted him and said "This is a funny tumour because it has got limbs!" The Nurses laughed but the Doctor said "Be quiet!" and he hit me again on my head. Then, another time, the Doctor asked the Nurses what they thought the scars on my side were and I said "Unless the Nurses have done Plastic Surgery they would not know" and again he hit me on my head. I laughed because he was joking with me.

I had a very easy pregnancy and there were no problems except that I was concerned that the baby might have a cleft palate. I had hardly any sickness and at eight months the Gynaecologist gave me a date for my baby's birth by Caesarean Section.

Back on the ward I was attending to a toddler who was very ill when the cleaner came waddling to me in the cubicle and asked me in her broad accent "Are you alright, my baby?" She always called me 'baby'! When the toddler died the cleaner was at my side and she stayed with me while I laid the baby out. I think she liked me as she was always kind towards me. I think she knew that I was expecting a baby.

Two babies were admitted to the ward suffering from meningitis and both babies died. It was very sad for the parents. One day a baby boy was admitted for tests on his stomach. He was screaming a lot. He was not allowed any fluids to drink at all and he would not stop crying. As I was holding him I felt the Lord say to me "Feed him, he is hungry." So I did give him a feed and he wolfed it down.

David wanted a place of our own and we found a nice flat in Walsall. David would never have a mortgage because he did not like owing money. David did not want me to do any more nursing because of the baby. As the baby was very active inside me I did not see any problem although I remained concerned about the baby's mouth would be like. The time had arrived to give in my notice. We decided to go home to Wales to visit my relatives in Rhyl and Prestatyn and my Mother arranged a party in a pub in Ruthin so that people could meet David. When I tried to tell my Father that I had passed exams in Colchester he just ignored me so my Aunts called me over to go and sit by them.

Louie and David Brighton

My parents lived in 'Hendrerwydd', next door to their pub which suited them. One evening after a night out my Father was slumped in the chair. My Mother was trying to get him to his bed so I went to help her. As I went to get hold of his arm he hissed at me and shouted "Get out of my sight!"

My Mother said "Louie, go to bed. You are upsetting your Father." Then David went to help my mother and my father said to him, 'Hello, David, it is nice to see you'.

Then on another evening my mother attempted to attack me after they had been out drinking. David was furious with her. I told him "It's alright, David, I am used to it!" I think poor David was glad to leave there and to get back to our home!

I had always wanted to go to Rome in Italy and when David had two weeks holiday off we went for a holiday. We went around the sights where St. Paul had been and we also saw the prison where Paul was held in chains. I could not eat the food in the hotel but we found a cafe and I liked the toast that they served. We went on a coach trip to Pompeii, an ancient city that was near to the volcano, Vesuvius in Italy. I did not like travelling on the plane. To me it seemed very eerie and I was glad to get back home.

When we arrived back my friend, Rene was very close to having her baby. The people at the church knew that we were having a baby and David always came to church with me. However I was still very concerned deep down inside about the baby's mouth. One day my sister rang to ask me if I would like to have her maternity dresses, and I immediately answered her "Yes!" I decided to visit and to see my parents in Ruthin but after a few days I remembered that I had an appointment with the Gynaecologist which meant that I would have to return to Walsall.

My Mother told my Father that he would have to give me a lift to Chester but I could see that he was very annoyed. He said to me "Get in the car and don't speak." By the time we started out it was dark and also my Father wanted his dinner before we set out. Then, after a while of driving down a dark lane my Father suddenly stopped the car and said "Get out, I am going no further!" I was left in a dark lane with a heavy suitcase and eight months pregnant. I dragged myself to the main road and found a bus stop.

After waiting for what seemed a long time it started to rain. Then a car stopped and a young man opened the car window and said that there were no buses until the morning. He asked me where I was going and I answered "Chester."

I had started to think that I would have to walk to Chester! The young man got out of his car, came round to me and put my case in the boot and said "I will take you to Chester." Now I believe that was the Lord sending me an angel. I arrived in Chester and the young man drove off after seeing me inside the station. He looked a very pleasant young man.

My friend Rene had a baby boy and three months later I was admitted to the hospital to have my baby by Caesarean Section. When I came round after the anaesthetic David was standing by my bed and said "We have a daughter and her mouth is normal." I thanked the Lord. I did not see my baby for two days and I did not know why but a Nurse brought her into my room in an incubator.

Then, one day, a Nurse came into my room and said to me "You made me cry!" I asked her why and she told me that before I came round from the anaesthetic I was asking about the baby's mouth. She was a Theatre Nurse and told me that I had a very pretty baby. I was in a lot of pain and Pethidine was prescribed for me. Eventually I was moved on to the Main Ward.

One evening David came and told me "I have the electric bill to show you." I said "David that is the last thing I want to see!" All the other mothers had flowers and boxes of chocolates but they said that my husband was attractive looking! We called our baby Rachel because that was David's favourite name. After twelve days I was discharged from hospital and we took our baby Rachel home.

Rachel was a very good baby and always slept at night. But I had a terrible accident when Rachel was only three months old and still a very small baby. My friend Rene and I took turns each week to visit each other on a Wednesday. One day I was on my way to Rene's home in Walsall and by the church there was a steep hill. At the bottom of the hill I saw a big white van parked but I did not see a car coming on the other side of the road. As I stepped into the road a car crashed into Rachel's pram. The poor baby shot up into the air and fell head first into the gutter. Her pram was smashed up. I just stood there in the road and the driver of the car came running over to me and said "Pick up your baby." but I could not move. I did pick her up eventually.

Then I started to shout at the driver and I said "Look what you have done to my pram. It's Christmas and I've no money."

The driver asked me where I had bought the pram from and I told him it was from Mothercare. Then the driver said "You carry your baby and I will carry what is left of the pram to Mothercare."

When we got to the shop the driver explained what had happened and the shop girl rang the Manager who came and gave me a new pram. I did not take Rachel to the hospital but I carried on to my friend's house. Rene was a Sister in the local hospital and when I told her about the accident Rene examined Rachel's eyes and said that the pupils of her eyes were normal. When David came home from work I told him about the accident and he was not very pleased at all. He said that I should have taken her to the hospital but as she was talking in baby talk and appeared to be happy I did not bother to.

One day Rene took me to see her friend. She was a young girl called Kay who had a little boy and another baby on the way. Then, to my surprise, Kay started to tell me that a Mr. North was coming to their Fellowship Church. He was the very powerful preacher who I had met in Liverpool through a friend.

During that time David and I made arrangements to have Rachel dedicated to the Lord Jesus. David and I went to the Assemblies of God in Walsall but one Sunday night I felt that the Lord gave me a desire to go to the Fellowship Church which was held in a flat by a Mr. and Mrs. Paul Evans. They were a young couple. The people who attended the Fellowship Church were Christians and it started to grow. I was quite content in my own church although I was still being plagued by terrible nightmares.

One night during my sleep I hit David across his face and he jumped out of bed and shouted at me. I told him that I had had a nightmare. They were usually the same dream about faces with no noses, ears or lips. I was also nervous about Rachel going near any fire and even to this day I will not use a chip pan because many years ago when I was in hospital I saw a badly burned face due to a chip pan fire.

Apart from all that I was quite happy in my life and also in the church. I started to go to the Women's meeting and, one afternoon, the speaker was coming towards the main door when she saw me holding Rachel and remarked "O, that's a baby! I thought you were holding a doll!" People in the church thought that Rachel was very pretty.

One day, while changing Rachel's clothes, there was a knock at the front door and when I opened it there was a young man who asked me "Can I look in your home?" so I answered him "Yes." After he had a look round I made him a cup of tea. Then he started to tell me about his problems so I told him about the church. He asked me where my husband was and I told him that he was at work. Then he said "You have a pretty baby." And then he left.

The next day the police came round the houses to ask if we had seen a young man. I said "No." It turned out that he had broken into houses in the area. David was annoyed with me when I told him about it. The next thing was when David was working a late shift I was washing up after putting Rachel to bed. I looked up and there was a face looking at me through the kitchen window. So I went and asked him if I could help him. He asked me if I would make him a cup of tea and toast. He was a tramp. Before he left he asked me for 50p for a bed at the Salvation Army so I gave him my last bit of money. When I told David he was not very pleased and asked me if I was going mad so I answered him "No, I just felt sorry for him." The next day I heard that the neighbours had rung the police to complain about the tramps in the area.

Rachel was doing well and was a healthy baby. The doctor told me that I had an alert and bright baby. When she was six months old she was talking very well. One day my sewing machine wouldn't work so I had a man in to repair it. While he was working I went to get some money to pay him and when I came back he said "I thought there was another adult in the room and when I looked all there was a baby talking." When Rachel was three years old I took her to a nursery for toddlers. She was very happy there but the only problem was I had difficulty getting Rachel to eat.

Rachel would only eat Heinz baby food so I took her to the doctor's surgery who told me that Rachel was very healthy and not to worry.

During that time David lost his job. He was in the RAF for five years as a wireless operator. After the RAF he had a job for the Post Office phones but after a few years he was made redundant. I prayed that he would find another job as we were finding it hard to make ends meet. I remember one night for our meal I had some sausages which had nearly gone bad but I cut round them and fried them to nearly burnt we ate them with plenty of tomato ketchup and they went down well! Another meal that we had was chicken that was nearly bad but I cooked it until it was nearly burnt. I think I must have had a stomach like a horse!

Also I used to do a lot of sewing with my machine. I used to make dresses and blouses for Rachel and me. My Grandma Baker had taught me to knit and crochet. I also did a lot of baking, such as big fruit cakes. My speciality was Christmas cakes which always contained brandy! Rachel was happy in nursery and David got a new job with the West Midland County Council on Spaghetti Junction, Birmingham. I started to miss hospital work so I discussed the matter with David and I told him how I felt so we decided that I should apply to the local hospital. Shortly afterwards I received a letter asking me to go for an interview. I felt very apprehensive while I was waiting outside the Head Nurses' office. When at last I was called in for my interview I was face to face with two men who appeared very pleasant. They told me that they received excellent high standard references from my previous Matrons and then they asked me questions about my experience in nursing. They then offered me a Ward Sister's post. Of course I immediately replied "No!" A look of surprise came over their faces! The reason was that I could not imagine myself in an office and chasing Nurses during their work on the ward. I also had to think about Rachel because she was only three years old. After questioning me some more the Nursing Officer gave me a Staff Nurse's post which suited me. Rachel would be going to the hospital nursery which was for the children belonging to hospital staff.

I walked to the hospital with Rachel skipping along for my first morning on duty. We had a forty minutes' walk to get there. Rachel was all smiles as I took her into the nursery but I noticed that the other children were crying when they were left but Rachel said:, "Go to work, Mum, or you will be late."

I reported to the Ward Sister who appeared quite pleasant. After making beds I was given dressings to do. One poor patient was suffering from open cancer in her legs and the dressing was very unpleasant. During February of that year, after I had been there a few weeks a flu epidemic broke out and some patients died and a lot of the staff were off sick. The Night Sister was amused because I kept turning up on duty every morning. When I finished my shift I went to collect Rachel from the nursery and she did not usually want to leave. Rachel would say to me "It's not time yet, Mum." but once we were on our way home she seemed happy.

One morning while having my coffee break with two Nurses I saw through the window the nursery staff taking the little children for a walk. I opened the window but the Nurses said to me "No, Rachel will be upset if she sees you." I said "Oh no, watch this!" and I said hello to Rachel. Her answer was "I'm going for a walk, Mum. You go back to work." One day when I collected Rachel from the nursery I took her to the ward because the patients wanted to see her. After the struggle to get her away from the nursery we went to the ward and the Ward Sister made a fuss of her and put her Nurse's cap on her head. Then Rachel went round all the patients and said "I Rachel Brighton. I three years old."

The day arrived when she started school in the Infant's department because she was four and a half years old. The only problem was that that I did not realise the effect it would have on me. During those years we went to a Christian Fellowship and Rachel went to Sunday school. I never met Rachel out of her school, which was called 'The Blue Coat School,' even though it was very near to where we lived. One day when Rachel came home from school she told me "Mum, I have given my heart to Jesus." She went down onto her knees to talk to Jesus. She was five years old. Because I had such an aversion to schools, David always went to the parents' evenings to meet the teachers. Rachel did well in school. She enjoyed it and appeared to be very happy. She had a lot of friends and because she was an only child I let her have her friends to come to our home for tea. She also had a boyfriend. He was a nice little six-year-old. When he came for tea he was very polite. One day his Mother came to see me and told me that he had asked his Father for extra pocket money to buy Rachel Brighton an engagement ring, which he did. They were happy together.

Back at the hospital I was not so happy! The reason was that one of the Nurses told me that the Staff did not like me, but in my mind I knew that the Lord would turn the tables, which He did. It was the middle aged Nurses that I found to be a problem. I could not quite understand their accents and because of that they accused me of being stand-offish or even posh. The real truth was that I had no confidence but the patients seemed to like me. If the staff didn't like me, I thought "Tough, it was their problem, not mine!" In my mind I decided to put my head down and work hard.

Eventually things changed. One day I was put on the Surgical Ward for a few days. Then, shock of all shocks, I was put in charge! During the day there were seven operations that I had to report on so I decided to pray for them. One of the young men who was supposed to be very ill sat up and remarked "I'm hungry!" Then towards evening as I was trying to work out some charts and the medication for each patient, I was struggling to decide what to do a Nurse was by my side and started to do all the things that I found difficult. The strange thing was that she did not speak at all but she looked very pleasant.

When the Nursing Officer came to do a ward round I said thank you for the extra Nurse. She gave me a strange look and said "I did not send you any Nurse." I asked the two Nurses with whom I was working if they saw a Nurse with me attending to the operation cases and they answered "No!" So I said "You must have seen her because you were quite near to me!" Again they said that they had not seen a Nurse and they asked me if I had been taking some drug. I replied "No, I do not take drugs!" I was able to put into the day report what the Nurse had written. It was a complete mystery!

I started on a new ward and on the first day the Ward Sister gave me a look of disdain. Little did either of us know at that moment what was to come! One day the Ward Sister told me to collect blood from the blood bank for a patient. Sister handed me the form to fill in but I had a problem with filling in forms so I decided to ask someone in the main corridor where I should go for help but to my surprise there was no one in the usually crowded corridor. Then suddenly a tall man with black hair approached me and beckoned me to follow him, which I did. He led me up a flight of stairs into a large room. Then he took the form off me, filled the form in and handed me the blood. Also I had to sign for the blood. I noticed that he didn't speak and when I turned round to thank him he was not there. I didn't hear the door open or close. When I went back down stairs the corridor was busy again with people. It was all surreal! The ward Sister was surprised that I was back so soon. For many days after I was looking out for that man and also for the nurse who came to help me on the ward. I even asked at the reception by the entrance on the main corridor but no one knew. I thought at the time that it was a complete mystery. I am convinced that they must have been angels sent to help me in times of need.

Back on the ward one of the doctors that I got on well with was Asian. He always appeared to be nice and happy until one day a new patient was admitted on to the ward. The ward Sister asked me to go with the doctor to examine the patient. All was well until the Doctor took out his stethoscope and showed me the ends of the tubes that the Doctor puts in his ears. I could see that the ends were black and white which were different colours from usual. Without giving it too much thought I immediately said "All are precious in His sight." Which are the words from a song "Jesus Loves The Little Children, All the children of the world..." by C. Herbert Woolston. I noticed an immediate change in the Doctor's face; he looked very annoyed and asked "Whose sight?" I answered him "Jesus Christ. He died for us." He looked very severe and he just walked away from me. He went to see Sister and told her that he did not want to examine the patient with me anymore and then he left the ward. Sister looked surprised and asked me what was going on. She said "Nurse Brighton, I think you have just lost a friend!" I told Sister what I had just said to the Doctor and Sister raised her eyes up. I felt a bit sad that I might have lost a friend. At that time I was also ignorant about his religion. But worse was to come!

One evening I was going off duty with another Nurse who lived near me. It was 9:00pm and very dark and as we were walking under a bridge I noticed two men coming towards us. I recognised one as being the Doctor. My companion started to chat cheerfully to them. Then suddenly the Doctor who I knew put his hands around my neck and said to his friend "I could kill this Nurse!" He really hurt me and as I felt the pain in my neck I heard my companion shout, "Leave her, let her go!" Then he let me go and walked off.

It was a good thing that someone was with me. The next day I had bruises all around my neck. When the Nurse who I was with the night before saw my neck she told me to report him. I did not report him but I have never forgotten the incident.

During the time that I was working on the wards I always tried to witness to the patients. One morning the Ward Sister took me into the dressing room and said to me "I do not care what you do in your private life but keep your religion off my ward!" Little did I know that Sister was going to change my working life!

One morning while I was making a bed with Sister the patient was reading a book which Sister took an interest in. When they had finished chatting about books the patient asked me "What book are you reading?" My answer was "Anne Frank." This was the story of a young girl from Holland who hid from the Germans in a in a secret annexe because she was Jewish. Eventually she and her family were arrested by the Gestapo and sent to a concentration camp called Bergen Belson. She died there two months before Holland was freed from Germany by the Soviet armies. The Sister with whom I was working was an Austrian Jew and she told me that her Father and Anne Frank's Father were cousins. Also Sister's Father was a Professor and he had realised that what the German Nazis were planning for the Jews so he left Germany and came to England. Eventually Sister started training to be a Nurse in Walsall, West Midlands. Sometime later she married a Mr. Yates and went on to become a Ward Sister.

Then, one day, Sister said to me "Nurse Brighton, I want to speak to you" In my mind I was trying to remember what Sister thought I might have done wrong but to my surprise Sister said "I need a favour. I trust you. Would you come to my home and I will speak to you." We arranged a time for me to go but I also told her that I would have to bring Rachel with me because she was only seven years old and David was working. I told Rachel to be on her best behaviour.

When we arrived at Sister's home she made us something to eat and drink. Sister appeared to be completely different from how she was on the ward. She was friendly towards us and not at all strict.

After we had chatted for a while and Rachel had asked a lot of questions Sister asked me if I would help her in her home and I said yes.

During that time I was helping a Doctor called Ruth who was a missionary in India for many years with her husband. I was friends with their daughter, Rachel, who was a trained Nurse and Midwife.

We used to go on bike rides together. Rachel and I were in the same church and fellowship. One day Ruth asked me if I would help a lady missionary who was in Africa but had now retired. She needed help to have a bath. There were also two other elderly ladies who needed help. All that extra work meant that I was getting very tired although I knew that the Lord was with me. Then, one day, we had a new patient admitted with gangrene in his leg. It was crawling with maggots and we had to dress the leg. I remember that it was a very hot day and I was thinking that I was just about to collapse when suddenly a very strong breeze came through the open window. The Nurse who was with me said "Where did that come from?" I knew that it came from the Lord.

One morning while helping an elderly lady she asked me if I would help another lady, Miss James. I said that I would go to see her. Then Miss Robinson said "Make a fuss of her cat and you will be alright." I went to see Miss James but, oh dear, I had not realised what I would be letting myself in for! When I went into her home she was in bed. I introduced myself to her she looked very severe and asked me my name. When I told her it was Louie she said "What was wrong with your parents that they called you a man's name?" I did not answer her. Then she said "You are not from Walsall. Where are you from?" I answered "Prestatyn, North Wales" she said "You are never Welsh!" So I said, "No, Miss James." Then she said "When you work for me I shall expect you to go into all the corners and I don't like your name so I am going to call you Rhyl." She had a very deep voice which was a bit posh. When she asked me what work I did, I told her I was a Nurse she sat up in bed and said "I don't like Nurses." I said "I am sorry to hear that, Miss James." She was condescending in her manner towards me but strangely I began to like her. I felt it was a challenge for me when she decided in her mind to let me help her. During that time I was still working in the hospital.

One day when I was on duty one of the Nurses asked me if I was ill because I looked terrible and then David started to comment on how tired I looked and told me to either give up nursing or cleaning for the elderly. Then, one day when I was at Anne's home cleaning out one of her cupboards I heard the Lord saying to me "This is the way, walk in it." I decided to give in my notice at the hospital. The Nursing Officer did not want to accept my notice and I knew that I would miss some of the nursing staff because we did have some fun on the ward. When I told my friend Doctor Ruth she thought that I had made the right decision. In some ways I felt a bit sorry but David was pleased because it was getting more difficult to look after Rachel as David was working shifts.

So after that I was helping five elderly ladies and the most difficult one was Miss James. One day she wanted me to take down the lamp shades to clean them. I was standing on the top step of the ladder and I was feeling terrified in case the ladder collapsed or I dropped the glass shades. Miss James started to insult me by saying I don't know what your husband saw in you; you are all bone and you are scarred. I replied "Neither do I, Miss James, perhaps he needs new glasses!"

At that time in my life I did not know what David saw in me so I was inclined to agree with her. Then one morning she accused me of taking her whisky. I said "Miss James, whisky is the last thing on this earth that I would drink. It reminds me of my Father!" After that it was a dress that she thought I had taken but I told her that I was a size 10, not an 18, and I just burst out laughing. Another day she asked me to go with her in a taxi to visit her long-time friends from childhood. When we arrived at their home to my surprise they called me 'Rhyl' and told me that I must be a Saint to stay with her because three others had already left her but I knew through prayer that the Lord wanted me to stay where I was. The next day Miss James told me that her friends did not believe that I was a Nurse and that they did not like me. My answer was "Miss James, I did not come here to be liked. I came here to help you."

Miss James asked me one day "How about giving me a bath?" After tea I went to give her a bath but it was an awful struggle. Miss James was a tall, well sized lady who suffered from emphysema, a lung disease.

I managed to get her into the bath but I could not get her out of it. She was going very blue and, try as I might, I could not lift her because she was too heavy for me. When I told her she was too strenuous for me and I would have to get help she started to get distressed and bluer so I asked the Lord to help me and then I just got hold of her around her waist and pulled. Miss James said "Rhyl, where did your strength come from?" I answered "The Lord!" then she put her hands around my neck and shook me.

One day she asked me to leave my husband and live with her but I told her "Miss James, I will never leave my husband!" One evening I had a premonition that something was wrong so I went to Miss James and found her on the floor in a lot of pain. I told her that I would ring the Doctor. I managed to get her into bed and when the Doctor arrived he wanted her to go into hospital but she refused. The Doctor said "You can't stay here alone." She answered "Rhyl will stay here with me." The Doctor was a bit confused and asked; "Rhyl?" Miss James got hold of my arm and said "This is Rhyl!" The Doctor looked even more confused and asked me "Are you able to stay with Miss James?" I said that I would and then she said to the Doctor "When I snuff it I want Rhyl to lay me out. I have spoken to the solicitor about Rhyl."

Miss James had never worked in her life. She came from a very wealthy family who owned a lot of property in the Midlands. She did not like men or children but she loved animals and she was eccentric. My friend, Doctor Ruth, knew Miss James from childhood. One day, after praying for Miss James, Ruth said to me "I will go to see her and tell her about you." The next thing was that Miss James did not appreciate Ruth telling her about me and when I next saw her she said to me "Rhyl, if you were as bad as Ruth told me you were it is a pity that your Mother did not put your head in a bucket of water!" I started to laugh because I could just imagine my Mother putting my head in a bucket of water!

Then, one day, the Doctor rang me up because Miss James was dying and she wanted to see me. When I went to her I could see that she was dying. She started to tell me that she had been a swine to people and I said "Yes, Jamie, I can well believe you!"

Then I said to her "If you confess your sins to the Lord Jesus He will forgive you and if you accept Him as your Saviour you will be saved from hell and you will have peace in your heart and mind."

The next day Miss James died and I was quite upset. The Doctor rang me to do the laying out of her body. After her funeral and cremation I cleared her house as the Solicitor asked me what I would like from the house. I asked for the photos as they were of Rhyl and I still have them. She also left me £500 which came at the right time for us as we had moved into a new house.

I went to visit my mother in Ruthin for a few days and David took Rachel to Brixham in Devon. I travelled on my bike and it took me 6 hours. David had made out a map for me but I took the wrong turning and ended up on the motorway. The drivers in the cars all looked at me and then I saw the Police! I managed to avoid them by going into a field. After that incident I carried on to Llangollen and I arrived sooner than I expected. Then I cycled on to the Horseshoe Pass to the amazement of some young men who were riding on racing bikes.

Eventually I arrived in Ruthin and by that time I could hardly walk. When I reached my Mother's home I was thanking the Lord for a safe journey but my Mother thought that I was mad and told me so. The next day my legs were agony. My Mother was then living alone as my Father had died in 1977. I never cried and I never missed him. When I told my Mother that I had given up working in the hospital she said "After all those years!"

When David rang he made me promise that I would go back to Walsall by train. Of course I said "Yes." but I had no intention of going home on the train! The journey back to Walsall started off badly because it was raining heavily and blowing a gale. Again I took a wrong turning and ended up in a farm. Three Alsatian dogs came running towards me but I wasn't nervous because I love dogs. One was running in front of me and the other two were at either side of me. I remember bending down to scratch the dogs' ears. When I got back to the main road I saw a sign which said Wrexham 8 miles. I decided then that I would go to Walsall by train. The station porters helped me with my bike and David was waiting at the station for me. He said "I am glad you had the sense to come back by train."

After the death of Miss James I missed her greatly. My friend, Doctor Ruth, asked me if I would go and visit another of her friends. A lady called Doctor Gillum, a retired doctor. She was a lovely lady; the complete opposite of Miss James. She lived in a big house and to my amazement, her house was full of cats and plants! The cats were everywhere, on the gas stove, in the fridge and also in the toilet! Her cats had all been wild once. One day when I went to see her there was a man on the roof of her house. When he came down the ladder he said "Well, Doctor, you do have a problem. It is a cat and her kittens." But the Doctor did not seem to mind because she loved cats. Then, one day, I found a little black kitten in our drive. I knew where he had come from and when I told the Doctor she said that I could keep him so I called the kitten 'James' after Miss James. The only problem was that we already had five cats! David did not mind all those cats and he wrote poetry about them.

Then one morning a young man who lived next door came to me with two tiny kittens and asked "Louie, will you take these kittens?" so I replied "Simon, I already have five cats and also a dog!" Then he said "Two more won't make much difference, then!" What could I say? I accepted them and then we had seven cats and one dog. Fortunately David and I loved animals. Oh what fun we had with the dog and the cats but then we soon found out who was the boss – the cats! Poor Kim did not stand any chance, especially over the fire. The cats would hit her across her face but she survived.

Our next door neighbour, who was the image of Stephen Fry in his face and body, had a Staffordshire bull terrier called Bod. He was in a dog kennel and was chained up day and night even in the cold weather. Of course, I was, and still am, a dog lover and it upset me especially when the poor dog was howling during the night. I used to go out to the dog with a warm blanket and some dog food and afterwards she would go to sleep. Next day when I saw the dog's owner, John, I asked him if I could look after his dog and if he would allow his dog to play with Kim, our dog, in our garden. John's answer was "Yes, but don't blame me if she bites you and beware of the way she might react to your dog because bull terriers don't like other dogs but they love people." I told him that I would take full responsibility. Fortunately for me the dogs played well together.

Then, one day, while the dogs were in the garden, the bull terrier jumped over our garden wall and ran into the main street and I was so worried in case she got run over. Then, I prayed for the dog to come back and walked around the streets looking for her. There was no sign of the dog so I went home and just as I got in there was a knock at the door. I opened it to find the men who had come to read the electric meter. I asked him if he had seen a Staffordshire bull terrier on is rounds. He said "Yes!" He told me that he had taken the dog to an animal rescue centre. When I told him that I was looking after the dog for my next door neighbour and that the dog had escaped from the garden he assured me "I will get her back for you" He did and I gave him £5 for his trouble.

Then, one evening when I was taking Kim, our dog, for a walk I saw a tall Asian man with a Doberman called 'Kharthen'. Kim ran towards his dog and as the man started to put his dog on the lead I shouted "No! Do not put him on his lead because my dog is friendly!" Then the man asked "Who are you? Usually people are nervous of my dog." So I told him who I was. His name was Sarvish and his parents owned a shop in the High Street. Then, of course, we got to know each other. He was a Christian and went to the Pentecostal church. When I told him that I also was a Christian he said "Yes, I know."

So one Sunday evening I went with him to his church and then another evening he came with me to the fellowship. His relatives were Hindu. My friend Doctor Ruth was not very happy about me being friends with Sarvish. The reason she gave was that we were both married. When I started to protest and told her we were just friends through the dogs, Ruth said that other people would not see it like that. Then the Pastor of his church told us that it was wrong to be seen together. Sarvish told him that I was not interested in him, only in his dog and he was right.

One evening when we were walking the dogs I saw a young black man with two Rottweilers. The problem was that Khan always guarded my dog Kim and as the dogs were approaching us Sarvish said "Louie, pray!" I already was! Then one of the dogs went into the play position and the other dog looked as though it was laughing! While I was making a fuss of the dogs the owner said to me, "People do not seem to like me and my dogs because I am black."

I told him that it was the dogs that made people nervous due to reports in the media causing people to worry about different breeds of dogs. So I told him not to worry but to take care of the dogs.

During that time David and I were not financially well off and David was still working. I decided to apply to a Nursing Home for work.

After my interview with the Matron I was accepted. I was very happy there. I worked as a Staff Nurse for two years on days and one year on nights. Working nights was a physical challenge for me and I started to lose weight. I went down to six stone. Rachel used to come to the home to talk to the residents and they liked her. She was 12 years old.

One day the Matron of the home told the staff that a clairvoyant was coming. Of course I was not very happy about that news and I told some of the staff that it was demonic and that I would not be there that evening to hear the clairvoyant. I am afraid that those spoken words did not go down very well with the staff. A resident who was very confused told the Matron that I had locked her in a cupboard, which of course I had not. Fortunately for me the Nurse who was working with me that night was able to say that was untrue. Then, to my surprise, one morning, the Matron rang me up to tell me that I was no longer needed at the home. In other words, I had the sack. After being dismissed I could not believe it because it was so surreal. When I told David he said "You are better off leaving the home!" But my friend did not see it like that and said that I should report it to the tribunal. I did not want all that trouble so I decided in my mind to accept it from the Lord Jesus. Not only that but I knew that clairvoyance could ruin a person's life because I had enough personal experienced of it in my past.

After leaving the Nursing Home I continued to help my elderly ladies and also Doctor Ruth who appreciated me. Doctor Ruth thought that my Mother was a brave lady for taking me to hospitals during the war years. Ruth also knew about the surgery that I'd had on my mouth. She kept telling me to write a book. At that time I did not take any notice about writing a book. I did not know it then that David and I would experience a big change in our lives because at the time our lives were going well. We were still attending the Fellowship in Walsall and I thought that we would be there for the rest of our lives but the Lord Jesus had other plans!

One day I received a phone call after which my life completely changed. Praise our Lord Jesus!

During my daily life at Walsall, West Midlands, I was quite happy. Then, one day, David became ill with very high blood pressure. The

Doctor put him on sick leave. At that time he was still working on the Spaghetti Junction and he was also on call even during the night.

Then one evening when I was getting ready to go out I asked David to wipe up the dishes after our meal. When he started to dry the dishes he collapsed on the sofa still holding the wiping-up towel. So I remarked "David, I only asked you to wipe up!" When I told Doctor Ruth she said that David had had a TIA stroke. Eventually when David went for an appointment to see a Specialist he told David that he would no longer be able to work due to very high blood pressure. David also had many hobbies such as painting country scenery and also making ships using table legs or pieces of wood. He made old ships like 'The Golden Hind', 'The Cutty Sark', 'The Victory', and 'The Bounty'. I still have these ships which take me some time to look after due to all the rigging ropes on them.

Then one evening when I was in the church meeting it was announced that there was to be a big meeting taking place in a marquee in Birmingham for all the churches in the Midlands so in my mind I decided to go. Oh dear, I did not know what was coming! Off I went with people from my church. We arrived at the big marquee which was packed with people from other churches.

Usually I felt tired during the meetings especially during the sermon but one evening when the preacher was speaking I was suddenly aware of what he was saying. I heard him say that if there was something in your conscious mind or subconscious mind the Lord will bring it to your conscious mind to be prayed for and to repent for and ask for healing. During that meeting I did not think that I had anything to repent of or forgive for but when I arrived home I decided in my mind to ask the Lord if there was anything. As I was on my knees praying I thought I heard a voice saying what about Rhyl and Prestatyn. I started to think about the awful memories I had of Rhyl and Prestatyn and how I hated the schools I was supposed to attend but I had not and about the hatred I had for the teachers. At that time the only love I felt was only for the Doctors, Nurses and hospitals. I was in awe of them and most probably looked upon the Ward Sister as my Mother.

I also felt hatred towards the Manager of the Scala Cinema who was called Saronie which was not his real name. I had resentment towards my Father who was born in the house in Fforddisa that we were then living in. My Grandmother had thirteen children in that house one of whom was my Father. Four of my Grandmother's children died in early childhood.

One night I was dreaming and in the dream one of my Father's sisters told me to go back to Prestatyn. Then I went to stay with my Auntie who was living in Fforddisa and was trying to sell her house but without any success. Then I knew why my Auntie went into a Nursing Home and her family put the house up for rent. I asked if I could stay in her flat for two nights which I did.

Then on the Sunday I decided to go to church. When I reached the Church of England church in the High Street in Prestatyn I changed my mind and then I started to walk over the railway bridge into Victoria Road and past the Police station. I had intended to walk as far as the Ffrith but then I saw a church across the road. It was called Calvary Pentecostal Church. I walked in and sat at the back of the church with a hymn book. After a few songs a young man started to pray and prophesy. Some of the prophecy went like this: there is someone in the church who is in indecision about moving into a house. This is the way for you to move. I could hardly believe what I was hearing but I realised that the Lord was speaking to me.

When I went back to Walsall I had to discuss the move with David. To my surprise, he was all for moving to Prestatyn but I thought that it would be hard for him leaving all his friends and different groups that he attended There was a lot to sort out on David's side but nothing on mine. My Auntie was pleased to hear that we were going to rent her house in Fforddisa. After we had made all the arrangements which went well we came to live in Prestatyn within a month. Our dog, Kim and our cat, Paddington came with us.

I did not know it then but I was going to be confronted with my past childhood! We settled down well and were happy in the house. It was the Lord's plan for me to receive healing from my past. One day while taking our dog Kim for a walk I came across a church called Deva Chapel. When I read the notice board I realised that it was the prayer meeting that evening and I decided to go.

During the prayer time I started to pray and I was the only woman in the meeting who prayed. I also remember that a young man who was playing the piano came over to me and asked me my name and where I had come from and also said that they had been praying for a long time for women to pray in the prayer meetings. On the Sunday morning David came with me to the church. He liked the church and the people seemed to like him but he also liked the pub next to the church called the Jolly Sailor. He enjoyed a pint. During that time Rachel was still in Walsall in the West Midlands and she rang one day to tell us that she was expecting a baby. She also said that she and the baby's Father were coming to stay with us for Christmas. He appeared to be very nice and polite; however I did not feel very happy about the news of the baby as Rachel was not married but I had to accept that.

After a few weeks of attending Deva Church which seemed to me to be like a Brethren church I heard about the Community Church while taking the dog for a walk. I decided to see what it was like and one Sunday I went to the meeting which was held in the old Scala cinema. I liked it immediately as the meeting seemed to be more filled with the Holy Spirit and I also attended the mid-week meetings. One Sunday morning during the meeting a young man stood up and requested prayer for his friend who was ill. After some prayer I believed that the Lord would heal the young man who was in hospital. The Lord was changing me too and I was remembering all the bad memories of childhood and I started to cry. Then I told the leading brother of the church that I did not like children. He told me that I had been damaged by them but while I was nursing I loved the children in the hospitals and also when I was a patient. Then, one day while walking over Vale Road Bridge, I had some kind of a flash back. It came to my mind that I could smell burns and a strange kind of taste came into my mouth. Tears came into my eyes and ran down my face and I said "Lord, what was all this about?" I remembered going to Emmanuel School after I had come back from Gloucester, after seeing all the terrible sights of burns when I was a child in hospital.

One day I decided to visit the young man who was ill in hospital and I felt that it was right in the Lord Jesus to take him something that I had written.

When I arrived on the ward the male Charge Nurse brought him out to see me in the visitor's room. His name was Colin and he knew who I was as he had heard about me. I told him how I was healed from a mental breakdown. When Colin was discharged from hospital he came to visit me at home and told me that he was having a prayer meeting at his house and he invited me to attend. I went along and met a lovely lady called Gwen Morris. I enjoyed the prayer meetings at Colin's home.

Then one evening I had a phone call from a Social worker in Walsall asking me if I would have my granddaughter and I replied "Yes, I would." Also my Auntie died and my Cousins who owned the house that we were renting wanted it back again. That meant David and I had to find some place to live. It was a very difficult time but through it all I knew and felt that the Lord was with me

One day when I was reading the local newspaper called 'The Visitor' I saw that a man called Harry Thomas was going to show slides of pictures of old Prestatyn and Rhyl. I made a decision that I would go. I went along to the show in the old Scala picture house by Harry Thomas. He showed slides of old Prestatyn during my Grandmother's time. To my surprise Harry showed a slide of my Grandmother's house on Marine road, Prestatyn, where I was born. I told Harry that I was born in that house and a few weeks later Harry gave me a big photograph of the house. It was also a boarding house for visitors. During the coffee break two ladies came to see me and said "We remember you when you were a little girl in your Grandma's house." I cannot adequately describe what I felt at that time as it was not a feeling of pleasure! I found it very painful. My memories were affecting me mentally and I was always in tears. Poor David could not understand my crying and said "Louie, that was years ago!" but to me it seemed like yesterday.

Then one evening after leaving the Scala a lady walked home with me and asked me where I lived. I told her "Fforddisa." As we started to walk through the Bryn Rhosyn estate which had consisted of council houses when I was young, I asked the lady what was her address and she answered "27, Central Avenue." Then I told her that I lived in that house when I was a young child. The lady invited me into the house and a strange feeling came into my mind.

I walked to a wall near the kitchen and said to the lady "Under the wallpaper there is a dent in the concrete wall where my Father threw a carving knife at me!" The lady did not say anything and then I left and went home in tears. I recalled that the knife had just missed my neck and that my father could have killed me.

During another evening while watching Harry Thomas' slides he showed a picture of an old jeweller's and watchmaker's shop called 'Hughes Bros'. That was the shop where my Father bought a watch for my Grandma when she was twenty one years old. Grandma gave me that watch when I was sixteen and I still have it. It is 115 years old and it is still going! When she gave it to me she said "I want you, Louie, to have this watch because when I first saw your poor face you went straight into my heart." That was just as well because Grandma paid for some of my operations and also an Auntie, who was my Mother's eldest Sister and who was a Music Teacher, paid for others.

Harry Thomas was very interested in my watch and still is! One day he asked me to bring the watch to his evening slide show and while showing the slide of the jeweller's shop he showed the audience my Grandmother's watch.

During the following few weeks the Community Church in Prestatyn came to an end. I felt very sorry because I had loved the church but the Lord had other plans. I started to go to Calvary Church on Victoria Road in Prestatyn but I could not settle down. Also my sister who was born after me died of cancer. Then one day I had a phone call from Rhiannon's Social Worker telling me that Rachel's partner was making threats to harm me and if he came I was to ring the Police. I took no notice because I knew him and I was mental health trained but I knew the Lord would protect me.

Also, due to my Cousin, we received a letter from the council to say we had been allocated a rented flat in Pentwyn, Prestatyn. When we went to see the flat I fell in love with it and David signed the forms to say that we accepted the tenancy. Soon afterwards the Social Worker in the Midlands sent Rachel and Rhiannon to live with us. It was hard but David loved children, especially Rhiannon. He was a very good Father and Grandfather. Rachel got a job in a hotel called the Grange which was opposite the sea front in Rhyl.

I remember one evening near Christmas time when I was on my way to a meeting and the Grange hotel was all lit up with Christmas lights and decorations. Because Rachel worked there I was able to go inside with Rhiannon and it was beautiful. Actors used to stay there when they were appearing in the pantomime at the Rhyl theatre.

One evening during Harry Thomas' picture slide show he showed slides of the Prestatyn Carnival in the early 1950's. The carnival was run by Mrs Kay and I was in the Morris dancing and acrobatic troupes.

Louie (doing the splits) in Mrs Kay's Dancing Team

To my surprise that night Mrs Kay was sitting behind me and when the lights came on I turned round to her and asked her if she knew the Bakers. Then Mrs Kay said "You are Louie!" A strange feeling went through me but it was not a feeling of pleasure because she had not wanted me in her dance team.

Rachel had to work shifts in the Grange Hotel so David and I looked after Rhiannon while she was working. Then Rachel obtained a flat in Rhyl so I used to stay at the flat overnight.

One Sunday morning after praying about which church I should go to I decided to go to Rhyl Baptist Church. I took Rhiannon, who was two years old, with me. After singing and saying a prayer a lady who was sitting near me took Rhiannon to the crèche for the very young children. There was also another little two year old girl called Ida Owen who became best friends with Rhiannon. They are still friends to this day. Rhiannon was very happy in the church. A young man called Andy Hughes was speaking and leading the meeting. After the service I spoke to Andy and when he told me that he lived in Central Avenue in Prestatyn a strange feeling went through me so I told him that I lived at number 27. One evening when I was in their house I ended up giving my testimony. Then Andy said to me "You must write a book!" Lots of people in my past had said the same thing to me so this is what I have done and I know this is the Lord's will.

One evening during Harry Thomas' slides I heard two ladies talking. They were looking at a large photograph and then one of the ladies said "There is Philip Baker!" So I asked to look at the photo. It was a school photo from Bodnant School in Marine Road, Prestatyn. Then I saw my Father on the picture, a tall fair haired boy. Then the ladies said how lovely he was which made me think "What went wrong?" I thought quietly to myself "It was most probably me!" and I felt a strange feeling of guilt.

One evening I went to a prayer meeting in the home of Colin Gent in Prestatyn. After the meeting Colin told me about a Plastic Surgeon called Gary Parker who worked in the Maxillofacial unit at Glan Clwyd Hospital which was our local hospital. He was an American Doctor who attended our church in Rhyl. I went to hear him speak at our church one Sunday evening. As I went towards him, even before I could speak to him he put his arm out to me and said, "Double cleft lip and palate." I told him I had a 'Pharyngeal flap.' an Abbe flap and a Pedicle flap for my palate. I also told him that I was trying to write a book about my life. He said to me "I want to be the first to read it!"

The last time I saw him in the church I asked him "Do you make fun of the children with cleft palates?" He looked a bit taken aback and said "No!" Then I told him about the Plastic Surgeon, Emlyn Lewis, who was my Surgeon and always made fun of his patients with cleft palates. Gary is a Christian and after finishing his training at Glan Clwyd Hospital he had a call from the Lord to join the hospital ship, the Anastasis, run by an organisation called 'Mercy Ships.' He has operated on hundreds of poor people who have congenital abnormalities in Africa. I greatly admire Gary for the marvellous way the Lord has led him and the things he has accomplished because of the power of God in his life. It is the Lord Jesus and it is marvellous in our eyes.

One day a friend had sprained her ankle and we went to my flat to get a bandage. On our way back I met a nice lady called Elan Roberts. She asked me what I was doing with the bandages. When I told her, Elan asked me where my friend lived but I had to say "Sorry, Elan, it is Welsh and I don't speak or understand Welsh." Then Élan said "No one will ever know what you went through!" Then I thought to myself "What does she know?" I had never spoken about my mouth or my operations. It turned out that years ago Elan was a District Nurse in Prestatyn. Also she had delivered my youngest brother at home. I was brought up to dislike the Welsh. My parents did not like the Welsh and my Father went into a rage when I told him that a Teacher at school had said that because I was born in Prestatyn I was Welsh. He screamed in my ear "You are English, not Welsh!" Then I remembered how much I had hated the Welsh teacher, Mr. Glyndwr Richards. I always took my knitting and a cigarette to his class. Of course, he put a stop to that! He told me to go to Miss Lewis who I also hated. Of course I did not go to Miss Lewis, I just went to the toilet and smoked my cigarette and waited for my friend Shirley.

I was still plagued with nightmares. I sometimes had to pray for the dreams but they always returned with a vengeance. Then, one Wednesday, a lady called Jean Boswell came to speak at the meeting. Jean offered people to have prayer. There was a lady in the church called Rhiannon Lloyd and one Saturday she led a meeting about healing. I decided in my mind that it could take all night!

One Sunday morning in church Rhiannon Lloyd sang in Welsh and I could feel the Lord very near to me. It was like I was being washed from hatred. I could feel it all leaving me. Rhiannon did not know about this.

After receiving prayer for deliverance from the nightmares I was having from Jean Boswell and after attending the meetings on healing run by Rhiannon Lloyd I knew that the Lord wanted me to forgive the children and the School Teachers in the schools that I had attended during my childhood and the hell that I went through because of my cleft palate. After Rhiannon and another young Christian lady had prayed for me I decided in my mind to visit the schools and I also felt the Lord leading me to be healed for that time in my life.

The first school on my list was the Convent school which had been run by Nuns on Russell Road in Rhyl. It was demolished in the early 1970's and is now a housing estate called St Mary's Court. As I walked into Russell Road I noticed the old school wall where the school had been and I started to remember the awful way that I was treated. I was called, 'Devil child'. A little boy called Richard and a little girl called Cathleen were my friends. The school was all girls but I was only there for six months because I had to go into hospital in Gloucester. When eventually I went back to the school Richard had left. I was very upset and when I told my Grandma she told my Father who said that I was to leave the Convent School and go to Bodnant School.

This brings me onto the next place that was like hell for me! After I had prayed for forgiveness at the Convent School one afternoon I went to Bodnant School in Prestatyn and I walked into a classroom. The Teacher looked at me and asked me if she could help me. Fortunately for me I knew a little boy in the school so I told the Teacher that I had come to meet Caelen and then I was told to wait outside. She most probably thought that I was a bit confused. The thing was that I was seeing another teacher called Ceri Ellis who told my mother that I would never be able to take the exam that children took at the age of eleven. I did not like Miss Ellis. I also remembered a big coke fire with a chimney in the middle going up towards the ceiling.

I recalled that one morning on a very cold day the bell rang for playtime and all the children went out to play. Because it was so cold I refused to go outside. Instead I went to the fire and put my hands on the surrounding fire guard. I would not let go of it when the teacher asked me to. So the teacher went to report me to the Headmaster who came into the classroom with his cane. He could not get me to take my hands off the wire guard. I could hear the children playing outside and then as they came back into the classroom after playtime but I still refused to take my hands off the wire guard. I expect the Headmaster realised then that he had a problem child on his hands. Part of the problem was that as I looked into the red hot coke of the fire I could see some of the burnt children that I had seen in hospital and I could also see the fighter pilots that I had known in the hospital. At the time I also had a problem with my speech which meant that the teachers could not understand me. I realise now that as a child and a young person that I did not receive all of the help that I needed.

Coming back to the present time I knew that I had to forgive the school and the Teachers so I prayed in the school and in my heart I forgave them. I loved Doctors, Nurses and the patients but I hated schools and Teachers! My next school was a place that had also felt like a hell pit for me, Emmanuel School in Rhyl. This place was the most difficult to come to terms with and to forgive the people there. I remembered again what I had gone through at that school and I felt my hatred once again towards the School Teachers. I decided to visit the school and as I went inside and walked through the corridors I could see the children in their classrooms which triggered my memory of one occasion when the Headmaster had entered my classroom and asked "Who would like to be a Nurse?" I had raised my hand up in response to his question and he retorted "You will never be a Nurse!" Then, I remembered Emlyn Lewis who told me that I had the makings of a good Nurse. I remembered telling the Headmaster then, how much I hated him and afterwards going to see the Headmistress and telling her that I hated her too.

As I continued to walk through the corridors nobody came to ask me who I was. I prayed that I forgave the school. There seemed to be so many things to forgive and so many people to forgive, including my parents.

I could only forgive through the work of the Holy Spirit and by the grace of God. Praise His name, we have a wonderful God!

Back at the church a week later a new Pastor arrived. His name was Rev. Dave Cave and I enjoyed his preaching very much. During that time our dog, Kim was suffering from arthritis and had difficulty walking. One morning while taking Kim for a walk she collapsed in the middle of Victoria Road. She brought the traffic to a stand-still and one driver opened his car window and asked me "Is it arthritis?" I had replied yes to his question and eventually I managed to get Kim home. When I told David we took her to the Vet who told us that she was suffering so David thought it would be kindest for her to be put to sleep, as they call it. Kim was 16 years old.

One day David and I went for a bike ride. While going along Gronant Road in Prestatyn I noticed a car and caravan coming alongside very close to me and the caravan hit my back wheel. I lost control of my bike and I went sprawling across the road and I ended up on the ground with my bike lying by the side of me. If a car had been coming down the other side I would have been killed. The strange thing was Gronant Road was usually a very busy road. When I eventually reached David he asked me what I had been doing because he had been waiting for ages for me. So I said to him "Didn't you see the caravan knock me off my bike?" David replied "No!" I thought in my own mind "Oh well, at least I'm still alive!"

Back in the church one Sunday morning the Pastor spoke about his dog. It was a Springer spaniel called Meg and he told us that at that time he had three Springer spaniels. Apparently Meg was a difficult dog who did not like being left alone. One evening the Pastor and his wife returned home to find that Meg had wrecked his office. After that the Pastor's Mother, Jenny accepted Meg but she became ill and had to be admitted to hospital and the Pastor found it difficult to cope with four spaniels due to his work so I asked David my husband if we could look after Meg while Jenny was in hospital and David said "Yes, we could" so she came to live with us. Meg took to David straight away and David loved her. Meg was a fun loving dog but we had to take her everywhere with us.

One day we took Meg to Conwy by train. Soon a lady came and sat opposite us in the carriage and started to eat a sandwich, but not for very long! Meg snatched the sandwich from the lady's hand and ate it! I felt terrible about it, but the lady was very nice about it, and told us that she loves Spaniels and thought Meg was lovely. Then one day while in town a little boy was coming out of a cake shop eating a cake and Meg snatched the cake out of the boy's hand. I apologised and offered to buy a cake for the boy. People seemed to love Meg with her red lead, collar and red coat, especially children who would always make a fuss of her.

One evening when I was taking Meg for a walk along the beach she disappeared. The tide was out and Meg loved to chase after the seagulls. When she came back she was covered in mud so I put her lead on and took her home. That incident reminded of Kim. It was an Autumn evening I had taken Kim for a walk on the beach. The tide was out but there were big pools around the beach. Kim must have picked up a scent of a smell in a pool because when she ran back to me she was covered in mud. So I took her to a big pool to wash the mud off her coat. Then I was aware of a man standing on a rock holding a very long stick. He shouted to me "Quick sand!" and then he threw his stick into the pool and disappeared. To this day I think that he was an angel.

One day someone was giving me a lift home and as we were turning into Pentywyn Road I saw a tall attractive young lady with a dog. The breed of dog was a Japanese Akita which I think is a beautiful type of dog. Then one afternoon I was going to a meeting with the Council about the trouble with some children with two other ladies and as I was walking along the drive I saw one of the houses in Tywyn Road had their garden fences down and then I saw two dogs in their big kennels. I was completely mesmerised! The owner of the dogs let me into her garden and brought a white dog out of the kennel for me to stroke. His name was Bear. They had another dog in the house called Scamp. He was a big dog and looked like a wolf. I fell in love with him.

By the time I got to the meeting it was over. My kitchen window overlooked my neighbour's garden. They had a little boy called Caelen. The mother was called Donna and she was a hairdresser. She became a good friend to me.

The first time Donna invited me into her home I was sitting on the settee and while Donna was making a cup of coffee the big dog was standing in front of me and he was growling. His face was almost touching my face and in my mind I was praying to Jesus. Donna said "That is his way of taking to you." After a time I got used to the dog.

One evening while taking Meg for a walk I made a mistake and took her lead off. She found a gap in a fence and ran onto the railway line so I had to go on to the crossing to get hold of Meg. Of course I was praying in case a train came. Fortunately Meg stopped to sniff around and I was able to put her lead on. Just as I got back onto the pavement an express train went past us on its way to London. When I told David he said that I should never have taken her lead off and that I could have been killed.

When I first came back to Prestatyn I wanted to get in touch with a friend who I knew on the estate where we lived. Her name was Margaret and she still lived in the same house. One evening I went to her home and I knocked at her door. Margaret opened the door and said "Louie Baker, we have just been talking about you, come in!" As I went into her sitting room there was another lady there from America who was staying with Margaret. They wanted to know what I had been doing in my life and because I had not seen Margaret for years I ended up giving my testimony. Then the lady asked me "How do you know that Jesus loves you?" so I said "The Bible says that He loves all people and that's why He died for us." I do not think the lady was satisfied with my answer because she asked "Yes, but how do you know He loves you as a person. We know your life and we know the way you were treated?" Then I told her how Jesus heals a person from the past hurts in their life. Margaret's friend told me that she was going to tell her son about me as her son was a Psychiatrist.

Life without David

Going back to Meg, our dog, she started to act strangely towards David. She did not seem to want him out of her sight because she was always following him and she also kept sniffing around him. I now believe Meg smelt cancer because they do say that dogs can detect it. David started to lose a lot of weight but he was still active and carried on making his ship 'The Victory' and going to 57th Club to do paintings. Then he had to go to the doctor's for a blood pressure test and also a scan which showed that he had cancer of the colon. He had a big operation followed by chemotherapy. It made him feel a bit awful but it didn't stop him going out. When two Nurses came to see him they could not believe that he had gone to Ruthin. Then he had another scan that showed that the cancer had spread to his lungs and liver. He never once complained but then soon after he died.

How I missed him especially as I then had to pay the bills myself. I had never had to pay a bill in my life! In my childhood my parents did it and then I worked for years in hospitals so I found it hard to pay the bills but now I have got used to it.

Going back to Meg, during the time that David was in hospital I had to take Meg with me when I went to visit David. I had to leave her attached to a rail in the hospital grounds. I remember that one day it was snowing and when I went to get Meg a lot of people were making a fuss of her as a lot of snow was on her head and red coat. Then, one day, I noticed a big lump under her body and she became very lethargic. The vet told me that it was cancer. Meg was 16 years old when she died.

After the death of David and also Meg in the same month, I felt very bereft and the flat felt like a morgue. Eventually with prayer I had to accept it and get used to it but I praise the Lord that I received a lot of support from my friends in the church but I felt at a loss in my life.

Then, one day while in prayer, I felt the Lord lead me to the elderly and I had the names of five ladies on my list. I was in school with one who taught me how to smoke. When I went to visit the ladies I took my Bible with me and I read to them but two of the ladies would not accept what I said to them about the Lord and I felt disappointed.

I also visited a lady who was a School Teacher and a Sunday School Teacher who was 94 years old but was still very alert. I was friendly with one of her Nieces from Walsall in the Midlands.

As time passed by I decided to make a last visit to Stoke Mandeville Hospital in Aylesbury, Bucks where I had had ten operations for a cleft palate. A friend of mine arranged everything for me including staying in a boarding house for two nights.

Eventually I set off on my journey by train. It was a long journey and I got a bit lost on the underground until I met a lady walking towards me. She noticed my brooch which was the RAF wings and had been a present that David had given me for my birthday. As the lady approached she remarked "RAF, how lovely!" She went on to say "You look lost!" I remember that the lady spoke in a posh English accent. I told her that I did not know which tunnel I needed for Aylesbury so she took me to the right tunnel.

After arriving in Aylesbury I got a taxi to the boarding house that I was booked into. The people who owned the house told me that I would need a taxi to get to the hospital but I walked there. When I eventually arrived after a very long walk it was a huge disappointment. The hospital had all changed as Aylesbury itself had! I went into the restaurant and had something to eat and a coffee and then I found the church inside the hospital. I sat down and said to the Lord Jesus, "Don't say I have come all this way for nothing!" Then I felt the Lord say "Go behind the hospital."

When I went behind the new hospital I found the old Nissen huts and then I found the driveway leading to the entrance of the Nissen huts. I walked up the long corridor, past the Spinal Unit and the old

Operating Theatre and then I arrived at the last hut which used to be Ward Six where I was a patient. I started to feel very emotional as I remembered all my friends and all the nursing staff that I had known. On the door of Ward Six was a notice saying, 'Clapper' which meant tongue and was a term for cleft palate.

As it was evening I made my way back to the boarding house in Aylesbury. The next day I decided to go back to the hospital and once again I made my way up to Ward Six.

As I put my hand on the door it opened and, to my amazement, a lady came out of a side room. She was a Speech Therapist and asked "Can I help you?" I told her that I was going down memory lane and explained that I had been a patient in Ward Six many years previously. I also said that no-one would ever know what that hospital meant to me. Then she said that my speech was very good and that they had made an excellent repair on my lip. As I made my way back down the corridor I could not stop the tears coming down my face. It wasn't that I was ungrateful; it was quite the opposite.

About one baby in seven hundred or a thousand is born with a congenital abnormality which is a failure of the palate and lip to fuse in the embryo. A baby can be born with just a cleft palate and a normal lip or with a normal palate and a cleft lip or a double cleft lip and palate like I had been born with which caused me to have twenty operations. I remember when I was ten years old and I was in hospital a Nurse had said to me "You will be scarred for life." The only problem is that in this day and age it is almost a crime to have scars or blemishes. I feel sorry for young people as they are bombarded with magazines featuring beautiful women and models. This can result in young people feeling that they are not good enough. Personally, I would rather have the beauty of the Lord Jesus Christ than the beauty of the world.

My daughter Rachel was going out with a young man and, after a time of living together in Wales, they moved to Newton Abbot in Devon. They went in their caravan to Devon and stayed in the grounds of a big house called RORA Christian Fellowship. It was run by Malcolm and Christine who helped Rachel and Gareth to get married and my granddaughter Rhiannon to be dedicated at the same time. It was a lovely service and a lovely reception and it was attended by the whole church and also friends and relatives, including me. I felt a bit sad because David wasn't there with me. I am sorry that after three years they separated but they still live in Newton Abbot. We used to go to conferences at the RORA fellowship and it was very powerful preaching by Mr. Norman Meeten and Bernard Hull. Then one week we went to a conference and the preacher was a Mr Parkyns who was a missionary in Africa. I stayed with Rachel who was working in a local supermarket but she did not like it so she had applied for a job in a prison. She got the job and she is still working there and getting on well.

Rhiannon is also doing well in the school that she attends in Newton Abbot. About two years ago I went by National Express coach to stay with Rachel for a week. By that time she was living in a cottage.

On my way back on the coach I had to change at Bristol. I got on another coach for Prestatyn and suddenly realised that I had left my coat on the previous coach. The driver told me that I would have to ring the lost property office in Bristol. When I got home I did that only to be told that I would have to go back to Bristol to collect it!

I decided to do that and went back to Bristol by train. It was quite a long walk to the property office and, of course, when I got there everybody else's coat was there but mine! I scolded myself "It serves you right, you should be more careful!" When I got back in the street I decided to go and visit the hospital where I had worked but of course Bristol had changed a lot since the time I was there. It reminded me of Chester as there were a lot of rows of bus stops and also a lot of people waiting for buses. I prayed that I would ask the right person, one who would know which bus I should catch for the hospital. The lady I asked said "Come with me. I usually get off the bus at the hospital." While walking around the grounds I started to feel very emotional as my memories came flooding back.

After a while I decided in my mind to go back into Bristol and find a restaurant and have a meal and then make my way back to the Temple Meads station. When I arrived in the station I had a strange experience. I needed to 'spend a penny' but I did not know where to go so I asked a lady who was walking towards me and she pointed to some very steep, narrow steps which seemed to go a very long way down. As I started to walk down the steps the lady was walking very close to my side. When I came out of the toilet, to my amazement, the lady was waiting for me. Then she asked me which train I wanted, so I told her Prestatyn. I followed her up the steps and through the barrier but, as I turned to thank her, she was gone! As I made my way onto the train, found a seat and sat down I started to think about the lady who had helped me in the station. I thought it was strange because she did not have a coat on, only a summer dress and the weather was quite cool as it was Autumn and she did not have a bag either.

I was on the Holyhead train and then I noticed a young man talking to another young man. He was looking at a book which I realised was a medical book for Doctors. I was sitting opposite him but I could hear what they were saying so I asked "Excuse me, are you a Doctor?" To which he replied "Yes." Then I asked him where he was studying and he told me "Frenchay Hospital, Bristol." I then told him that I worked there years ago. He asked me "What was nursing like in the old days?" I responded to him with the question "So you think I am old, do you?" He just laughed. He left the train at Chester leaving the other young man and me so we started to talk. I asked him where he lived and he told me that he lived in Meliden. I told him that I had a lot of relatives who lived in Meliden called the Bakers. I asked him if he knew them and he replied that he did and that he lived with one of them. It turned out that his girlfriend was my Cousin and that they had a baby girl! He then asked me if I knew Harry Thomas the historian and asked if I had been on his ghost walks. I told him that I had not because I was a Christian. He said "If you are a Christian, where do you think ghosts have come from?"

I told him "Demons, masquerading as people!" I told him what the Bible says and writes about such things. Then he told me then that Harry Thomas was his Uncle and that his mother owned the Diane Taxi. By that time it was 11:00pm and we arrived at Prestatyn. I was glad to get home. The Bible says that "We do not wrestle against flesh and blood but against principalities and powers of darkness in this world." Praise the Lord, He protects us and we are surrounded by His angels. Hallelujah!

I grew up with ghosts in my life and also with clairvoyance which ruled my life when I was young due to my Mother's interest in spiritualism. Praise the Lord, I was delivered from the lies of the devil many years ago and also delivered from the terrible effects on my life such as nightmares and clinical depression.

A clairvoyant is a person claiming to have the power to foretell the future events in a person's life. Of course, the real truth is that no person has the power or insight to foretell the future of another person's life. These things come from the devil and from demons. Also the person who is acting as a clairvoyant has demons too. I don't know my future but I know who holds my life; Jesus, of course!

I regret getting involved with clairvoyance and also with Ouija boards but I was brought up in those things and also the devil is out to destroy or even kill a person for going into his kingdom.

The danger of the Ouija board readings is that it can cause a person to attempt suicide.

> *'I tried the broken cisterns, Lord,*
>
> *But ah their waters failed*
>
> *And as I stooped to drink they fled*
>
> *And mocked me as I wailed.'*

I hope that this will be a warning to people.

I made the mistake of not having my eyes tested for three years and when I did eventually go to the Optician I discovered that I was only using my left eye. The Optician told me that I had to see an Eye Specialist at St. Asaph Hospital. When I arrived to see the Specialist in the Eye Clinic two Nurses gave me an injection. They told me that the side effect was that it turns your skin yellow. I said to the Nurse "Steady on, I have to get back to Prestatyn!" The Nurse asked me "Are you on your own?" I replied "Yes." After waiting a long time I was called in to see the Eye Specialist again and he was looking at photos of my eyes and asked me to sit down on a very comfortable leather chair. Then he gave me the news about my eyes. He told me that I had very poor eyesight and he had registered me partially blind. A lady came to see me and brought me a white stick and asked me if I wanted to have counselling but I said "No, because I am a Christian and I believe in the power of prayer." Also I thought of Pearl, my friend in the church who would be my Counsellor when and if I needed it.

When I was having my prayer time the Lord Jesus spoke to me in a verse from Scripture. It was "My grace is sufficient for thee for my strength is made perfect in weakness. Therefore will I rather glory in my infirmities." When the Eye Specialist told me that I could not drive I told him that I did not drive but that I rode a bike. To which he said "No, you must not ride, you must walk!" I rode a bike for years but towards the end I could not understand why I kept falling off near the kerb! David told me just to ride along the promenade near the beach but there were always a lot of dogs and people around which made me feel nervous.

Then, one evening David Landin was talking about bikes for 'Faster Pastors' in Africa. I felt the Lord tell me to give up the bike for His work so when I saw David in the church I spoke to him about my bike and David came to collect it and he sold it for Africa. In a way I felt a bit sad at having to give up my bike but I had to accept it.

I have had a few mishaps crossing the railway line. One time as I was crossing I thought I could hear a lorry which I knew was parked nearby but it was a train coming. However I managed to cross safely. Another time I was going to Coed Bell Cemetery in Prestatyn. I wanted to go to Bluebell Woods which are at the end of the cemetery but that meant I had to open big steel gates and I could not see to do it so I had to climb over the gates.

Once when I was in Scotland I did not see a small road and I nearly got run over and I ended up with three cracked ribs and an ankle fracture! One day I might have a guide dog.

Eventually the Eye Specialist told me that I could not have treatment for my eyes as they were too badly scarred so I had to carry on life with God's help and I know that the Lord Jesus has always been with me from the day I was born and He has kept me through many trials in my life. My one regret is that I did not let the plastic surgeon, Mr. Emlyn Lewis, who knew me as a patient in Gloucester and Chepstow that I had trained to be a Nurse.

Over the years in different churches people have told me to write a book. Andy Hughes, who was in the church at Rhyl, kept asking me, "Louie, have you started to write now?" Well, at last I have done it! This is a story about the power of God in my life. There is no way that I would have got through nursing exams without the Lord Jesus and I give all the glory to Him.

> *"The Lord shall preserve your going out and coming*
>
> *in from this time forth and even for ever more."*
>
> *Bless the name of Jesus.*

I do hope that what I have written will be an encouragement to people.

THE END